# Future Radio Programming Strategies:
## Cultivating Listenership in the Digital Age

### Second Edition

**LEA'S COMMUNICATION SERIES**
Jennings Bryant/Dolf Zillmann, General Editors

Selected titles in Broadcasting (James E. Fletcher, Advisory Editor) include:

Webster/Lichty • Ratings Analysis: Theory and Practice

MacFarland • Future Radio Programming Strategies, Second Edition: Cultivating Listenership in the Digital Age

Metallinos • Television Aesthetics: Perceptual, Cognitive, and Compositional Bases

Biocca/Levy • Communication in the Age of Virtual Reality

For a complete list of other titles in LEA's Communication Series, please contact Lawrence Erlbaum Associates, Publishers

# Future Radio Programming Strategies: Cultivating Listenership in the Digital Age

## Second Edition

**David T. MacFarland**
*A. Q. Miller School of Journalism
and Mass Communications
Kansas State University*

LAWRENCE ERLBAUM ASSOCIATES, PUBLISHERS
1997   Mahwah, New Jersey                London

Copyright © 1997 by Lawrence Erlbaum Associates, Inc.
All rights reserved. No part of the book may be reproduced in
any form, by photostat, microform, retrieval system, or any other
means without the prior written consent of the publisher.

Lawrence Erlbaum Associates, Inc., Publishers
10 Industrial Avenue
Mahwah, NJ 07430

**Library of Congress Cataloging-in-Publication Data**

MacFarland, David T.
   Future radio programming strategies: cultivating listenership in the digital age / David MacFarland.
      p.   cm.
   Rev. ed. of: Contemporary radio programming strategies. 1990.
   Includes bibliographical references and index.
   ISBN 0-8058-2105-8 (alk. paper). — ISBN 0-8058-2106-6 (pbk. : alk. paper)
   1. Radio programs—Planning.  I. MacFarland, David T. Contemporary radio programming strategies.  II. Title.
PN1991.55.M33     1997
384.54'42'0973—dc21                        97-7737
                                              CIP

Books published by Lawrence Erlbaum Associates are printed on acid-free paper, and their bindings are chosen for strength and durability.

Printed in the United States of America

10 9 8 7 6 5 4 3 2 1

# Contents

**Acknowledgments**     xi

## Chapter 1
### An Overview of The Book     1

    What The Title Means    *1*
    What This Book Offers    *2*
    Organization of The Book    *4*

## PART I
### RADIO'S ARENA, ATTRIBUTES, AND AUDIENCES     7

## Chapter 2
### Radio's Arena     9

    What Business Is Radio In?    *9*
    Choosing Radio    *11*
    Consistency    *14*
    The Challenge of Change    *16*
    Major Points    *25*

## Chapter 3
### Radio's Attributes 27

    Mendelsohn: The Positive Values
       of Mass Entertainment    27
    Stephenson: The Pleasures of Play    30
    What Radio Does Best    32
    Lessons About Entertainment Values
       from Computer Games    34
    Major Points    37

## Chapter 4
### What Radio Audiences Want 38

    Fantasies and Daydreams    38
    Pleasure as Product, Not By-Product    42
    Body Rhythms    45
    Structure    48
    Appeals    50
    Other Audience Needs and Desires    51
    The Flow Experience    56
    Major Points    58

## PART II
### FORMATS, SOUNDSCAPES, AND VOICES 61

## Chapter 5
### Formats: Developmental History, Audience Differentiation, and Recent Trends 63

    A Brief History of Radio Music Formats    63
    Audiences Attracted by Various Formats—
       A Historical Overview    69
    Recent Trends in Selected Formats    74
    Major Points    83

## Chapter 6
### Format Innovation and Management — 85

    Innovation of Format Elements   85
    Special Problems of Automated and
        Syndicated Stations   96
    The Primary Tasks   99
    Major Points   103

## Chapter 7
### The Structure and Appeal of Acoustic Space — 105

    The Listening Environment   105
    A Sense of Place in Acoustic Space   110
    Rate   113
    Major Points   117

## Chapter 8
### Air Personality: The Structure of Spoken Gesture — 118

    The Challenge of Radio Performance
       in a Visual Era   118
    Needing Arthur Godfrey Again   120
    The Announcer as Ideal Mate   127
    Announcers as Actors   128
    What is There to Talk About?   131
    Talk About the Community's Stories   135
    Major Points   138

# PART III
## MUSIC PROGRAMMING — 141

## Chapter 9
### Choosing Radio Music—Today — 143

    How Listeners Choose a Music
       Radio Station   143
    How Music Stations Currently
       Choose Their Music   148

The Standard Components
  of Record Popularity    155
Major Points    162

# Chapter 10
## Choosing Radio Music Tomorrow—
## By "How it Makes You Feel"    164

Research on How and Why
  Music Affects Us    165
Mendelsohn's Music Moods Research    171
Clynes' Music Moods Research    175
Major Points    181

# Chapter 11
## The Components of a Mood-Evoking Music Progression    183

Music Presentation Based on
  Mood Needs    183
Time    185
Space    193
Force    197
The Time/Space/Force Components
  of Radio Mood    202
Major Points    203

# Chapter 12
## Factors in MOST—Mood-Oriented Selection Testing    205

Using Clynes' Terms to Select
  Airplay Music    206
Time (Song Rhythms)    215
Space (Involvement Factors)    218
Force (Acceptance Factors)    219
Lyrics    220
Special Considerations    222
Appendix A: Complete List of Songs
  Tested in All Five Formats    225

Appendix B: Anecdotal Highlights—
   Adult Contemporary Format    227
Major Points    229

# Chapter 13
## Factors in MEMO—Mood-Evoking Music Order    231

Composite Mood Curve    234
Continuation    239
Popularity and the CMC    241
Using the CMC for Other Elements    242
Major Points    243

# Chapter 14
## Toward MERIT    245

Should Radio Lead or Follow Society?    245
A Glimpse of What MERIT Might Be:
   Mood-Evoking Respondent-Interactive
   Tracking    246
Major Points    250

**References**    251
**Index**    260

# *Acknowledgments*

I am gratified that there is a demand for a second edition of *Contemporary Radio Programming Strategies,* which has been renamed *Future Radio Programming Strategies, Second Edition: Cultivating Listenership in the Digital Age,* to more accurately reflect its focus on what radio programming people need to be thinking about today to compete effectively tomorrow. I have tried to respond to feedback to make this new edition timelier and easier to follow, without changing its usefulness to both professional broadcasters and students of the field.

All of the people who helped on the first edition still have my gratitude, but rather than reprint that long list here, I simply thank you all again. There would not have been a second edition without your contributions to the success of the first.

It has been a delight to work with everyone at Lawrence Erlbaum Associates, a company staffed with consummate professionals who have treated me with kindness, probably undue respect, and a sense of humor. Hollis Heimbouch was instrumental in negotiating a contract for the second edition, and Kathleen O'Malley patiently listened to my excuses for why the manuscript was late, and even laughed at my jokes. Linda Bathgate, Sara Scudder and Teresa Horton provided valuable editorial assistance, and Eileen Engel was an incomparable book production editor. All have been first-rate ambassadors for a first-rate publisher. I was pleased to get their expert guidance, and I'm proud to have the LEA imprint on my work. Please keep in mind that, in my experience, the company often graciously accedes to the wishes of its authors, and that is why the flaws that you will find in this book are all but certainly of my doing, not the people at LEA.

This second edition would not have been completed without the loving support of my wife Charlotte and the unselfish help of Kansas State University faculty colleagues William Adams, Charles Lubbers, Paul Prince and Tom Grimes. The innovative multimarket, multiformat music research reported here could not have been accomplished without the valued assistance of the National Association of Broadcasters, Paragon Research, Marlene Adkison of KTPK-FM in Topeka, RTV faculty friends Steve Smethers and Gary McIntyre, graduate alumnus Jason Adair, and undergraduate students Rick Darnell, Connie Weber, Jean Lebak, Gary Litchman, Ted Smith, Eileen Meyer, Jenny Jones, and Roger Burns. Finally, this book would have been published at least a year later had there not been the uncluttered concentration afforded by a semester-long sabbatical that was supported by Carol Oukrop, Director of the A. Q. Miller School of Journalism and Mass Communications, and approved by Peter Nichols, Dean of the College of Arts and Sciences at Kansas State University. I sincerely thank them all.

—*David T. MacFarland*

# 1. AN OVERVIEW OF THE BOOK

's on FMs, but considers other transmission channels, ːoadbroadcast satellites and the Internet. We are at the end of ␣␣n broadcast radio is the only significant method of delivering audio service simultaneously to a mass audience.

The term *programming* reflects my belief that the most important thing to manage in radio is the programming—that if you get the programming right, a lot of other necessary things will fall into place. That is what the people who pioneered Top 40 believed, and it still makes sense today. Prior to the advent of Top 40, many stations played what owners or announcers decided to air, with little regard to what listeners actually wanted to hear. Top 40 pioneers changed that, by trying to track music popularity as a way of satisfying public taste. The impulse to "let the people decide" with their requests and their wallets what music should be played was basically right, but the selection process has become corrupted in the intervening years. Thus, this book challenges the assumption that merely airing the most popular music is still adequate today. By asking "What is it that listeners really want?" this book attempts to take the next step beyond Top 40-type formats in which measures of music popularity predominate.

Finally, the word *strategies* should be an easy one for a broadcaster to feel comfortable with, because radio has been a viable business for more than half a century. For much of that time, radio practitioners were so busy making radio that the basic question "What is it that we are trying to do here?" simply fell by the way. If, through this book, the reader can begin to answer that question, conventional radio broadcasting may have a better chance of prospering into the 21st century. In modern times when new media appear, the older media adapt and manage to survive. But the pace of that change is accelerating, and the pressure to carve out a niche makes it tougher to produce a profit. I am convinced that in hard times, the companies that have taken the time to ask themselves "What is it that we are really in business to do, and what means are we going to use to achieve that?" will be ahead of the game for having gone through the process. It is radio's very "dailiness" that keeps too many program directors and managers from getting around to the apparently postponable but actually vital business of defining the station's mission.

## WHAT THIS BOOK OFFERS

The theater has had Aristotle for more than 2,300 years and Stanislavsky for more than four decades. Because the theater has these thinkers and others to point to, theater professionals are better able to express themselves. They can identify with one or another system of beliefs as they continue a search for a general understanding of values and reality. But

# WHAT THIS BOOK OFFERS

there are few such rallying points in the radio business. Ther whose specific contributions to radio are admired and emulatec particular gifts are hard to fit into a gestalt of fully defensible, fu beliefs.

*Fundamental beliefs* is what the reader will be exploring here—a common understanding of what the radio enterprise should be about—entertainment and information. The term *information* has grown to encompass so many things that it is almost fruitless to argue about what is and is not information anymore. Similarly, *entertainment* continues to be an elusive concept, one that appears to be heavily dependent on the eyes of the beholder. A major thrust of this book is to arrive at a set of fundamental beliefs about the values and the realities of the radio business in regard to entertainment programming—a set of beliefs that may or may not be right, or true, or forever, but that might at least provide a basis for developing programming strategies.

Most other books on radio programming describe the formats and programming that already exist. This edition does that, too, but then it starts with a clean sheet of paper and the question "What do listeners really want from radio?" Some of the answers to that question are derived from uses and gratifications research in the mass media. Instead of focusing on what mass media do to people, the uses and gratifications perspective seeks to discover what people do with mass media. The functionalist viewpoint of such research basically says that a medium is best defined by how people use it. That is also the approach of this book.[1] Having looked at some of the audience research that comes from sources other than the standard ratings companies, the book then goes on to demonstrate new ways that formats, production procedures, and announcing styles can meet audience needs and desires. Although the book concludes with several original methods for selecting and presenting airplay music based on the audience's moods and emotional needs, the book does not insist upon a singular, formulaic approach for constructing or modifying a music format. Instead, it attempts to involve you, the reader, in thinking through the process of format development. Rather than merely observing a format element's obvious *form,* there is an attempt to make you a partner in appreciating the underlying *function* that that element should perform.

To borrow a concept from computer programming, this book is not intended to provide algorithms (a precise series of steps that lead to a precise outcome), but rather heuristics. *Heuristics* are exploratory, sometimes trial-and-error problem-solving techniques that deal with probable (not

---

[1] For a further description of uses and gratifications mass media research, see Rubin, A. M. (1986). Uses, gratifications, and media effects research. In J. Bryant & D. Zillmann (Eds.), *Perspectives on media effects* (pp. 281–301). Hillsdale, NJ: Lawrence Erlbaum Associates.

guaranteed) outcomes given a certain relationship. A book that takes a heuristic approach does not attempt to establish mathematical formulas but rather seeks to explore likely relationships, including the inevitable exceptions. The practicing broadcaster, and the student about to enter the field—who comprise the dual audience for this book—will not find all-purpose solutions here. Instead, you will find new ways of thinking about programming and its effects. Those new ways of thinking should then lead the thoughtful reader to develop his or her own strategies for a given station. Throughout the book, the assumption is made that the reader either already is—or intends to be—a radio professional. When a reference is made to "your station," an FM running some kind of a hit-based music format is usually the imaginary model.

## ORGANIZATION OF THE BOOK

Part I of the book considers radio's arena, attributes and audiences. Chapter 2, "Radio's Arena," looks at the highly competitive environment radio finds itself in today, both in terms of audience fragmentation and the new technologies that challenge radio as a delivery system. Chapter 3, "Radio's Attributes," explores the several things that radio does better than any other medium. Chapter 4, "What Radio Audiences Want," discusses the expectations radio listeners have today, and lists needs and desires not usually considered in audience analyses.

Part II examines formats, soundscapes, and voices—the basic components of radio. Chapter 5, "Formats: Developmental History and Recent Trends," looks at the way all hit music formats have evolved out of Top 40, considers audience differentiation and niche programming, and summarizes the current "state of the art" of the major U.S. radio formats. Chapter 6, "Format Innovation and Management," investigates how format innovations come about, and suggests how some present-day formats fall short of meeting the full menu of listeners' needs. Chapter 7, "The Structure and Appeal of Acoustic Space," considers the parameters of sound and production elements, and argues that too much of radio happens without regard to an acoustic sense of place. Chapter 8, "Air Personality: The Structure of Spoken Gesture," explains the ways in which actors and announcers share technique and invites performers to be more cognizant of factors of time, space, and force.

Today, the majority of listeners turn to radio primarily for music. Thus, Part III, on music programming, begins a close examination of program content, beginning where the average listener begins: with music. Chapter 9, "Choosing Radio Music—Today," explains how listeners choose music stations, and how music stations choose records for airplay. It focuses on the primacy of popularity in all airplay decision making, and offers definitions and alternative understandings of terms such as *popularity, liking, favorability,* and *familiarity.* Chapter 10, "Choosing Radio Music—Tomorrow," delves deeply into research on how music evokes certain emotions and generates certain moods in listeners; it lays the groundwork for the consideration of the uncommon music selection and presentation sytems in chapters 11, 12, and 13. Chapter 11, "The Components of a Mood-Evoking Music Progression," pulls together many of the elements introduced in the earlier chapters, to show how airplay music can be selected on the basis of mood. Chapter 12, "Factors in MOST—Mood-Oriented Selection Testing," demonstrates the elements of a non-popularity-based system for selecting or rejecting any given piece of music. And chapter 13, "Factors in MEMO—Mood-Evoking Music Order," displays and describes use of the composite mood curve, a comprehensive system for ordering and presenting all of the elements in a music-oriented station's programming.

Finally, chapter 14, "Toward MERIT," offers some of the elements of an evolutionary format that depends on—and in turn promises to generate—high audience involvement.

A list of major points follows every chapter in the book except this first one. The major points summarize the important arguments of the chapter but necessarily condense the discussion. Readers who would like an "executive overview" of the book can consult these pages but should keep in mind that important detail will be missing.

The book builds many of its later cases and assumptions on material that is presented earlier. The logic, viewpoints, and arguments are intended to be cumulative. Therefore, the sections and chapters are best read in the given order.

# PART I

# *Radio's Arena, Attributes, and Audiences*

This first section of the book considers radio's arena, attributes, and audiences. Chapter 2, "Radio's Arena," looks at the competitive environment radio finds itself in today and the ways management and staff need to respond. Chapter 3, "Radio's Attributes," explores the several things radio does better than any other medium. Chapter 4, "What Radio Audiences Want," discusses the expectations radio listeners have, and lists needs and desires not usually considered in audience analyses.

# CHAPTER 2

## Radio's Arena

### WHAT BUSINESS IS RADIO IN?

The answer to the question "What business is radio in?" is not as obvious as it seems. This is not a matter of images or public relations. Rather, it is a question of actualizing a positioning statement; of discovering the unique thing that radio does that other media do not do as well, if at all.

It is a cliché that a fish never realizes it is in an aquarium until it jumps out and dies in the air. When you are working in the radio business, it is very hard to see what it is that radio does best. It is easier to figure out what other businesses do well, even if they do not think of those attributes as strengths. As a way of understanding the problem of "examining your own navel," take the example of the daily newspaper.

**The Local Daily Newspaper Example**

Today, many communities offer a wide choice of news sources. There are national newspapers like *USA Today,* and the traditional big-city dailies. There are local radio and regional TV newscasts. There is often news on a cable system. There is news on the Internet. With such heavy competition, it is much to the credit of local daily newspapers that their circulation figures remains as strong as they have. Of course, newspapers offer advantages that radio does not have: tangibility (you can hold the product in your hand); visuals (there are photographs and artwork to illustrate the stories and the ads); and programmability (you can "edit" the paper for your own tastes by choosing only stories that interest you, and you can in any order). These are three examples of positive attributes unique to newspapers. But a local daily newspaper has something else that it ought to think of as an asset rather than a liability: a delivery organization that places a product "in the hands" of a sizable chunk of the local citizenry every day. That is the one characteristic that a successful local newspaper has going for it that no other information provider can claim: a force of people that regularly blankets the town with hand-carried delivery service. From my perspective, as a person steeped in radio and television, I find it curious that local newspapers do not do more to capitalize on the one thing that really sets them apart from every other information-providing medium. Instead of grumbling about circulation as a necessary evil, why haven't most local newspapers thought of circulation as a potential profit center? Why haven't they gotten rid of the term *circulation*, and replaced it with the much more all-purpose term *delivery*? Why haven't they started to think of ways to upgrade and professionalize the circulation department so that it is able to deliver a lot of other non-first-class-mail printed material that is now just hung on doorknobs or is sent via third-class mail? The newspaper's carriers pass virtually every house in the city anyway. Why shouldn't the newspaper get really good at the delivery business, and make money at it?

Local daily newspapers know they are not alone in supplying local news, but most have not asked themselves "What is it that we do that is *unique* to local daily newspapers?" One answer, "local delivery of printed material," usually does not occur to someone who thinks he or she is in the news business. The same is true with radio. By the end of this section, a case will have been made that one of radio's necessary evils is actually its greatest strength. That is why it seems useful to spend time exploring the roles radio seems to play and the attributes the listener-consumer ascribes to radio.

## Listeners Do Not Care About the Radio Business

The way radio industry people tend to divide up their world (management, sales, engineering, programming, etc.) does not occur to the listener in the least. Listeners do not even care about programming—as a science or an art. As is argued later, listeners do not even listen *for* formats, although they listen *to* them because that is what is offered. The radio listener tunes in for a certain set of gratifications that radio provides. However, most of the time, radio is not unique in providing those gratifications or does not provide them consistently enough to suit some listeners.

In his essay about "the new languages" (nonbook media), Edmund Carpenter (as cited in Ohlgren & Berk, 1977) made the point that the newspaper, by juxtaposing various items that might interest the reader, puts him or her into the role of the producer instead of merely a passive reader.

Rather than using a chronological or linear approach as would be for novel, the newspaper presents items simultaneously on the page, for the reader to choose. In contrast to the effort the newspaper reader expends is the dial-turning, button-pushing behavior of the radio listener searching for a particular kind of content. Dial-turners and button-pushers wish they *could* be the producer. The only control available to such a radio listener is through station-hopping—or plugging in tapes or CDs instead.

## CHOOSING RADIO

People today do not have to settle for listening to a radio station that is not exactly what they want. At home, cable TV and VCRs give them plenty of ways to escape the lock-grip of the television network schedule. As MIT professor of media technology Nicholas Negroponte said in his book *Being Digital* (1995), consumers with computer access to services like the Internet do not have to put up with having information (or entertainment) "pushed" at them. Instead, people or their digital agents can "pull" the specific information and entertainment they want to get, and avoid the rest (p. 170). It is demand access consumerism—people getting what they want to read, see, or hear when they want it. If radio does not provide the programming that fulfills similar needs, then cassettes, or CDs, or the Internet can, and people will turn to them. Programming consultant Ed Shane (1991) wrote in his book *Cutting Through* that today's listener tunes to an average of 3.2 radio stations, and that in focus groups especially the men reported putting their receivers on "scan" and letting them go. Burger King's old slogan "Have it your way" obviously sank in with the baby boomer generation, according to Shane.

In recent years, home music listeners have bought increasing numbers of CD changers compared to single-play decks. In 1994, the Kenwood brand offered MoodMaker PC software with its CD changers so that home listeners could catalog and search all the music in their collection, and even play music from the changer based on several criteria—including the user's own ranking system ("Boot Up the Future with Mood Maker Software," 1994). In effect, Kenwood was offering a simpler version of the same sort of computerized music selection and rotation systems that radio stations were using.

The cassette decks and CD players both at home and in cars are enormous threats to some radio formats but especially to those that lack human involvement, topicality, and localness. A station can still afford to be a "music utility," but only if it hammers away at the "more music, less talk" theme in all of its promotion, and backs it up with actual percentages that the listener can understand as proof. How many radio stations have you

## The Least Objectionable Program (LOP) Theory

Decades ago, former TV programmer Paul Klein developed a Least Objectionable Program (LOP) theory that suggested that TV viewers did not tune in for the best show, but rather—because they were watching TV anyway—they would watch the least objectionable program that was on. The theory suggested that the way to satisfy such an audience was to supply the lowest common denominator of inoffensiveness.

Klein's LOP theory is not in vogue in television programming any more, because delivering "tonnage" (huge, homogeneous audiences), as the three commercial networks once did, has given way to delivering qualitative, targeted categories of consumers. Radio has been delivering qualitative, niche-market audiences to advertisers for far longer than has television. But the tonnage versus qualitative argument does not negate the "lowest common denominator" part of Klein's theory. Supplying the lowest common denominator of inoffensiveness has long been one of the hallmarks of much of radio's network and syndicated programming. Moreover, the majority of U.S. music-formatted stations offer a music mix that is intended to have mass appeal. One of the factors in achieving mass appeal is the avoidance of negatives, and for decades, radio programmers have been seeking to minimize tuneout by eliminating or minimizing objectionable elements. That attitude coincides with the common radio management desire to achieve hassle-free consistency. It may not be exciting radio, but at least it will not offend anyone.

It is ironic that stations whose audiences may be largely comprised of LOP listeners may think that those same listeners are highly loyal to that station. The contest winner tells you yours is her favorite radio station because she just won something! But ask her which is her favorite pair of shoes, and you will usually get a greater level of emotional involvement.

## The Least Objectionable Lunch

There are people who go to a McDonald's restaurant for lunch, not because it is the best food in town, but because when you only have a few moments, McDonald's provides a familiar product that is served up quickly and is consistent over time. You know what to expect at any McDonald's, and that is its chief virtue. Nobody can argue with the success of McDonald's for featuring consistency and standards. But what you eat is one of the basic, eternal needs in life (food). What you listen to (if anything) is a clear choice. It is not something people have to do every few hours or even every day.

If what your radio station provides is not programming people really want to have, then something is wrong. In other words, if they settle for

ion because it offers the least objectionable program served up in
t consistent way, then you will eventually come to be regarded as
more a utility than an entertainment medium. And whereas the public
may view monopolistic utilities such as the local telephone company or
cable TV with a mixture of admiration and contempt, because your radio
station is not the only franchise in town, they will not even bother to get
mad at your station when it is ineffective. They will just tune to another,
play their own music, or shut off the radio. By offering the least objectionable programming, your station risks becoming irrelevant.

**What's New With You?**

It is not that you want to run a radio station that is completely inconsistent. A basic program consistency can draw and hold a core of people who are searching for that LOP. But think of this: How many major new items have been added to McDonald's menu? When did they start serving breakfast and staying open late? How many times have they remodeled their stores? How many dozen different commercial campaigns have they had? Now ask yourself: How many major new items has your station added to the programming in the last 10 years, especially if you air a syndicated service? Have you gone after and won over an audience that was out there all along but had never been served that way before (like McDonald's did with breakfast)? How many times has your listener sensed a remodeling and freshening of the total sound when he or she has tuned your station?

## CONSISTENCY

Now we confront an oxymoron—that is, a pairing of two normally opposed words. The oxymoron is *consistent quality*. Consistent quality is one of the selling points of radio automation systems, and one of the buzzphrases used to promote syndicated program services of all kinds. "Play our stuff," the flyers say, "and you'll enjoy consistent quality." But the two words do not belong together in radio. Quality radio programming must always include inconsistency if it is going to work tomorrow as it does today. Not only is "a foolish consistency . . . the hobgoblin of little minds," it is also the hobgoblin of radio formats.

**Positioning: Information, Format Structure, and Dependability**

A dissertation by David E. Kennedy (1981), titled *Listener Perceptions as Dimensions of Radio Station Positioning: A Multivariate Analysis,* studied the ways radio listeners perceived competitive radio stations and "positioned" them in their minds with respect to one another. (*Positioning* is defined by Al

Ries and Jack Trout, 1986, authors of an important book
not so much what you do to a product, but what you c
the prospective user.) Kennedy's research provides three fa
the stations he studied: information, format structure, an
*Information* characteristics that aided the stations' positic ......u to
being in touch with what was happening in the area, providing desired
daily information, and having enjoyable announcers. *Format structure* characteristics included having games and contests that invited participation,
and an acceptable number of commercials (Kennedy, 1981). *Dependability*
was defined by Kennedy as referring to

> a sense of expected consistency; in other words, the listener knows what to
> expect on the station when he or she tunes to it, because the station has an
> overall consistent approach toward its programming. Consequently, the lis-
> tener can "depend" on the station, and thus doesn't grow tired of it. (p. 93)

The key idea in the foregoing paragraph is that the station should have "an overall consistent approach toward its programming." Like television's CNN Headline News that repeats every half hour, or the Weather Channel that presents the local forecast at :08, :18, :28, :38, :48, and :58 every hour, you know the general framework of what is going to happen. But *within* that framework, there should be plenty of novelty. How long would anybody watch the news or the weather if only 5% to 10% percent of the content were different from day to day? But that is what we expect people to do in regard to LOP-type radio music formats.

The first edition of this book described the case of an AM station in Cedar Rapids, Iowa—WMT—that had managed to achieve a 30% audience share and a number-one ranking among the top revenue-producing stations in the country with a morning show that featured patriotic tunes, classical music, and poetry reading, and that mixed farm reports with reruns of old-time radio comedies and tunes by Mama Cass. It appealed to its older target audience by being consistently inconsistent. Of course, the station adhered to a program schedule, but in any given program, almost anything could go on the air. The only predictable thing about the day-to-day content was that a listener today probably would not hear much that duplicated what had been aired yesterday.

## Mass Appeal Need Not Mean Doing What the Other Guys Do

The handful of AMs like WMT that managed to hang on to their traditional listeners became the beacons of hope for the many AMs whose audience declines matched the decline in overall AM listening over the last couple of decades. But some of the leading FM stations also rejected the program directors at Top 40 and "progressive" format stations turned up a list of both positive and negative impacts.

> Accounting for their feelings that radio suffered little at the hands of music video, programmers said (in order of response frequency) that: (1) radio was a different medium with very different use characteristics (it is portable and people listen to it at different times and places than they would normally watch TV); (2) that music videos had some initial novelty that subsequently wore off; (3) that radio is simply immune to any effects from music videos; (4) that music videos' content qualities are different insofar as radio is more imaginative while the visual content in the videos destroys the listener's/viewer's creativity with the song; (5) that the age groups typically targeted by music videos are younger than those targeted by radio; and (6) that videos affect other leisure time activities more than they do radio. (Strover, 1987, p. 2)

Strover's research is sound, but not so the program directors' wishful thinking that it reports.

Point 1: A Street Pulse Group telephone survey of music consumers found that 75% of their sample watched music video programming (MTV, VH-1, The Nashville Network, etc.) Fifty-eight percent said that they usually sat and watched the programming (rather than using it as a background music source). An even larger 66% of respondents under age 18 said that was how they used the video services. Fully 88% of the sample watched for at least a quarter of an hour, and 66% watched at least a half hour per viewing session (Shalett, 1988).

Point 2: There is not much proof that the novelty of music videos has worn off—rather, video viewing is now a normal, habitual event. A study that surveyed San Jose, California, high school students, record store patrons with an average age of 18, and bars with big-screen music videos found that the average time all groups watched music videos was just under 3 hours a day—more on weekends, less on weekdays. The high school students watched almost 3½ hours a day. The San Jose study also found that MTV was being used for relaxing and passing the time—the video music service was being used like radio (TV listening instead of foreground viewing) (Wallis & Malm, 1988).

Point 3: Radio—especially radio that leans heavily on current hit music for its appeal—is *vulnerable* to replacement by music videos, not "immune" to such effects. One study (Melton & Galician, 1987) found that 43% of teenage MTV viewers watched MTV at times when they formerly listened to radio, in spite of the fact that radio was thought to offer better songs and more musical variety. If forced to choose, two thirds of the teenagers in that study said they would choose MTV over radio.

Point 4: It is probably true that "the visual content in videos destroys the listener's/viewer's creativity with the song," and research with college students seems to bear this out: Those preferring radio over MTV as a music medium said that watching a music video channel limited their own interpretation of the song (Melton & Galician, 1987, p. 39). However, it should be noted that a theatrical movie sometimes destroys the creativity that the reader brought to the book on which it was based, but for any given title, far more movie tickets than books are sold. It has sometimes been said that the mass audience generally opts for the medium that requires less "work." A better perspective is that the mass audience generally opts for more stimuli than fewer. Watching movies requires less work than reading books; but, watching music videos actually requires more work than listening to the radio. However, both movies and music videos supply more stimuli than books or radio, with the additional stimulation acting as a reward for the extra attention demanded.

Point 5: Although it is true that many of MTV's viewers are teens and people in their early 20s, these are the very people who used to spend those years making a habit of radio listening. And the popularity of country music videos shows that the appeal is not limited to rock devotees.

Point 6: A study by Gary Melton and Mary-Lou Galician (1987) showed that although both radio and video music helped their college student respondents to pass time, forget about problems, relax, and shift moods, music videos did a better job than radio in helping viewers to keep up with the latest fads and fashions, get in touch with feelings, and share an experience with friends. Moreover, the young people in the study were more likely to find music videos helpful in escaping the real world, relieving tension, and getting in touch with feelings.

In addition to providing competition for the rock/alternative music listener, MTV-style videos were the vanguard of a new style of storytelling—one based more on quick sense impressions rather than traditional linear narrative. Researchers Gary Burns and Robert Thompson (1987) said that:

> the central myth of rock video, in our view, is the rejection of the "dominant" mode of consciousness—rational, scientific, unemotional—in favor of an alternative mode. The conventionalized form and motifs of rock video reflect this rejection. The alternative mode is irrational, expressive, playful, visually charged while tied to music, and self-conscious. (p. 22)

Ronald W. Roschke, whose paper "Dream/Brain/Text:The Media–Brain Connection in Mental Processing of Texts" (1987) discusses the relation of dreams to stories in detail, made this comment about MTV during an interview:

MTV is daytime dreaming. It is bringing you a nighttime state in the daytime. MTV is an especially powerful storyteller because of the visual elements, but all of pop music succeeds best when it tells a story. Pop music does not lecture. The stories in popular music are very dense constellations of associations. Lectures are tight, self-contained intellectual units that are smooth on the outside and have all of their hooks pointing inward to connect internally. Stories are bristly and have many of their hooks on the outside so that it works like Velcro™—you throw this Velcro™ ball at that Velcro™ board but it doesn't bounce—it sticks to all kinds of other associations that people have. MTV, and to a lesser extent, pop music as heard but not seen, is Velcro™ communication with all of these extended subliminal hooks. These kinds of Jungian and Freudian symbols are perhaps new as a TV music form, but they have historical roots stretching far beyond just popular music: apocalyptic literature worked the same way in the ancient world. Music that tells a story that we can relate to is music that has its hooks on the outside. (R. W. Roschke, personal communication, January 24, 1985)

In the quote just cited, Roschke said that "MTV is an especially powerful storyteller because of the visual elements." Perhaps this is because those visuals—maybe especially when they seem chaotic to the linear-oriented viewer—are providing the counterpoints and the surprise connections that are the hallmarks of dreaming. As becomes apparent in the next chapter, by operating as a repository of dreams and fantasies, music services like MTV are poaching one of radio's prime attributes. Roschke's ideas appear again in this book's final chapter about dreams, stories, and society as they relate to the development of an audience-responsive radio format—one answer to the impact of music videos.

According to Straw (1988), another effect of music videos has been the reinstitution of the power of the single song. Because it is too expensive to make a video of more than one song from an album, that single song becomes the pivotal one for the entire album's promotion.

MTV's original viewers were attracted to the channel in spite of the generally poor sound reproduction ability of most mono television sets when the service premiered. That has changed in the intervening years, with an increasing number of high-fidelity stereo receivers now available in U.S. homes. The improvement in audio reproduction makes MTV and other video music services even more of a threat to music on the radio that is intended for home consumption.

## Digital Audio

In the first edition of this book, I made some dire predictions about audiences defecting from analog radio in order to enjoy the full frequency range and freedom from noise and distortion offered by home playback of CDs.

I was wrong. I should have noticed that the audience for home video seems content to watch VHS tapes that have poor resolution, blotchy color, and grainy audio. By analogy, I should have understood that an increase in audio fidelity would not matter all that much. I had gotten caught up in the general hype about the wonders of digital-quality sound. Since the first edition, my students and I conducted a simple survey at a local record store that asked which features of CDs were most important to people. Good fidelity and lack of noise and distortion were not high on the list. What people liked most were the ability to program selected tracks, the fact that the discs were less likely to be harmed by mishandling than cassettes or LPs, and the ease of storage.

Also in the interim, a system was demonstrated that would allow broadcasting of digital audio in the same bands broadcasters now use for their analog service. When the general changeover to digital broadcasting occurs sometime in the next few years, the shift may be greeted with more of a whimper than a bang. Contrary to what I said in the first edition, analog FM stations may be around for a long time to come. However, most AM stations will have every reason to jump to digital, because it will offer the chance to increase audience shares rather than see them continue to erode.

On the other hand, successful FMs will see many bottom-line reasons to maintain their analog signal. As former talk-oriented AMs convert to digital and begin airing high-fidelity music, we may see additional FMs converting to the news/talk category. FM may prove to be the perfect channel for the human voice (which is what some industry people have said—wishfully—about AM). The human voice demands neither the dynamic range nor the frequency response that music does. Voices on FM can sound very natural. As pointed out by the late veteran radio programmer Rick Sklar (1988), high commercial loads are more compatible with talk than with music: compare up to 18 commercial *minutes* on a talk station with as few as 7 *units* on some FM music stations. In the future, the analog FM music-format station could try to compensate for its lack of musical fidelity compared to digital by surrounding the music it airs with the elements that radio has traditionally handled well: entertaining talk. Just as some AMs have succeeded by generating audience involvement through their air personalities rather than relying on the music, in the same way the analog FMs of the future could move farther from being "music utilities," and could instead recommit themselves to "show business" as the only business to be in.

But the heading "digital audio" now refers to a much wider range of delivery systems than it did in 1990. Several of these new "channels" deserve a closer look.

Special audio services delivered via cable have not seemed to make much of an impact, but the same services received via direct-broadcast satellite certainly have done so. There are about 200 subcarrier audio services on C-band satellites—many of them radio station and network audio feeds. Then there are the newer, specialized music services such as DMX and Music Choice. Eddy Hartenstein, the president of DirecTV—a highly successful direct-to-home, small-dish, satellite broadcasting system—is delighted that one of the most popular services he offers is Music Choice, a 28-channel menu of digital audio. The president of Digital Cable Radio, the programmer of the Music Choice service, says that when DirecTV sold the service on an a la carte basis for a couple of months (rather than bundling it with basic programming), it outsold every other service offered (Beacham, 1995b). DMX is available to 40 million listeners spread across the planet, and offers up to 120 different audio channels, some as niche-targeted as "Swiss Folk," "Chinese," and "Flemish." Even the venerable Muzak company entered the residential music market by partnering with subscription TV program provider EchoStar to deliver 30 channels of digital music (Fuller, 1996).

The satellite-delivered music services are still examples of "push"-type media. The "pull" media—services that are ordered up individually—are centered around computers, and there are rapid developments in this field. For example, software such as RealAudio allows instant playback of Internet audio content, rather than waiting for it to download. Thus, what RealAudio offers the computer user is the chance to receive audio-on-demand, along with links to a series of on-screen visuals (Beacham, 1995a). Radio stations have begun to use such software to distribute their audio around the globe via the Internet, but so have other purveyors of audio such as record companies, and groups like the Internet Underground Music Archive, an organization that tries to expose alternative music using neither radio nor record company channels.

Radio Broadcast Data Service (RBDS), the subcarrier technology that has been marketed to consumers as Smart-Radio, offers a way for standard broadcast listeners to find a station by format, receive paperless coupons, and read scrolling messages about what is coming up next. RBDS (also called RDS) is at the heart of experiments with radio-on-demand. It was Alan Box of EZ Communications who pursued the idea of equipping computers with radio receivers and using the RBDS subcarrier to cue a computer to store non-real-time content on a hard drive for later retrieval by its owner. Greg Riker, director of advanced consumer technology at Microsoft, worked with Box to test the concept in 1994 in Seattle. By using information about what was upcoming from several stations' RBDS data stream, and comparing that with a computer profile of the information and entertainment desired by the user, the system was able to save a personalized program that could be played back at the user's convenience. Obviously, such a system will also make it possible to target commercials only to the most likely buyers (Chichester, 1995; Wilke, 1994). It will be a simple matter for the software to scan the offerings of lots of stations, meaning that a higher chance of the user getting the desired content—but at the radio station of zero station loyalty. For all intents and purposes, will be little difference between the future broadcast radio "listener" just described and a software "smart agent" searching the Internet for desired content.

In addition, the Smart-Radio components can be included in a computer, to deliver stereo radio and digitally transmitted text and data to the desktop. Listeners at their computers can select call letters or station frequency; they can choose by music format, artist's name, or title of a song; and they can preset up to 99 stations ("Smart-Radio Targets PC Users," 1995).

RBDS/Smart-Radio depends on the audience buying new radios for broadcast reception, and, at this writing, sales have been rather slow. And the tasks of Internet searching and setting up the software for a RBDS-based system assume that ordinary people want to go through that much work to hear specific content. Some do, but others will be happy to continue to receive what good programmers send out to the general public. As Gary Fisher, Vice President for Advertising Sales and Affiliate Marketing for the Sony Warner Networks said at an Arbitron-sponsored think-tank on the future of radio in 1994:

> Recent history has shown that when radio has tried to become technology-driven rather than programming-driven . . . the results haven't been that pretty . . . the ad dollars, no matter how complex the landscape, will continue to chase the audience and the audience will continue to chase after the programming . . . . Build it and they will come—or build it and they will cume. (p. 16)

It is clear that digital audio is moving from scarcity to ubiquity; someday, it will be analog audio that is rare. But in the meantime, while analog and digital audio coexist, there will be an even greater number of competitors for the radio listener's ears. How many minutes a day will be devoted solely to radio? The answer will not lie so much in the technical improvements to audio reproduction as in improvements to the product the audience is seeking—programming that is responsive to the listener's needs.

## The Role of Radio in an Increasingly Visual Electronic Society

Whatever the future shape of radio's technical facilities turns out to be, and regardless of how many challengers there are for the audience's attention, it is clear that radio broadcasting will continue as an important component of the U.S. mass media for a long time to come. However, it is also clear that that role is changing.

I believe that the agenda-setting and cultivation functions of the mass media are today carried out most pervasively through entertainment rather than through news and public affairs programming. (That is one reason why radio news operations are not covered in depth in this book.) Just the music aired each day on radio, and on MTV and its clones, makes hundreds of millions of impressions about lifestyles, mores, social problems, and the like, tying in to our personal stories at a level of consciousness that is near dreaming. What our society believes, and what it aspires to, is today shaped as much by the songs on the nation's playlists as by newspapers and news magazines. For people under 21, and certainly for those under 18, one of the most powerful "editorial" voices in the United States is MTV—because of the lifestyles and the attitudes the network portrays. Radio now often plays a supporting role to television in the generation of opinion among teenagers, but because of its sheer ubiquity, radio is still influential.

In an increasingly visual age, MTV has become a significant part of the young generation's ritual drama entertainment. Someday, music videos without lyrics (instrumentals) may be as prevalent as those with words, because visuals will tell the story—because the visuals themselves are what critic Kenneth Burke (1966) called the "visible tangible material embodiments" (p. 362) of the actual objects. There need not be description. When watching video, we think we see the thing itself.

## Video and Computers Are Changing the Commonality of Community

Marshall McLuhan suggested in the 1960s that television was creating a global village with itself as the communal fire, and events such as the 1969 moon landing—which was viewed by billions of people around the world—seemed to bear that out. Then, with the "cocooning" of the 1980s, many villagers chose to stoke their own fires via the videocassette recorder (VCR), by timeshifting network fare, or by playing rental tapes. Now, in the mid-1990s, as we practice what one futurist called "armored cocooning," some have retreated even from the TV and VCR; the extent of the commonality of a mass media video event is now in question. Today the electronic hearth might be a TV connected to a satellite dish that receives several hundred channels. But it is increasingly likely to be a video monitor connected to a PC on the Internet.

Some have argued that the Internet represents a whole new kind of electronic community. But genuine community includes the sharing of a space and the possibility of touch. It almost always involves speech. In some ways, the cybercommunity of people typing messages to each other via the Internet is not very different from the medieval monasteries in which individual monks copied manuscripts. The bottom line is still the n of words and the solitariness of each lone respondent.

sential to appreciate how things have changed for radio, and for society at large, because we are now living in an age dominated by electronically generated visual information. We have perhaps found it easiest to ignore the most obvious change: Today, many Americans spend a substantial part of their day at work or in school viewing images on a computer screen, then in the evening spend still more time viewing images on a television screen. In the computer age we have—with very little fanfare—added a second "screen" to our lives, and have allotted considerable time to watching it. Note, too, that the computer is the second consumer electronics item that supplies both audio and video—the television set being the other. That fact may also contribute to a sense that radio is a "partial" or "incomplete" medium.

For radio, the implications of that additional screen time can be profound. Consider first that the computer screen is viewed close up as compared to television, and thus the images occupy a much greater percentage of the field of view. That results in a sense of immersion, which is made more complete by a pair of desktop speakers connected to the computer's sound card. By supplying both audio and video, the multimedia computer effectively displaces traditional radio listening from the workplace and from the home entertainment area. But it also accustoms the user to that greater sensory immersion. Immersion in a visually and aurally rich environment becomes the norm. By contrast, radio is like the TV or the computer with the brightness turned all the way down.

Computer software is designed to give the user a sense of control over the objects the computer manages. As graphical user interfaces such as the MacIntosh operating system and later Microsoft Windows became de facto standards, users became acclimated to perceiving situations and producing changes in them by manipulating visual presentations. We no longer type codes, or punch function keys, or type in words. We move little icons instead. Usually, we are not reacting to sounds, and at this writing, most of us are not interacting vocally with a machine equipped for speech recognition, except in a limited way. We do not interact with our computers by using speech and music, which are the languages of radio.

The change the computer has made in what we can do with what we see has also been very profound. Computers bring a new way of thinking about the physical world. No longer are curious children concerned with taking apart real physical objects if they can see them taken apart and put back together in exploded views on a screen. The manipulative skills that used to go into turning a screwdriver now are put into moving a joystick or mouse to produce changes in visual icons. Visual icons can be featured on a computer screen all the time it is running, just as network logos appear continuously on a corner of the TV image. If radio ran its logos—its station IDs and jingles—continuously, nobody would listen. A͟i does not have an aural equivalent of the ideogram; a written symͰ represents an idea or object directly, as a computer icon does. The r ͺuse-driven or touch-screen-selected icons that operate computer software today may be precursors of a time when we will do much of our communicating via ideograms, avoiding the written and spoken word altogether. But even if that day is far off, this point is supremely important in the future of radio: Today, children learn to use their hands to make changes in what they see. They press buttons on a TV tuner and the picture changes. Yes, they can adjust stereos and tune radios that way too, but only in this age has it become so easy for children to manipulate their visual environment so exactly. In the previous 50 years of TV, all it was possible to do was change channels and alter the volume. Cable brought more channels but still no interaction. VCRs brought more choices about content and when it was viewed, but still no interaction. Computers bring all of that, plus interaction. Today, computers invite users to create their own visual environments. Not just choose a picture, but create an environment.

Music videos, digital audio, an increasingly visual society. This is the arena in which radio today and in the future must compete for its share of the public's attention. And it is in this context that the rest of this book unfolds.

## MAJOR POINTS

1. It is sometimes difficult to tell, when working in a mass medium, just what its special niche is. For example, the unique thing local daily newspapers do is door-to-door delivery.

2. Today's listener has many choices beside radio, so when he or she turns to radio, it is as a demand-access consumer—someone who is accustomed to getting what he or she wants to hear when he or she wants to hear it.

3. The station that is most vulnerable to replacement by cassettes and CDs programmed by the listener is the "music utility"—unless the station backs up the usual claims of "most music" with clearly stated proof. A "What's your favorite medium?" survey can tell you how replaceable by cassettes and CDs your station is.

4. *Mass appeal* need not mean doing what the other guys do. Mass appeal stations do not have to settle for the lowest common denominator. Narrowly targeted stations can succeed if they continuously ask themselves "What does the listener really want?"

5. *Consistent quality* is a pair of words that do not belong together in radio. Quality radio programming must always include inconsistency if it

is going to work as well tomorrow as it does today. Consistency eventually leads to boredom.

6. For many younger listeners, the strong visual imagery of most music videos makes radio airplay seem weak by comparison. As TV increases its share of music listening time, radio audiences in cars and other places where TV is not feasible will take on added importance.

7. What our society believes, and what it aspires to, is today shaped as much by the songs on the nation's music video playlists as by newscasts, newspapers, and magazines. For people under the age of 18, MTV is one of the nation's most powerful editorial voices—and they never air any editorials per se. Among teenagers, radio now plays a supporting role to television in the generation of opinion.

8. The human speaking voice is reproduced well on FM, so FMs may eventually displace AMs in doing talk programming, especially when music-formatted stations go digital.

9. Satellite-delivered music services, real-time digital audio on the Internet, and radio-on-demand systems are all potential competitors for the traditional broadcast radio listener.

10. The "armored cocooning" of the mid-1990s features an "electronic hearth" with either a television set connected to a satellite receiver, or a computer connected to the Internet. Either way, the extent of the commonality of mass-mediated experience has begun to wane.

11. Today, children learn to use their hands to make changes in what they see. Both with TV tuners, and with computer joysticks and mice, children can manipulate and even create their visual environment with great precision. This capability is unmatched by radio.

# CHAPTER 3

# *Radio's Attributes*

Among the objective answers to the question "What does radio do?" are these. It plays music. It tells the news. It predicts the weather and warns about traffic. It raises issues of public importance. It puts another voice in the room. As a result of those objective functions, the subjective perception is that it entertains (music), informs (news), empowers (weather and traffic), socializes (public issues), and befriends (companionship).

If we look at what audiences use radio for, one cluster of answers keeps occurring: entertainment, relaxation, and enjoyment. Dolf Zillmann and Jennings Bryant (1986) suggested that entertainment may be "crudely defined" as "any activity designed to delight and, to a smaller degree, enlighten" (p. 303). Thirty years ago, two researchers published books that were among the first to acknowledge—and even celebrate—the fact that mass media audiences are usually in it for the fun. These two books are worth an extended look at this point in our discussion of the business radio is in.

## MENDELSOHN: THE POSITIVE VALUES OF MASS ENTERTAINMENT

Harold Mendelsohn published his landmark book *Mass Entertainment* in 1966; but its lessons are still largely unlearned even by the broadcasters who underwrote the research through a grant from the National Association of Broadcasters. In its 200 well-written pages, Mendelsohn laid out every argument broadcasters would ever need to defend themselves from the charge that their programming was deleterious, wasteful, trash, and so on. But more than being a defense of the value of mass entertainment, Mendelsohn's book was an explanation of the positive values to be derived from entertainment delivered by mass media. Because the majority of the airtime of most radio stations is devoted to entertainment rather than hard information or high culture, it is important to have Mendelsohn's ideas in mind before proceding with the present discussion.

In his first chapter, Mendelsohn examined "The Attack on Entertainment" and made the case that the majority of Americans rejects the negative valuation put on entertainment by the more "responsible" sectors of society. Mendelsohn (1966) said that "It is from the gratifications that the mass population receives from entertainment that our knowledge about the phenomenon must spring—not from the assumptions of our guardians of social values" (p. 33). Clearly, Mendelsohn's point of view is with the consumer of the mass media, just as it is in this book.

## "Relaxation," Not "Escape"

In a second chapter that explored the sociological functions of mass entertainment, Mendelsohn said that "In sociological terms . . . in contemporary American society mass entertainment is equated with the 'good life'" (p. 50). In refuting those sociologists and psychologists who think that those seeking entertainment are actually trying to escape negative factors in their daily living, Mendelsohn said "For the most part . . . the pursuit of entertainment in modern America can be seen more as a 'running toward' what Americans have defined for themselves as 'the good life' rather than as a 'running away' from an allegedly unrewarding social-economic life" (p. 51). A later part of the chapter dealt with *relaxation*—a term that is highly associated with radio listening by virtually all audiences.

> The word "relaxation" is not synonymous with "idleness"—either sociologically or psychologically. Rather, "relaxation" suggests a mere diminution of action—not an absence of it; it suggests a slackening rather than an abolition of work; an abatement of activity rather than a cessation of it. "Relaxation" . . . implies a sort of fruitful idleness that is not *completely* divorced from work and serious pursuits. (p. 70)

### Listening as Work Accompaniment

It is a given that a huge amount of radio listening is done as an accompaniment to actual work; the point to be added here is that the listener who identifies just listening to the radio as a "relaxing" activity may actually feel guilty that he or she is not paying attention to some job that needs doing. Although there is evidence that people (especially better educated people) feel more guilty about having "wasted" time with television than with radio, it is important to realize that radio listening is often thought of as work accompaniment rather than as entertainment in its own right.

Thinking of radio listening as work accompaniment—even if the listener is not actually working but believes he or she ought to be—is different from thinking of radio as a "background" audio service. Radio as work accompaniment can be very much a foreground service, with lots of talk and personality. This is true because much of the work that radio accompanies is performed by people toiling as individuals, and not even necessarily in the workplace, but in the car, in the home, or in an office cubicle. Whereas TV viewing—especially in the evenings—often takes place with a surrounding group, most radio listening is done individually.

## Solitary Versus Social Listening Experiences

The individuality of the experience of listening makes radio audiences more like readers of printed matter than like television viewers. The listening experience, like the reading experience, is almost always solitary. Yet, as Mendelsohn said of all media:

> it is quite evident that mass entertainment allows the individual to share with others a wide variety of events of common interest and concern. The seeker of mass media-derived entertainment uses the entertainment experience to bind him with others who are similarly disposed. (p. 77)

The next day at the office, there is talk about what the guy said on the radio, what they wrote in the paper, what she did on TV. And yet, radio—because it is heard individually—lacks some of the impact of those media that are experienced with a social group, such as the movies. Mendelsohn said:

> All of us have experienced the sense of embarrassment that accompanies a loud outburst of laughter when we witness something funny while we are alone. This inhibition about the expression of elementary emotion is relieved by witnessing others doing the exact same thing. In an entertainment audience the cues for releasing emotional reaction are reciprocal, and consequently they enhance the enjoyment process. We need not feel embarrassed about a sudden surfacing of our deepest feelings in situations where we can see the same process occurring all about us. (p. 79)

We have such group experiences at the movies and attending the theater, and to a lesser extent when watching television with others. But because we generally listen to radio alone, we probably feel more inhibited about reacting to some of what we hear. This needs to be qualified, however.

...entioned being embarrassed by laughing out loud when ...same time, many of us would be glad to be alone if the emo-...experiencing causes us to cry. The difference is one of social ...example, in our society, laughter is usually a group experience, wh... ears are private. And although crying may not seem to be as pleasurable as laughter, the opportunity for the private release of such deep emotions may well be one of radio's assets. Both Mendelsohn and I have more to say later about radio reinforcing a listener's moods, but for now it is important to affirm that, because radio is not usually listened to in a social group, and if it hopes to have the emotional impact of media such as television and film, radio probably needs to work harder at helping the individual to express otherwise repressed responses.

## STEPHENSON: THE PLEASURES OF PLAY

In the first chapter of his book *The Play Theory of Mass Communication,* William Stephenson (1967) commented that he was puzzled when he began his research in 1958 that so few people were studying mass communications entertainment, rather than mass communication as an agent of persuasion. Stephenson thus shared the same view as Mendelsohn: that mass entertainment is worthy of study. Information theory alone, according to Stephenson, can explain neither the "social control" that is manifested in the formation of public opinion, nor the "convergent selectivity" on which advertising is based. What Stephenson proposed to fill that void was his play theory. Stephenson said, "Communication is not just the passing of information from a source to the public; it is better conceived as a recreation of information ideas by the public, given a hint by way of a key symbol, slogan, or theme" (p. 8). Stephenson asked, "What, indeed, does a person say to himself; what conversations does he carry on in his own mind? This is likely to be crucial in any consideration of the effects of mass communication upon him from whatever source" (p. 9). Stephenson's concept that communication is "a re-creation of information ideas by the public, given a hint by way of key symbol, slogan or theme" is important. It underscores the subjectivity of the mass audience, while also stressing that there are common symbols and themes that may trigger common responses.

### Socially Controlled Publics and Existential Mass Audiences

Later, in the chapter on air personalities, the late Arthur Godfrey is cited for his breakthrough idea that radio announcers should not try to address the mass audience the way a platform speaker talks to a crowd but rather should talk to each individual individually. Stephenson made a distinction

between the public (in the sense of a group that comes to a consei
ion under social control) and a mass audience, whose members
free to think as they please than ever before. The difference in announcing
styles, pre- and post-Godfrey (discussed later in chapter 8, this volume),
may be akin to the difference Stephenson drew between passing information to the public in order to form public opinion and letting the individual member of the mass audience, carrying on conversations in his
or her own mind, bring his or her own set of notions and experiences to
bear. He pointed out that in a mass-appeal periodical, as in all advertising,
"ideologies are ignored and personalities and social character are reinforced"
(p. 39). Stephenson said, "It is my thesis that the daily withdrawal of people
into the mass media in their after hours . . . is a step in the *existential* direction, that is, a matter of subjectivity which invites freedom where there had
been little or none before" (p. 45). Far from condemning the vehicles of
mass media entertainment as having a "narcotizing" effect on the audience,
Stephenson applauded the opportunity for the individual to exist for himself
rather than for the public.

## Definitions of *Play*

Stephenson also made an extended attempt at defining *play:*

> Playing is *pretending,* a stepping outside the world of duty and responsibility. Play is an *interlude* in the day. It is not ordinary or real. It is *voluntary* and not a task or moral duty. It is in some sense *disinterested,* providing a temporary satisfaction. Though attended to with seriousness, it is not really important. . . . Play is *secluded,* taking place in a particular place set off for the purpose in time or space: it has a beginning and an end. The child goes into a corner to play house. And play is a free activity; yet it absorbs the player completely. The player is unself-conscious if he plays with the proper enjoyment.
>
> Play has been explained by psychologists as abreactive, wish-fulfillment, instinctive, and much else. All that seems certain is that play is "fun." (p. 46)

It is worth examining Stephenson's points more closely for a moment before proceeding. Most people who listen to the radio do not think of themselves as "pretending" in the sense of stepping outside the world of duty and responsibility. This is because much radio listening is done precisely while performing some duty or attending to some responsibility. That difference is also important in the other factors Stephenson cited. Radio listening is not an interlude, because it is more likely to be an accompaniment. Like play, it is voluntary and disinterested. But it is not usually secluded—radio listening succeeds in part because it can be done almost anywhere. And it is not as absorbing as his description of play—at least not most of the time.

TV, or see only the words on paper as when reading a newspaper or magazine. A radio listener is still able to utilize the full field of vision, which is why radios (unlike TVs) are legal in the front seats of cars. And, although the radio listener can practice selective perception, and can decide just to hear rather than to listen actively, still, if anything is audible, the listener hears it all at once. To the listener, then, radio is encompassing.

## Radio Is Open-Ended

A third element (which radio shares with the printed page so long as it is without pictures) is a lack of closure. Stan Freberg made the case for radio's open-endedness against television's complete closure when on his late-1950s CBS radio show (and later for the Radio Advertising Bureau) he constructed a gigantic chocolate sundae in Lake Michigan. He tagged his famous sound effects tour-de-force with the statement "Radio stretches the imagination." A young guest asked, "Doesn't television stretch the imagination?" To which Freberg replied, "Up to 21 inches, yes!" The point is that television visuals (and the magazine or newspaper illustration) appear to be so detailed that they leave little for the viewer to imagine. Their specificity does not allow much viewer participation in the generation of imagery, because most of it is supplied. That is *closure*. Radio, on the other hand, is open-ended with regard to the listener's imagery.

## Radio Is a Fertilizer of Fantasies and Daydreams

As a result of making low attention demands, while being pervasive in the physical and psychological space around the listener, and being open-ended with regard to the listener's imagery, radio becomes a prime breeding ground for daydreams and fantasies. Consider this: No one sits down and works to come up with daydreams and fantasies. But daydreams and fantasies are a necessary and pleasant part of everyone's psychic existence. It takes a positive effort at concentration to keep them from happening. Left to its own devices, the human mind naturally slips into daydreaming and fantasizing. Ronald W. Roschke in his "Dream/Brain/Text: The Media–Brain Connection in Mental Processing of Texts" (1987) said:

> I would suggest that sleep-mode consciousness is *not* uniquely a property of sleep, but rather represents a way of thinking also accessible to the brain during its waking hours. The most obvious example would be the *daydream*. Although I am wide awake when I daydream, the quality of a daydream is more similar to a real dream than it is to waking consciousness. I am not aware of my daydream until it is over. I never find myself saying, "Oh, here I am going into a daydream." Rather, I suddenly realize that I have been daydreaming; my mind was off somewhere else. I was not attending to the

und me. In fact, in many ways my mind did exactly what it does
. What I was "seeing" was an image in my memory. My ego was
, in that room with those people. I was hearing what they were
uld "see" them. But the quality of sight is like that of a nocturnal
dream. It is a different kind of seeing from, say, looking at a picture. It is not
really an hallucination but more like the memory of an appearance. And yet,
it is not simply the *memory* of a scene either, for in my daydream I can see
things that I have never seen in "real life." New "memories" can be forged
out of existing images as they are woven together into a matrix. (pp. 164–165)

The very *in*attention that radio listening allows is the *modus operandi* of the daydreamer. If the radio professional comes to understand that radio's strongest asset is the way it can be ignored, and realizes that the business of radio is to provide fertilizer for daydreams and fantasies, then inattention will stop seeming to be a threat. It is shown later that dial-hopping—the behavior that drives programmers crazy in their quest to avoid tuneout—is merely the technique the listener uses to maintain a certain daydream or fantasy.

## LESSONS ABOUT ENTERTAINMENT VALUES FROM COMPUTER GAMES

Since the advent of arcade, home video, and computer games, the electronic game has become another competitor for the listener's attention. If we could understand how the better of those games allow an exchange of the best efforts of a game designer with the best efforts of a game player, it might be possible to try to emulate that exchange in a radio format.

First, we must define what we are *not* talking about. We are not talking about games whose main objective is shooting, gobbling, or escaping—in other words, games whose main appeal is conflict and competition and whose main skill is eye–hand coordination. To put it another way, we are not interested in a game that depends mainly on positioning (the familiar joystick) and "zapping" (the familiar FIRE button).

### Challenge and Control

It may seem arbitrary to dismiss such games because they were long the staple of arcade units and home video game cartridges. But these seemed to appeal most especially to children and especially to adolescent boys. Theorists have speculated that they may be zapping pimples, siblings, parents, teachers, or even the arms race as they hammer away at the controls. Whatever the object of disdain, it is clear that the conflict-competition

appeal is finding expression in a safe (non-ego-threatening)
which the player can attempt to gain enough skill to ultimately
overcome the adversary. Most such games are designed to i.
challenge of the action as the player's skills increase, with t.
arranged to pay bigger rewards at higher skill levels. Thus, the b _ginning
player knows that he or she will be eased into the game, that the middle
levels of play will be more difficult (but that increasing skill should match
them), and that the most difficult later levels can only be reached when
he or she has mastered the intermediate ones. There is a combination of
continually increasing *challenge* presented by the game, and continually
increasing *control* as exercised by the player. These are the prerequisites for
the "flow" experience, which is discussed in the next chapter. It is partly an
attempt to gain that sense of *control* that keeps the kid pumping tokens into
the arcade machines. It is difficult, but with enough practice, most such
games can be mastered, and thus the player is rewarded with the sense
that there is something in his life that he *can* control.

**Fantasy Fulfillment**

A sense of control is not the only prize video games provide. Fantasy
fulfillment is clearly another strong appeal. Willam Hawkins, founder of
Electronic Arts, a computer software company, said:

> A lot of people like playing with computers because they gain control . . . but
> at an emotional level it's a lot more interesting to think of situations where
> you're *not* in total control. That's what it's like when you're dreaming. At
> some level your mind is directing the action, but there is a feeling of helpless-
> ness. You can't alter the script; your brain won't let you. It will be like watch-
> ing a movie for the first time, except that you'll be the hero and have to make
> decisions. . . . Everything you do in life is a situation in which there are sepa-
> rate players involved, and there are separate decisions you have to make. . . .
> There's a competitive feeling and maybe there's a score—but maybe there
> isn't. That's the kind of fantasy fulfillment you can get out of a computer,
> which is what we're really after. (Hawkins, as cited by Eckels, 1983, p. 18)

If Hawkins is right about the appeal of fantasy fulfillment, then radio has
been on the right track for a long time. Because the only direct control the
radio listener can exercise over programmming is to turn the radio off or to
change stations, good programmers have attempted to thwart even that
limited amount of control by giving the listener reasons to stay tuned
longer. It appears that the best of those reasons to stay tuned would be
ones promising fantasy fulfillment—through the music, through the presentational style, and through features, contests, and promotions.

Perhaps the person who seeks pleasure in games is trying to achieve a temporary escape from the real world into a fantasy one, hoping to achieve a measure of control in the fantasy world that may be either greater or less than the control he or she has in real-life situations. This person is different from the news/talk listener. The news/talk devotee seeks a temporarily deeper connection with the real world and all its problems, partly out of the sense that simply knowing about something is the beginning of gaining control over it. Yet the news/talk listener may also be deriving fantasy fulfillments in hearing about people, places, and events he or she could not possibly have known otherwise, and in which the "situations where you're NOT in total control" (in Hawkins' words) are the norm.

### Hard to Master

When they are done well, both the fantasy-fulfilling music presentation and the situation-immersing news/talk presentation follow one of the prime rules of the video game industry: "make it easy to learn and hard to master" (Hawkins, cited by Eckels, 1983, p. 14). Ideally, anything that aspires to be mass entertainment should be apparently easy to engage on its surface, while the content provides plenty of challenge. (This follows the "challenge-but-not-*too*-tough" formula for the "flow" experience, too, as is seen in chapter 4, this volume.) Another way of saying that is, the form (or format) should be familiar and nonthreatening, whereas what the format conveys (the content) should be endlessly novel and at least moderately difficult to master. In radio terms, that means that when the format is really working, it disappears. The content takes over. This is congruent with the precept that the business of radio is *in*attention, in the sense that the framework should be so transparent that only the content shows. The listener must be engaged at the level of a pleasant, voluntary competition—like playing a game.

The point has been made that it is not enough for a game to provide fast action leading to a sense of control. A good game might also provide a high degree of fantasy fulfillment. But are even those two enough? According to one of the original gurus of video game design, Atari's Chris Crawford, most skill and action games are dismissable "as so much 'candy' that gives a quick thrill and nothing more" (Immel, 1982, p. 57). In pop music formats, much of that "candy" is in the music. Some people have even called adolescent-appeal music "ear candy." Other format elements can be candy, too: jingles, promos, contests, announcer chatter, even the news when it is actually comprised mostly of soft features. There is nothing inherently wrong with ear candy; we all have at least a slight sweet tooth. But a station that does not provide much substance is not going to attract and hold an adult audience for long. In other words, fantasy cannot be total escape, and escape never means blandness. Formats that do their best to be inoffensive wind up being unengaging because they offer too little challenge to the listener.

## Something You Walk Away With

Then what *are* the elements of a video game that appeal to an adult? Chris Crawford mentioned these: "something to challenge a mature person with a sense of judgment. . . . Computer games, or any game really, should have a point, should mean something, and should have something you walk away with. It should make you a better person." (Immel, 1982, p. 57) Crawford said that the best games blur the distinction between learning and entertainment. Indeed, software publisher Electronic Arts asked of magazine readers in its premiere advertising, "Can a computer make you cry?" A partial answer to that query was provided by the company's advertising brochure, which stated the following:

> We are learning, for instance, that we are all more entertained by the involvement of our imaginations than by passive viewing and listening. We are learning that we are better taught by experience than by memorization. And we are learning that the traditional distinctions—between art and entertainment and education—don't always apply. (*We See Farther,* 1983)

## MAJOR POINTS

1. As a mass entertainment medium, radio provides relaxation and work accompaniment, information, socialization, and companionship, but the unique thing radio does is encourage *in*attention.
2. Radio listening is not done for escape so much as for relaxation.
3. Stephenson said that mass media such as radio allow the individual an opportunity to exist for himself or herself rather than for the public.
4. Radio listening affords the simple pleasures of play—taking pleasure in being absorbed in novel fantasies and moods.
5. Radio is low-demand, aurally encompassing, and open-ended with regard to the listener's imagery.
6. Radio is best thought of as a fertilizer of fantasies and daydreams.
7. Dial-hopping is the technique listeners use to keep a certain daydream or fantasy going.
8. Radio can take lessons from video game designers. Video games offer challenge, control, and fantasy fulfillment, but most of all they are something that is easy to learn yet hard to master. There has to be substance, not just fluff. The best games give you something you walk away with.

# CHAPTER 4

## *What Radio Audiences Want*

Audiences are the target of a lot of research. For example, a survey found that 40% of men read on the toilet, whereas only 14% listen to the radio there (Allen, 1984). Format-oriented books about radio programming tend to treat audiences as different flavors of demographic pie—that is, they describe what kind of audience tends to be generated by which kind of programming. This chapter explores audiences from a consumerist standpoint. It takes a look at the listener's needs, desires, and expectations, some of them quite apart from the programming radio typically provides. Given the near-infinite variability of human nature, it would not be sensible to expect to find even a simple majority of radio listeners fitting most of the attributes that are described. Matching up formats with the listeners they generate is not the idea of this chapter. Instead, the idea is to describe what drives people to listen and respond to radio in the first place, by paying primary attention to human needs, desires, and expectations.

### FANTASIES AND DAYDREAMS

It is generally agreed that one of the entertainment functions of the mass media is to provide a means of escape from the real world, or, more positively, a means of relaxation through immersion in something else. The end of the last chapter stated that the real business of radio is to serve as a fertilizer of fantasies and daydreams. If so, then the following question might be asked: What are the daydreams that people commonly indulge in? A survey commissioned by the advertising agency D'Arcy Masius Benton & Bowles questioned 752 men and 798 women about their emotions, drives, and thoughts. The results under the heading "Have You Ever Imagined Yourself . . ." are shown in Table 4.1. A pattern begins to emerge in the table that shows men being more interested in risk-taking (note the prison camp escape difference) and athletic prowess (the Olympic medal), whereas women seem to be more interested in the caring that is shown in developing a cure for cancer and in the social acceptance that is reflected in winning an Academy Award™. These trends are borne out by another question that asked, "Which of these fantasy activities would you love to try?" (see Table 4.2). In Table 4.2, note that men continue to be risk-takers (hot-air balloon trip, African safari, white-water rafting, manned space flight, and skydiving) to a greater extent than women. Men's sexual aggressiveness appears to be about four times greater than women's in regard to visiting a nudist colony, and about six times greater in terms of a sexual encounter with a stranger. Women, on the other hand, like to imagine themselves in social situations that offer glamour and prestige (gambling at a Monte Carlo casino, having dinner at the White House, attending the Cannes film festival).

Interestingly, when asked what their greatest source of pleasure or satisfaction was, fantasies were not in the picture. Combining the scores for both men and women, 36% said their greatest pleasure came from their children. Twenty-eight percent said their greatest source of satisfaction was their marriage, 21% chose hobbies, 19% said vacations, 18% mentioned friends, and only 17% chose sexual relationships as their greatest source of pleasure ("Fears and Fantasies of the American Male," p. 48). Clearly, there is a considerable disparity between the actual sources of the respondents' pleasure and the sources of pleasure that they dream about. Media that supply a chance to daydream and fantasize help to bridge the

TABLE 4.1
Daydreams

|  | Men | Women |
|---|---|---|
| Saving someone's life | 77% | 75% |
| Finding a cure for cancer | 28% | 42% |
| Winning an Olympic medal | 43% | 24% |
| Accepting an Academy Award | 18% | 26% |
| Being President of the USA | 26% | 14% |
| Appearing on the cover of *Time* | 17% | 17% |
| Escaping from a prison camp | 24% | 08% |

*Note.* From "Fears and Fantasies of the American Male," 1987, August, *Men's Fitness,* p. 48. Copyright © 1987 by *Men's Fitness* magazine. Reprinted by permission.

TABLE 4.2
Fantasies

|  | Men | Women |
|---|---|---|
| Visit mainland China | 54% | 45% |
| Gamble in a Monte Carlo casino | 44% | 52% |
| Have dinner at the White House | 41% | 51% |
| Fly in a hot-air balloon | 48% | 39% |
| Go on an African safari | 54% | 33% |
| Camp in the wilderness | 53% | 31% |
| Go white-water rafting | 47% | 23% |
| Attend the Cannes film festival | 32% | 35% |
| Participate in a manned space flight | 44% | 20% |
| Appear on a TV talk show | 28% | 27% |
| Have a sexual encounter with a stranger | 31% | 05% |
| Go skydiving | 24% | 10% |
| Visit a nudist colony | 23% | 06% |

From "Fears and Fantasies of the American Male," 1987, August, *Men's Fitness*, p. 50. Copyright © 1987 by *Men's Fitness* magazine. Reprinted by permission.

gap between wishes and reality. That is why radio's job is to be a petri dish for daydreams.

**Pleasure Seeking**

A closer look at the *imagined* (fantasy) activities just listed shows that many of them have to do with the excitement of a challenging new situation. Conversely, those surveyed reported that the greatest sources of *actual* pleasure or satisfaction included children, marriage, hobbies, vacations, and friends—the sort of ongoing, low-key activities that might come under the heading of *relaxation*.

Fantasy, excitement, and relaxation are the three types of experiences that people typically seek in order to feel good, according to Harvey B. Milkman and Stanley G. Sunderwirth in their book, *Craving for Ecstasy: The Consciousness and Chemistry of Escape* (1987). Milkman and Sunderwirth explored the psychological and physiological reaction to mood-altering situations and to drugs in order to discover the actual sources of a person's pleasure—pleasure so intense that the seeking of it can become compulsive. For instance, although we tend to think that drugs are addictive, Milkman and Sunderwirth asserted:

> People do not become addicted to drugs or mood-altering behaviors as such, but rather to the sensations of pleasure that can be achieved through them. We repeatedly rely on three distinct types of experience to achieve feelings of

well-being: relaxation, excitement, and fantasy; these are the underpinnings of human compulsion. (p. xiv)

Later, the authors use the word *satiation* interchangeably with *relaxation*, and *arousal* as a synonym for *excitement*.

### Satiation/Arousal/Fantasy

Milkman and Sunderwirth defined each of the three types of ecstatic craving more closely. Those who seek relaxation/satiation might do such things as eat excessively, watch TV endlessly, or use sedative (depressant) drugs. Such people are looking for tranquility and ways to reduce their discomfort. Sometimes the discomfort they feel is their own hostility, and these behaviors provide a means of controlling it.

People who seek arousal actively confront a world they feel is hostile or threatening. To compensate for feelings of inferiority, they repeatedly demonstrate their physical or intellectual ability. Such people are often boastful and have an inflated sense of themselves. According to Milkman and Sunderwirth, "The sky diver's adrenaline rush is remarkably similar to the short, exhilarating jolt from a line of cocaine. Excessive risk takers often mix danger with drugs" (p. xiv).

Finally, people who crave fantasy often involve themselves in mystical or occult practices, and tend to make too much of accidental, random circumstances. They may seek a greater sense of spiritual or cosmic unity. Marijuana and hallucinogenic drugs are favored by such types.

### Receptive and Active Fantasy

Milkman and Sunderwirth, in their later chapter on "Mental Excursions," made a distinction between two types of fantasy:

> *Receptive* fantasy is the concentration on thoughts or pictures that have been produced by others, for example, watching television, reading a novel, or visiting a black-light poster display. *Active* fantasy is the production of images and thoughts that emerge spontaneously from one's own psyche. These may be highly representational and reality oriented, such as a person visualizing how to approach his or her employer, or they may be highly abstract and unrealistic, such as imagining the creation or destruction of the universe. (p. 122)

Without direct references to radio in that passage, Milkman and Sunderwirth nevertheless differentiated between the two fantasy modes in which today's radio broadcasting—and especially music—is perceived. For those who see music on video services such as MTV and then hear it on the radio, the mode is *receptive* fantasy, because such listeners are essentially replaying the video in their heads when they hear the audio. On the other hand, music that has either not had video connected with it or music whose videos have been forgotten may beget *active* fantasy, in which the listener develops images and thoughts from his or her own mind.

### The Radio "Connection"

Although radio listening is not specifically mentioned by Milkman and Sunderwirth, because it is one of the most pervasive of the mass media, it is an important source for fantasy, arousal, and relaxation. Dolf Zillmann and Jennings Bryant identified both *excitement* and *relaxation* as ends desired by mass media consumers (Zillmann & Bryant, 1986). Veteran communications researcher Percy Tannenbaum (1985) said "the basic element of entertainment is some heightening of emotional arousal or excitation" (p. 238). And research by Zillmann and Bryant (1985) into the arousal caused by both informative and entertainment television messages led to the development of an implicit continuum of stimulus categories and hierarchies, with the opposing ends labeled *nonarousing* and *arousing*. They found that nature films that emphasized grandeur were decidedly at the nonarousing end of the scale. Action, drama, comedy, and game shows tended to be moderately arousing, whereas highly violent and fear-evoking dramas were highly arousing.

In considering only popular music on the radio, it is striking that there have always been strong *fantasy* elements in lyrics about sex and romance, *arousal* in the strong rhythms and some of the lyrics, and *relaxation* in slow ballads and instrumentals. Radio talk has also featured all three types of experience: *fantasy* in the identification derived from imagining the fun-loving, personable disc jockey who plays your tunes, *arousal* in listening to other people's quirks or opinions on a telephone call-in show or in hearing a newscast, and *relaxation* in enjoying the familiar, consoling voice of a trusted local personality.

## PLEASURE AS PRODUCT, NOT BY-PRODUCT

So, radio stations are already supplying many of the mass-mediated sources of fantasy, arousal, and relaxation. The point is, they may not realize how much some of their listeners crave such experiences. To really be in the radio business is to be intentional about providing fantasy, excitement, or relaxation—or in some cases, all three. Fantasy, arousal, or relaxation are not by-products of radio listening; they *are* the product. The question then becomes this: How can radio assure that the listener experiences at least one of these pleasures? Fantasy, excitement, and relaxation are all complex concepts. A programmer cannot just put on a new record and assume that, say, arousal will result. Other audience behaviors and other programming factors will help determine that outcome.

## The Opponent-Process Model

One of the most basic of those audience behaviors, according to Milkman and Sunderwirth (1987), may be "the repeated pairing of opposite emotional experiences, and their underlying physiological counterparts." Some researchers believe that such pairings may be "the sustaining force behind all forms of human compulsion" (p. 104). This behavior, which is later referred to as the *opponent-process,* is a theory advanced by University of Pennsylvania psychologist Richard Solomon. Solomon's opponent-process theory of human motivation suggests that a life event that creates a powerful mood or feeling also causes an *opposing* biochemical process. The feelings of euphoria or happiness provided by drugs or life experiences are the things that initially motivate a person's behavior. But such mood-altering behavior continues (sometimes to the point of addiction) because the person tries to avoid the unpleasant sensations that result from the opposing biochemical process.

> In some addictions, for example, running, the initial experience of pain is followed by a highly pleasurable reaction, probably related to the release of pain-relieving endorphins. The addiction is maintained, at least in part, because runners develop a craving for the biochemical opposition to the primary activity. The opponent-process model may be used to explain the pleasure that some people apparently derive from inflicting pain on themselves or others, or from taking unnecessary risks through unsafe physical or sexual practices. (Milkman & Sunderwirth, 1987, p. 105)

Figure 4.1 shows what Milkman and Sunderwirth said is a predictable pattern of mood changes in a person who seeks alternating feelings of both arousal and satiation. The dashed baseline shows the person's typical style of coping with the world—neither aroused nor sated. The solid line shows the person's subjective feelings of arousal and satiation, rising above and dipping below the baseline. The dashed and dotted line shows the opposing biochemical process that was triggered by the rising sense of arousal—it is a sort of "mirror-image valley" to the peak representing arousal. The opponent biochemical process is what eventually brings the person "down" from the arousal peak. Milkman and Sunderwirth explained it this way:

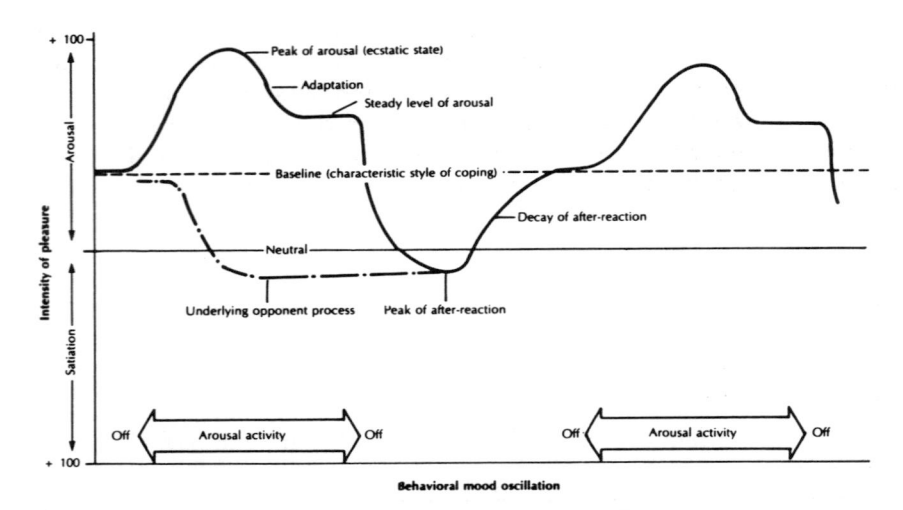

FIG. 4.1. "Opponent-process" model of mood changes (from Milkman & Sunderwirth, 1987, p. 106). Reprinted by permission of the publisher.

The peak of arousal intensity corresponds to the maximum state of biochemical excitement achieved during a risk-taking activity such as skydiving. The potent adrenaline rush, subjectively experienced as an ecstatic state, is followed by a period of adaptation in which the intensity of the pleasure declines, although the person continues to enjoy the exciting sensations of free-fall. Shortly after landing the diver feels a satiation aftereffect, the quality of which is very different (opposing) from the primary hedonic state. It is a sense of blissful relaxation, often bolstered by group celebration and alcohol intoxication. (Milkman & Sunderwirth, 1987, p. 105)

Note that the curve works for less hair-raising activities, too. What the skydiver experiences in a few minutes is experienced over an entire day by an alpine skier—arousal in skiing the mountain, satiation in the hot tubs and bars of *apres ski*. Milkman and Sunderwirth amplified the point this way:

A prolonged experience of stress and physical immobility from a traumatic automobile accident, for example, may be followed by an extended rebound of invigoration and euphoria. The opponent process leads to a waving pattern of mood alterations, which varies between people in terms of frequency and intensity. Some people seem to exist on a constant roller coaster of mood change, while others remain emotionally bland with only minor ripples in how they feel. (p. 105)

Milkman and Sunderwirth's assertions that ecstasy is achieved not by seeking some "middle-ground" mood, but by striving for peaks of arousal or satiation is supported by program-choice research done by Zillmann and Bryant (1985). Although they cited examples of people seeking positive, humorous programs to combat negative moods in order to achieve "excitatory homeostasis" (an equilibrium between under- and overarousal), they also stated that program selection "often serves the evocation of positive affect of the greatest possible intensity." Zillmann and Bryant also reported that their subjects "tended to overshoot the excitatory middle ground"—that is, they overcorrected for the mood they were trying to attain (pp. 172–173). It appears that few people want to live the life—or listen to programming—that deviates little from some flat-line average.

## BODY RHYTHMS

The mood alteration pattern described here is the product of (generally) conscious, willed sensation-seeking. But there are subtler mood swings that occur throughout everyone's day as a result of biological changes tied to "body time." Radio runs by the cliché "clock on the wall" that tells real time, and the arbitrary "clocks" that control radio's music and commercial presentation. Meanwhile, radio listeners are generally unaware of the program director's format "clock." Instead, the listener pays conscious attention to real time, remaining generally unconscious of the control being wielded by body time.

One of the better short treatments of the way body time operates is by Lee Weston. His book is titled *Body Rhythm: The Circadian Rhythms Within You* (1979). Weston was careful to separate his discussion of body time from the notion of *biorhythms*. Most scientists do not find much factual basis for biorhythm claims; on the other hand, the concepts of chronobiology, circadian rhythms, and photoperiodism all have strong scientific backing. The term *circadian rhythm* is the most commonly used term in the scientific community to describe the natural rhythms of the body, rhythms that keep a person in synchronicity with the world around him or her. Circadian rhythms are repeated daily. The 24-hour solar day is probably the primary "clock," according to Weston, but organisms can also anticipate changes in seasons by sensing changes in the length of daylight. This latter capacity is called *photoperiodism*. Both circadian (daily) rhythms and photoperiodic (seasonal) rhythms fall under the more general term of *chronobiology*—the way any living organism lives with and reacts to time cues.

### The Program Director as Chronobiologist

One of the things radio programmers need to develop is a greater sense of chronobiology. Once it is understood that the body reacts to time cues that cause us to think and feel and do certain things at regular times of the day and even at certain seasons of the year, then slavishness to either real time or to music "clocks" begins to seem arbitrary in both cases. Rather, the trick is to try to find out what abilities and moods the average listener has at various times of the day and at various seasons of the year, and then develop programming that coincides with them.

## Daily Rhythms

So far as the programmer is concerned, the most important rhythms are the daily, circadian ones. Some general findings have emerged from years of research by many different scientists. Among the general conclusions are these:

- When a person (males and females have similar rhythms) first arises from sleep, the person's mood is quiet, and distractions are not easily tolerated. Sensory perceptions are low. This would seem to indicate that listening to the radio—as a distraction—is not something most people really want to do *immediately* upon arising.
- Memory is best in the morning. It begins to slacken about noon, suggesting that oldies and nostalgia segments may work better in morning time slots.
- Mental skills such as number manipulation are best around noon. There is a measurable decline in the afternoon. Contests that require the listener to recall and use numbers might be best scheduled in the late morning.
- Many people feel like taking a short nap after lunch. If you wanted to program to complement that mood, you would play quieter music and have mellow announcing. To counteract it, your music should be livelier and your personalities more "forward."
- Sensory perception is at its peak in the early evening. This suggests that commercials that make strong use of sensory imagery will have greatest impact at that time.

These findings may not have direct application to every shred of music and every commercial message aired on the radio, because they are quite broad, but it seems wise to at least keep the general principles in mind.

## Rhythm Durations

Although most of the traits just described recur at about the same time, in younger people that time may be shifted toward the night, whereas it remains in the daytime for adults. In addition, a person's rhythms tend to shorten with age. According to Weston (1979): "Since younger people have longer free-running rhythms, they unconsciously want to stretch their rest–activity cycle and tend to become nightowls. Their parents, whose rhythms have shortened, favor the daytime" (p. 40). Thus, all of the "time-of-day" findings mentioned earlier may occur with an offset toward nighttime for younger listeners. Weston said that shifting the time when a circadian rhythm begins and ends is not too difficult, but changing its length is very hard to do. For example, it is possible to change the time when the usual patterns begin and end (as happens when traveling to a different time zone), but the length of each cycle is likely not to vary much. Therefore, it may be hard to pinpoint the exact time to start radio programming so that it coincides with the development of a given need in the listener, but once the activity is begun, the duration is easier to suggest. For example, Weston gave details of an experiment that tracked the intervals during which test subjects *consumed* various items. People lived in isolation in a room where food, drinks, and cigarettes were available. Without day–night time cues, their eating, drinking, and smoking tended to fall into a rhythmic pattern with an interval of 96 minutes (Weston, 1979). Weston said the 96-minute interval is close to a pattern found in sleep rhythms. But he also pointed out that during times of stress, or right after such events, the eating–drinking–smoking interval shrank to about 60 minutes.

**The 90-Minute Hour**

One conclusion that can be drawn from the aforementioned study is that relaxed listeners "consuming" the programming on a radio station might expect the programming to follow a cycle based not on the hour, but on 90 minutes. On the other hand, listeners subject to stress (perhaps in morning and evening drive) might feel more at home in a clock-like 1-hour cycle. The "sleep cycle" that Weston mentioned is explained by him further, with reference to an accompanying chart (see Fig. 4.2).

The term *REM* refers to a sleep stage in which there is rapid eye movement; the term *NREM* is a stage of nonrapid eye movement.

According to Weston:

> The first show of the night is brief. Typically, REM sleep lasts only about ten minutes the first time around. After it is over, the descent through the stages of NREM sleep begins again. The entire trip, going down from Stage I to Stage IV and coming back up, plus the ten-minute short-subject in REM, takes an average of about ninety minutes. Depending on the length of a night's sleep and individual sleep cycles, most people have four to seven such trips in the course of a night. (p. 54)

It is striking that both the daytime consumption patterns and nighttime sleep cycles start out at about 90 minutes in length. Weston was quoted earlier saying that the duration of circadian cycles is difficult to change.

48                    4. WHAT RADIO AUDIENCES WANT

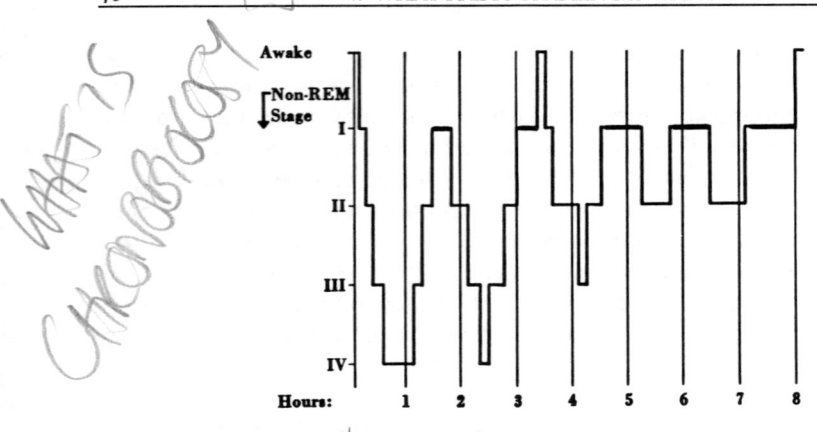

FIG. 4.2. The nightly sleep cycle, from *Body rhythm: The circadian rhythms within you* (Copyright © 1979 by L. Weston. Reprinted by permission of Harcourt Brace Jovanovich, Inc).

This suggests that listeners would normally be expecting radio to program to them in roughly 90-minute cycles, except during those times when stress reduces the period to about 60 minutes.

## STRUCTURE

The desire to be able to perceive a structure and order to the programming is generally acknowledged. And although there are stations that feature an apparently random or structure-free method of presenting music, no station goes so far toward randomness and chaos that they cut off songs in the middle, or air only the last 12 seconds of a newscast, or announce their call sign by picking alphabet letters at random. Thus, even so-called "freeform" stations still have a lot of structure in their presentation; they simply allow more leeway in music selection.

Long ago, Aristotle realized that there is pleasure in orderliness rather than chaos and that classic drama derives its impact in part from a certain wavelike structure that seems to move toward chaos, then return back to normalcy. And even though radio drama per se is not the subject, Aristotelian dramatic structure is shown later to have a lot to do with a listener's expectations about "what happens when" on the radio.

### Aristotelian Structure

The four elements of dramatic structure outlined by Aristotle millenia ago can be expressed in today's terms as exposition, development, building to a climax, and resolution.

*Exposition* is factgiving or backgrounding. In a drama, it is the journalistic five Ws and an H that begin to inform us about character (who), action (what), time (when), place (where), motivation (why), and method (how).

*Development* is the interweaving and deepening of the threads that were spun in exposition. This is the "entanglement" stage in a dramatic story. In modern parlance, "the plot thickens." Often at this stage, events are set in motion that can only lead to a later climax. Or to put it another way, there is in the development stage the creation of inevitability.

*Building to a climax* is a phrase that today carries heavy sexual overtones, but in the case of much popular music, that is probably appropriate. The orgasms that Aristotle talked about were more often intellectual than physical. The high point of the dramatic action was supposed to result in a purging of the pity and fear the audience had built up during the development and the build to the climax.

The *resolution* is the time after the climax when all the threads that came apart during the development and build to the climax are knit back together and life returns to something close to normal (see Fig. 4.3).

Because very little of modern radio programming is comprised of dramatic shows—and especially not Greek tragedy!—Aristotelian dramatic structure may appear to have low utility in describing what a listener expects from radio listening. But as is shown later, the wavelike form of Aristotelian dramatic structure does correspond well with the rising and falling rhythms of certain music presentation systems. And most individual songs are designed to be fairly close to the Aristotelian model.

The reader should especially compare the graph in Fig. 4.3 of Aristotelian structure with the Milkman and Sunderwirth graph of opponent-process mood changes (see Fig. 4.1). In both, there is a build-up to a climax, the peak of arousal, then a short "shelf" period following the peak that is less intense but still arousing, and finally the period of resolution/satiation. Maybe one of the reasons dramas constructed along classical lines are effective is because they tap into the opponent-process that is apparently so basic to human physiology and psychology. Or to turn it

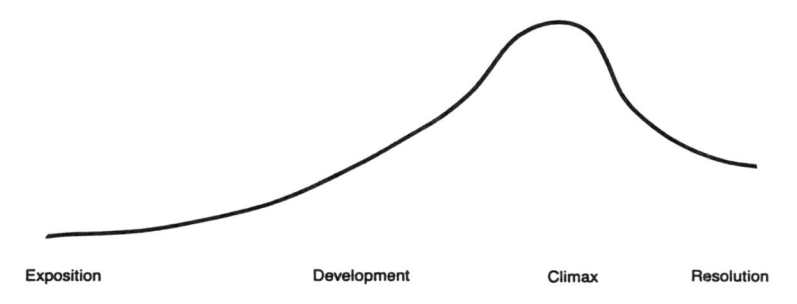

FIG. 4.3. Graph of Aristotelian dramatic structure.

around and look at it from a cultural perspective, maybe millenia of dramatically poignant life experiences have conditioned us to desire (or have caused us to induce) psychologically and physiologically intense experiences in everyday life. Either way, whether noting the dramatic parallels to psychophysiological behavior, or the similarity of physical responses to ancient dramatic patterns, the message about radio listeners is this: People enjoy the wavelike, opponent-process pattern. Later chapters explore ways to make it an important part of programming structure.

## APPEALS

Back when radio was (like television today) comprised of individual shows, rather than one continuous program of music, it became apparent that although two programs had virtually the same dramatic structure, they still varied from each other in popularity. Clearly, certain appeals were present in the more popular show that were absent in the less popular one. Decades ago, professor Harrison B. Summers of Ohio State University developed a list of major appeals, minor appeals, and modifiers that seemed to describe the motivations, drives, desires, and needs that people fulfill by listening to broadcast programs. Speech and rhetoric researchers had been working with similar terms for centuries, and in the sense that radio broadcasting began merely as a way to "speak at a distance," (cited in Lichty & Ripley, 1969) it is not remarkable that many of the same appeals seemed to apply during radio's first network heyday. Today, the terms (amplified by Lichty & Ripley, 1969) are still good descriptors of why shows are popular with audiences, especially in television. The major appeals both attract a listener's attention and then reward the listener for having paid that attention. A case can be made that the greater the number of major appeals that are well-presented in *any* broadcast program, the greater chance that show has of succeeding.

*Major Appeals:* Conflict/Competition, Comedy, Sex Appeal/Personality, Information, Human Interest
*Minor Appeals:* Sympathy, Affiliation, Nostalgia, Acquisition, Importance, Involvement
*Modifiers:* Beauty, Credibility, Originality

Lichty and Ripley's list of appeals is probably not exhaustive, nor is it immutable. As society changes, the appeals are bound to change with it. For example, some otherwise well-adjusted students have described television car crash scenes in which there is much smashing, twisting, explosion, and general destruction in the "beautiful" appeals category. And some appeals are stronger in the obverse: The very *in*credibility of Superman, for instance, is part of the charm. (We willingly accept the fantastic premise because it satisfies our daydreams.) A textbook on persuasive speaking is likely to list dozens of "motive appeals," such as pride, loyalty, reverence, dependence, achievement, authority, and adventure. But, almost always, the Lichty and Ripley list has at least one term that is a good descriptor of the reasons people listen to broadcast programs—which reasons are entirely different from why they buy a product or subscribe to a service.

## OTHER AUDIENCE NEEDS AND DESIRES

### Maslow's Needs Pyramid

Except for the classification into major appeals, minor appeals, and modifiers, Lichty and Ripley did not attempt to build a hierarchy of appeals in the way that psychologist Abraham H. Maslow advanced his now-famous five-step classification of human needs. In Maslow's scheme, a human being must largely fulfill physiological needs before beginning to try to fill safety needs; in turn, safety needs have to be fairly well satisfied before considering belongingness and love needs; those have to be fulfilled before the individual can strive for esteem needs; and finally, if most things are under control, the person reaches self-actualization, in which he or she realizes full potential as a distinctive human being.

### Esteem Needs

It is interesting to note that the radio (and television) media work most obviously on the middle three of Maslow's levels, satisfying safety, belongingness, and esteem needs at the same time that many programs and especially the commercials purposely raise questions about our adequacies in those areas. Professionals in psychology are seeing increasing numbers of people with low self-esteem, perhaps as a result of the separation of the worker from the finished product, perhaps as a consequence of measuring worthiness by disposable income. Whatever the causes, it seems safe to say that audiences are probably seeking from the media ways to enhance feelings of self-worth, and ways of receiving honest emotional reassurance, without being exploited in the process.

A sense of self-worth has to be based on realistic self-examination. This would seem to be at odds with the beginning premise of this book, that radio serves best as an incubator of fantasies and daydreams. By definition, these are fiction, not fact. But radio's lack of specificity, its open-endedness, means that the individual listener brings his or her own imagery and predispositions to the dream. Unlike television, which supplies specific visual detail that may be far different from the viewer's own reality, radio draws on a combination of the listener's reality and his or her fantasies to construct what might sometimes be a more practical dream for that individual.

## The Audience and Control

Scan the magazine racks at any newsstand and you will see that what American readers are interested in today is control. Our society wants to learn how to overcome an increasingly pervasive sense of helplessness to manage the circumstances of our lives. For instance, there is a whole section of home handyperson or "do-it-yourself" project magazines. Their message is that you do not have to depend on someone else for what you need. The ultimate expression of that impulse is the survivalist magazines, ranging from those with an environmentalist's viewpoint all the way to those frankly rating which weapons will do the best job of blasting away your neighbors if they try to get into your bomb shelter. Then there are the diet books—the magazines that promise control over your own flab. And there are physical fitness magazines—do-it-yourself *to* yourself. There are consumer products rating magazines that promise you will not be as likely to get ripped off if you read them first. There are computer magazines that help you to feel less confused in that bewildering field. And business opportunity journals offer the hope of financial independence. The magazine stand's message is that you do not need to be stuck in your present circumstances, that you can have clout, that you are not helpless.

Another popular magazine genre—the one dealing with video in all its forms—has the same message and an additional one. It is important to notice that whereas there are perhaps a dozen highly visible magazines having to do with video, television, satellites, and VCRs, there is not one dealing with radio. *Audio* is well-represented in the stereo/music area, but there is no national consumer magazine that deals exclusively with radio.

The programming choices available to a cable subscriber or satellite dish owner are usually made explicit through several different kinds of locally printed program guides, some available as newspaper sections, others available free at checkout stands, and so on. But because most music-format stations provide the same service all the time, newspaper radio guides are usually not very specific about programming, and some newspapers do not print radio guides at all. One content analysis of Radio-TV columns published in 1980 found only 12% contained an item about radio (even though there were 10 times as many radio as TV stations on the air; Adkins, 1984, p. 358). As a result, radio stations that do offer an eclectic mix of programming often feel compelled to produce their own guides, which generally do not have circulation or impact comparable to newspaper TV sections.

There is one overriding message being spoken by the video guides, VCRs, multichannel cable systems, satellite dishes, and places to rent lifts up mountains in the winter chill just so that they can go through the work of skiing back down.

When a person is out for a motorcycle ride or goes skiing just for the fun of it, the gratifications he or she gets from interaction with the machine or the skis are in some way analogous to the ones he or she gets when listening to the radio just for fun.

Riding a motorcycle or skiing a mountain are exercises in the laws of physics and the factors of aesthetics—an unreeling of the vectors of time, space, and force. Although time, space, and force are all quantifiable in a physics lab, they can also be identified as attributes of aesthetic experiences. Because these vectors are used throughout the rest of this book, we need to begin to understand them now.

### The Rewards of Exploring Time/Space/Force

Why ride, ski, or listen when you do not have to? One answer is, to explore your relationship with space over a given unit of time while using only the appropriate amount of energy (force). Many skiers derive considerable satisfaction merely from the fun of making smooth, graceful turns. Many motorcyclists enjoy the way their bikes react to changes in the pavement, and how they respond to the throttle and the brake. In both cases, it is about feeling in control.

What modern industrialized people often seek is the 100% closed loop between ourselves and the environment or the machine. What we want in an increasingly mechanized world, and one in which nature holds the final cards, is the sense that we are in control of the powers that are in control of us. Skiing and motorcycling do that. The participant decides when and where to go. When you point your skis downhill or twist the throttle, *you* decide where and how fast you move. It is a closed loop.

### The Listener's Agenda: Enjoying the Process

When a person goes skiing or motorcycling, he or she is at least partly responsible for the outcome. The participant has an agenda. But with an entertainment event, the audience is not responsible for the outcome. The audience does not arrive at the entertainment event with an agenda beyond simple enjoyment. Turning on the radio is a singular event, but listening to it is an ongoing process. Processes or procedures (like skiing or operating a motorcycle) can be interesting in themselves, without reliance on additional content for enhanced enjoyment. Doing the procedure has intrinsic rewards that surpass whatever the extrinsic ones might be. Put simply, in riding motorcycles, getting there is more than half the fun or else you would go by bus. (Downhill skiing does not even pretend to be a form ion; it is purely for giggles.) Unwinding a twisty road or a ... your way is better than having someone unwind it for you.

The problem with some radio programming is that somebody else does unwind it for you. The disc jockey or automation system is driving the bus. The listener just sits and looks out the window. Without the sense of personal participation—of an energy exchange taking place in time and space—the radio listener becomes detached, passive, and a candidate for tuneout. Live concerts and theatre exist because the audience *wants* to sacrifice its usual control for the uniqueness and electricity that comes from observing the risk and open-endedness of ephemeral experiences. Most TV programming (except breaking news and sports) lacks such electric anticipation. Talk radio is ephemeral, like theatre. But most music radio repeats the well-known song, often accompanied by the obvious introduction. One of radio's attributes is that it is a low-demand medium. But *demanding* little is not the same as *offering* little. There needs to be the chance for audience participation.

A well-programmed radio station can move the audience in time and space, requiring from them (and also supplying to them) appropriate amounts of energy (force). It can give listeners a sense of control, perhaps over some of the programming, but surely over some aspect of their private lives. It can increase awareness of where the audience exists in time and space. And it is a highly credible service all the while—functional, but not only that; amusing, but not only that either.

## THE FLOW EXPERIENCE

Process is the most fun to do because it results in the "flow" experience. An article titled "The Fun in Fun" (Furlong, 1976) explored the work of Dr. Mihaly Csikszentmihalyi at the University of Chicago, who studied activities that are intrinsically rewarding. He found that when we are deeply involved in these activities, the feeling we get is a sense of flow. *Flow* is the elementary reward in what we enjoy. The person in flow

> loses a self-conscious sense of himself and of time. He gains a heightened awareness of his physical involvement with the activity. The person in flow finds, among other things, his concentration vastly increased and his feedback from the activity enormously enhanced. (p. 35)

The increase in concentration during a flow experience is not willed—it comes automatically. Sometimes people in flow report altered senses of time and space, so that an individual is able to be aware of his or her actions, but is not aware of that awareness. The challenging nature of

the activity does not allow time for the individual to beco.
about his or her performance. The individual does not judg
from the perspective of a third party. In fact, self-criticism se
flow.

And yet, clear feedback of some kind is essential for flow
racquetball player knows right away whether or not his ...er shot was good—and that there is not time to get neurotic about why it was not better. The same is true of surgeons and performing pianists. But, Csikszentmihalyi pointed out, the nonperforming artist must derive his or her feedback from "an internal sense of rightness. The feedback is not an end in itself, but rather, a signal that things are going well. The person does not stop to evaluate feedback" (Furlong, 1987, p. 36).

The radio performer is in the odd position of being involved in a public performance before an audience (like the pianist) but with virtually no way to get reliable immediate feedback. The radio announcer stuck in a studio must derive flow from that elusive "internal sense of rightness."

A flow activity cannot be too simple or easy, because that leads to boredom. Nor can it be too demanding, because that leads to anxiety, which also stops flow. And the way it is done correctly should be unambiguous, like a tennis shot that lands in-bounds but where your opponent cannot return it.

### Can Radio Listening Be a "Flow" Activity?

Is radio listening ever a flow activity? If a person in flow "finds his concentration vastly increased," how does that fit with the concept that the business of radio is to promote *in*attention? How can a person be both inattentive, almost dreamlike, and also be concentrating deeply? The answer is, people do not pay just one consistent level of attention to radio. The level of attention in part varies with the person's state of arousal/fantasy/ satiation. It varies by overall mood. It varies by time of day, and is affected by where the person is and what else they might be doing. *Inattention* and *concentration* are flipsides of the same listening coin.

For the radio listener, where is the "enhanced feedback" that flow activities offer? When radio demands so little of the listener, where can there be a sense of having met a challenge? The answer this time lies in smiles, frowns, laughter, and even tears. These are mere kinaesthetic responses, but they are also a kind of feedback. They are feedback in the sense that they confirm to the listener his or her participation in the listening event, and through that, a kinship with the host or singer, or a synchronicity with the spirit of the music.

The flow experience from an activity like radio listening is likely to be short-lived. In most music formats, it lasts either as long as the song, or as long as the jock's entertaining chatter. The music progression that is proposed later allows the possibility of more sustained periods of flow.

### Kinaesthetic Responses

Can processes be fun merely to observe (watch or listen to)? Yes, if the observation of a process can provoke in us kinaesthetic responses. *Kinaesthesia* is the sense whose end organs lie in the muscles, tendons, and joints. These sense organs are stimulated by bodily tensions; thus they are sometimes called "the muscle sense." In kinaesthesia, the capacity for sensation that we think of as the aesthetic sense is tied to bodily reactions. Laughter and tears are kinaesthetic responses. So are goosebumps or sweaty palms. You have these reponses most often when you are actually doing something (skiers and motorcyclists grin a lot), but you can have them as an observer, too. Evoking a kinaesthetic response in a listener has to be one of the highest goals of the radio arts. To do so is to create "the willing suspension of disbelief"—to cause the listener to forget that what he or she is really responding to is a conglomeration of wires and circuit boards in a box!

But of course, the radio listener at that moment is not hearing the technology of the receiver. Instead, he or she is listening past it, through it, as a participant in an experience where performer and listener are joined in a kind of communion. Just as the kinaesthetically involved listener is mindless of the radio receiver as a technology, so it is in the flow experience that some participants report having no sense of the place in which the activity occurred.

On the other hand, skiers and motorcyclists are consciously employing the vectors of time and force to explore space, often to achieve a heightened awareness of their relationship to it. Could it be that radio listeners, too, seek a certain set of spacial cues that serve to heighten the probability of kinaesthetic involvement? That question is answered in the next section.

### MAJOR POINTS

1. Men and women differ in their fantasies, with men more interested in risk-taking, and women more interested in caring and social acceptance.

2. Both men and women claim their greatest sources of actual pleasure are their children, marriage, hobbies, vacations, and friends. Media that supply a chance to fantasize help to bridge the gap between wishes and reality.

3. Relaxation (satiation), excitement (arousal), and fantasy are among the underpinnings of human compulsion.

4. Fantasy, arousal, and relaxation are not by-products of radio listening. They *are* the product. The expectation that at least one of these pleasures will be satisfied is the real reason people tune in.

5. The opponent-process model states that every life event that causes strong feelings or moods also triggers an opposing biochemical process. The result is a wavelike pattern of mood alterations that vary among people in terms of frequency and intensity.

6. The PD needs to take chronobiology and especially circadian rhythms into account when scheduling radio programming.

7. When relaxed, people tend to follow a 90-minute consumption cycle (a length like that of sleep patterns). This cycle shortens to 60 minutes when under stress.

8. Aristotelian dramatic structure (exposition, development, building to a climax, resolution) displays a wavelike pattern similar to both the nightly sleep cycle and to the opponent-process behavior model.

9. The greater the number of major appeals (conflict/competition, comedy, sex appeal/personality, information, human interest) that are offered by a program, the greater the chance the show will succeed.

10. Radio concentrates on the three middle levels of Maslow's Needs Pyramid (safety, belongingness, and esteem), satisfying them at the same time that commercials question our adequacies. Audiences seem especially to be seeking ways of enhancing feelings of self-worth and of receiving nonexploitative reassurance.

11. The radio station that succeeds in an era where computer games, home-programmed media, and even self-help magazines all promise more control is the one that actually does try to involve the listener in helping to determine programming.

12. The *process* of listening to the radio can be rewarding if the listener has a sense of interaction employing the vectors of time, space, and force.

13. The ultimate interactivity is the flow experience, in which the kinaesthetic response of the listener simulates the completion of the (otherwise missing) feedback loop.

# PART II

## *Formats, Soundscapes, and Voices*

In this section, the reader should gain a greater awareness of how present-day radio formats have developed, of production values and management procedures as they relate to formats, of the acoustic spaces in which radio happens, and of the part that the human voice plays in them. Chapter 5 provides an overview of how modern formats have evolved, explores some of the factors that cause audiences to prefer one format over another, and summarizes recent format trends. Chapter 6 considers the production "glue" that holds a sound hour together, and the way a music format needs to be managed. Chapter 7 concentrates on the way differences in the sound space cause changes in recorded music, in announcing, and in production. Chapter 8 pays special attention to the human voice as a physical presence in that space, making gestures through speech.

# CHAPTER 5

## Formats: Developmental History, Audience Differentiation, and Recent Trends

In a 1969 speech, one of the two or three people most responsible for the advent of format radio, Gordon McLendon (1969), said:

> I have always been a listener, concerned almost entirely with what came out over the radio. Nothing has ever happened to change me in all of those years, and I feel now as then that it is the programs, which come out over the radio loudspeaker . . . that are all that matter in the end. (p. 1)

This chapter leads off with a short history of radio music formats. By taking a look at how music has been presented on radio for the past 40 years, we can begin to understand which assumptions and "rules" make sense and which need to be challenged.

### A BRIEF HISTORY OF RADIO MUSIC FORMATS

#### Music-and-News

By the mid-1950s, with the dual threats of television stealing radio audiences and newly built radio stations increasing competition for the audiences that remained, radio programmers were in a frame of mind to try almost anything to keep radio afloat. For decades, radio stations had tried to be all things to all people. But as the total listening audience began to shrink because of television's increased popularity and availability, and as more and more new radio stations came on the air, programmers realized that differentiation might be a way to attract audiences. The continued success of stations such as WNEW in New York seemed to indicate a possible direction. For decades, WNEW had programmed a music-and-news format, and had done reasonably well with it even against the network flagship stations in the Big Apple. As both radio network programs and radio network station audiences defected to television, WNEW and stations programmed like it had managed to maintain their audience. The apparent reason was that the music-and-news format did not demand long-term or high-level attention from the listener, as the typical dramatic shows on the networks did. A listener could enjoy a few moments of music and a little news while he or she did other things. The music-and-news format—because it placed low demands on listener attention—could accompany lots of other activities. Instead of competing with television head-to-head it could fit into the moments when the listener was not available to watch TV because some other activity took precedence.

**Countdown Shows**

"Your Hit Parade" had been a radio network staple since the 1940s. And independent music-and-news stations had often featured listings of the popularity of current records, and carried "countdown" shows that played the Top 40 or so songs that week. Audiences for the countdown shows, where only the popular songs were played, seemed especially strong. So it is not surprising that programmers working for some of the major chains of independent (non-network-affiliated) stations, such as those owned by Todd Storz and Gordon McLendon, adapted the Top 40 countdown concept and turned it into a continuous format. By playing only the 40 or so most popular records, they were catering to what the audience had already proved they wanted to hear. The concept of the hit-oriented playlist had been born.

**Top 40 and the Limited Playlist**

The success of the general Top 40 concept led many stations to try it. The proliferation of stations all playing the same music inevitably resulted in an attempt at differentiation through refinement. For instance, on some stations, certain records were restricted to being played only in certain dayparts, when the target audience for that music was most available. But the most important concept in developing the limited playlist came through a chance observation, about 1957. As the almost legendary story goes, station owner Todd Storz and programmer Bill Stewart had been sitting in a bar in Omaha, and they had been observing the behavior of both the patrons and the staff in regard to the tunes they played on the jukebox.

Not only did the patrons play the same favorite tunes over and over, but, as the place began to close, they saw a cocktail waitress going over to the jukebox and dropping her own money in to play the same few songs yet another time. Shortly after that, Storz and Stewart went back to Storz's Omaha AM station, KOWH, and installed a refinement of the limited playlist concept that prescribed differing levels of record rotation. Then as now, music rotation systems were designed to assure that the most popular hits were repeated more often than the less popular songs. The reasoning was, people wanted to hear the most popular songs more often than the less popular ones, so even though a station might call itself a Top 40 station, it would really only play about 30 records, and of that 30, it would play the top 10 far more frequently than 11 through 20, and so on. The ultimate outcome was a station like WMCA in New York, that went to a surefire list of only the top 10 songs, playing them over and over again, 24 hours a day. Listener fatigue set in pretty fast with just 10 tunes, but WMCA had positioned itself as a sort of "hit utility"—if listeners wanted to hear the megahits, all they had to do was tune over to WMCA and one would be played soon enough. WMCA's extremely limited playlist and very tight top-hit rotation was the exception rather than the rule. Most Top 40 stations played 20 or 30 records, but they repeated the top hits more frequently than the lesser ones. And because of the meteoric rise in ratings enjoyed by the first stations to use the limited playlist/music rotation concept, literally thousands of other stations adopted the Top 40 format.

The story about the waitress in the bar that resulted in adding record rotation systems to Top 40's limited playlist is a charming one, but Storz and Stewart may not have extended the analysis of their observation far enough. For one thing, to be working in a bar, the waitress had to be a legal-aged adult. She was thus demographically different from the teenagers whose taste began to dominate record sales in the late 1950s. But even more important is the point that she did not play 40 or 30 or even 10 records, but only 3 or 4. For her, there was something about those few records that continued to work, even after hearing them all evening. Put another way, she was rejecting dozens of records that were also hits. It must be asked, why would she do that, if a song's being a popular hit were the main reason for enjoying it?

It is likely that the waitress replayed her three or four favorites because of factors intrinsic to the records, regardless of their position on the charts. If so, then all the formats that have developed around the limited playlist and record rotation schemes emphasize the wrong thing—the hit ranking of a record, rather than the factors intrinsic to the song that cause it to appeal to the listener. "Hot clocks" and music rotation systems assume that those appeals are present in all hits, but later sections of this book demonstrate that records sometimes become hits because they fill the needs of a certain narrow format niche, because they have been designed to appeal especially to teens, or because they are co-promoted by record companies, key radio stations, and trade magazines. Those are all factors that may have nothing to do with the intrinsic rewards the listener finds in the song.

**Differentiation Via Oldies**

Once most Top 40 stations had installed some form of the limited playlist featuring heavy rotation of the top hits, the need for further differentiation arose again. The only two obvious choices were to shorten the list *a la* WMCA, or to expand it. Most stations chose to expand it by adding oldies. Oldies (or "gold" as Top 40s often called the songs) were hits of the past. They had proven their popularity. Originally, the theory was that oldies were as safe to play as were the top hits. Unsafe songs were the new ones. Thus, although at one time in the 1960s record companies were releasing hundreds of singles each week, only three or four were added by most stations, and they added those only when the songs had proved their popularity at some other station or in some other way (record sales, name value of the artist, etc.) Even though albums are far more important than single records today, the number of new songs added each week is still quite low at many stations. A survey of New Rock stations by *Radio & Records* in 1993 found that the length of the average playlist had shrunk from 54 to 51, and the number of new adds per week had dropped from 6 to 4, in just 1 year's time (Alexander, 1993a).

Eventually, most Top 40s were playing a selection of oldies, but music research began to reveal that some oldies were suffering from "burnout" and needed to be rested or retired. In what seems a case of selective perception, the radio industry discovered decades ago that past popularity was not *ipso facto* a guarantee of present-day listener appeal, and yet record popularity rankings continue to be the major factor in selecting music for airplay. There is more detail about selecting music for airplay in Part III of this book.

**Differentiation Via Presentational Style**

As "rock and roll" became "rock," and as other pop music genres such as Country evolved, stations also began to differentiate themselves on the basis of their presentational style. The music, of course, was the most important element. Some stations emphasized the more mellow, soft sounds in rock, and some reverted to the sounds of the big band era and the days when Broadway musicals and the movies were the major source of pop tunes. Some did not go that far, but did call themselves "Adult Contemporary" stations, which means that they played mostly current hit songs but omitted the more challenging records appealing only to teenagers. Another group of stations played primarily cuts from albums, realizing that rising album sales were signaling that people wanted to hear certain artists, not just certain songs. However, most of these Album-Oriented Rock (AOR) stations have played it safe by airing only familiar artists and songs that have an airplay track record.

For the listener, the obvious "bricks" in the structure of a music format were the songs being played. But as music lists tightened and the same hit music was played on competing stations, the "mortar" that went between the music became more important in differentiating one signal from another. What happens between songs (commercials, announcer chatter, weather, community calendars, traffic reports, promos, public service announcements, and station identifiers such as liners and jingles) is what gives a radio outlet its "stationality"—a term coined by programming consultant Ed Shane.

## Station Identification Jingles and Image Packages

In heavy competition for listeners' attention, developing a consistent station image became important. Station identification jingles were heavily used by early Top 40 operators to solidify the impression that their stations were bright, lively, energetic, even irreverent places on the dial—far different from the staid, slow, proper sound of the old-line network affiliates they were competing against. The network affiliates' call letters and dial positions were well-entrenched in older listeners' minds, so that they were easily recalled when ratings services inquired. Top 40 operators knew that to show up well in the ratings, they had to make their call letters and dial location just as memorable. For a while, the Storz station group awarded prizes to the disc jockey who got the most call letter mentions into his airshift. As a result, the call letters got attached to everything—the weather, even timechecks. But dropping-in the call letters that way did not necessarily keep the call letters in the "top of mind" position the way a singing jingle could. Thus, Top 40 pioneer Gordon McLendon recruited local Dallas musicians like Tom Merriman (the founder of TM Productions, now TM/Century) to record multiple station ID jingles for his KLIF Top 40 outlet. Such ID jingles did for Top 40 stations what singing commercials had done for products like Pepsi-Cola decades earlier—make the item unforgettable by infiltrating a jingle into the listener's mind that could not be deleted. The earliest jingle packages were custom-made for just one station, but eventually, they were syndicated to other stations. One of the most successful early station ID syndicators was Bill Meeks' PAMS, whose release #27 is considered by some aficionados of the genre to be a classic among Top 40 station ID packages.

In addition to stations IDs, such "image packages" also included musical introductions for news, weather, sports, traffic reports, bulletins, community bulletin board features, and more. Even the chart position of the music to be played was announced via a musical intro. At Storz's WQAM in Miami, the temperature was sung several times an hour thanks to a package that included a jingle for every conceivable south Florida temperature.

Today, station identification jingles are shorter, and typical packages have fewer elements. It is thus more difficult to project "stationality" through the jingle package, and listeners are more likely to suffer burnout on heavily repeated jingles and liners. And although jingles generally coincide with the format of the music being played, because they are syndicated nationally, they may not have much of the flavor of the local community.

A point little noted by others who write about radio programming is that in the heyday of the Top 40 format, there were simply many more elements happening per unit of time than had ever been heard on the radio before (or since). Jingles were used as intros, outros, and separators, and thus allowed the disc jockey to catch his breath in the midst of Top 40's frenetic pace. By continuing the music between the records, and even between commercials and other elements, jingles contributed strongly to the excitement of the Top 40 format.

## Slogans and Station Characteristics

As formats have proliferated, the major factor discriminating one from another has been the addition of qualifying adjectives to describe the major music genres. In defining their music, stations generally want to appear to advertisers as if they were highly inclusive of many types of listeners, without falling into the trap of trying to be all things to all people. Thus, some of the terms the industry uses are *purposely* obfuscatory. Radio researcher Rob Balon studied the differences among the buzzwords and slogans radio people employ and the terms the public actually uses to describe stations. For example, he found that the term *Hot Hits* for a contemporary hit radio (CHR) format was identified by listeners most often by the old term *Top 40*. Two popular terms, *Magic* and *Power,* turned out to be benign in their ability to describe the music, but very good for recall. On the other hand, *fresh, mix,* and *variety* seemed to be good music descriptors, along with *easy listening, rock, rock and roll,* and *oldies.* Balon reported: "[The term] oldies is so strong that I've seen successful Gold stations begin using the word and immediately gain a cume increase, because the audience can relate to the product. But 'classic' isn't a listener word" (Denver, 1988b, p. 42).

Another Balon study (1988) of listeners' "top-of-mind" awareness of the characteristics of Adult Contemporary stations in the top 50 U.S. markets, asked 500 respondents what came to mind first when the station's call letters were mentioned. Although Balon's focus was on the problems that loomed for stations that received many "don't know" responses, it is interesting to note that the most mentioned responses were ones with a music *mood* rather than a music *popularity* orientation. Such answers accounted for the top 46% of responses in the study of market-leading Adult Contemporary stations. Specifically, the responses were *soft and mellow rock,* 22%; *mellow music,* 14%; and *variety,* 10%. Lesser responses included the popularity term *oldies,* 8%; the mood term *easy listening,* 6%; and *Joe morning guy,* 4%.

## AUDIENCES ATTRACTED BY VARIOUS FORMATS— A HISTORICAL OVERVIEW

There have now been several decades of research into the kinds of audiences that are attracted by various radio formats. A look at a few of those earlier findings provides a framework for considering current trends later in this chapter.

A study of contemporary radio formats by Lull, Johnson, and Sweeny (1978) tried to construct a generalized demographic profile of audience types attracted by each of several formats receivable in the Santa Barbara, California area. Marital status was found to be a good predictor of format preference, with listeners to news and soft music stations most likely to be married, and Top 40 and album rock listeners least likely. Geographic stability was also a characteristic of news listeners, whereas rock listeners were least likely to have remained in a single location for the 2-year period preceding the survey.

### Electronic Media Habits Related to Various Radio Formats

Two of the three authors of the preceding study produced a follow-up to it (Lull, Johnson, & Edmond, 1981). This time, they studied consumption of other electronic media by listeners to each format type and found that how much attention was paid to *other* media was an accurate predictor of which radio format would be preferred. For purposes of the study, *electronic media* were defined to include movies as well as records/tapes and television. Table 5.1 cross-lists five radio formats with the mean number of minutes per day spent with radio, TV, and records/tapes, and the mean number of movies viewed in theatres in the previous 3 months.

Table 5.1 shows the AOR audience listened to less TV but spent far more time with records/tapes and with movies than other segments of the audience. AOR listeners also listened to the most radio in this study. Combined listening to records/tapes and radio exceeded 4½ hours per day for the AOR listener. On the other end of the scale, Beautiful Music listeners

TABLE 5.1
Radio Format Preference by Electronic Media Consumption

| Format Preference | N | Radio[a] | TV[a] | Records/Tapes[a] | Movies[b] |
|---|---|---|---|---|---|
| Top 40 | 77 | 124 | 178 | 54 | 3.4 |
| AOR | 153 | 188 | 90 | 92 | 5.1 |
| Adult Contemporary | 34 | 164 | 175 | 27 | 1.9 |
| Beautiful Music | 69 | 167 | 176 | 16 | 1.4 |
| All News | 20 | 130 | 129 | 26 | 2.5 |

Note. [a]Radio, TV, and Records/Tapes expressed in mean minutes per day with each medium.
[b]Movies expressed in mean number viewed during the past 3 months. From "Radio Listeners' Electronic Media Habits" by J. Lull, L. Johnson, and D. Edmond, 1981, *Journal of Broadcasting*, 25(1), p. 28. Copyright © 1981 by *Journal of Broadcasting*. Reprinted with permission.

TABLE 5.2
Format Preference and Selectivity Rank

| Format Preference | Selectivity Rank |
|---|---|
| Top 40 | 2 |
| AOR | 1 |
| Adult Contemporary | 3–tie |
| Beautiful Music | 4 |
| All News | 3–tie |

spent the least time listening to records/tapes and also viewed the fewest movies.

Not reported in Table 5.1 but mentioned in the text, was the topic of selectivity. The authors noted that some listeners had developed media habits that reflected a desire to spend time with media over which they could exercise a choice as to content. (Recall the discussion of control and the desire to be your own "producer" in chapter 4.) This desire was seen in the significant positive associations on the time spent listening to records/tapes and the time spent viewing movies (Lull et al., 1981). Table 5.2 shows a "selectivity" or "self-programming" ranking for the five given formats, based on the number of minutes of records/tapes listened to, or the number of movies viewed. What Table 5.2 suggests is that AOR listeners, although they tended to spend the most time with radio, also spent the most time programming their own music. This may be because they tended to be highly involved with music anyway, not necessarily because they were disenchanted with the way their AOR station programmed it. Beautiful Music listeners, on the other hand, seemed the most pleased to take what radio offered. Also found was a clear tendency for younger listeners to program their own music. The study did not predict whether a generation of young listeners who were in the habit of programming their own media would revert to depending on radio programming for their music needs as they grew older, as Beautiful Music listeners did in 1981.

In the mid-1980s, the National Association of Broadcasters (NAB, 1985) commissioned a study on the psychographics of radio listeners titled *Radio W. A. R. S: How to Survive in the 80s*. Among the findings were that AOR and Nostalgia listeners both thought of themselves as music experts; that Adult Contemporary fans were less involved with their station than any other listeners, and Country devotees were the most loyal; that AOR listeners often chose their station on the basis of peer group pressure; that Urban Contemporary listeners were the heaviest listeners (in this study) and also the most likely to use radio to change their mood ("The Psychology of Formats," 1983).

### ARTS '82 National Music Preferences Study

The *Radio W.A.R.S.* study was both appreciated as "thought-provoking" and disdained for the simplicity of its methodology and findings. In the same year, the results of a useful survey of music preferences by Fink, Robinson, and Dowden (1985) was published in the journal *Communications Research* and thus received much less fanfare among broadcasters. The study reported the results of a nationwide U.S. survey of music preferences that had been conducted in 1982 by the U. S. Bureau of the Census for the National Endowment for the Arts under a grant to the University of Maryland Survey Research Center. Known as ARTS '82, the survey consisted of more than 17,000 interviews conducted with people aged 18 and older across the United States. The data for the section on music preferences were based on a sample of 5,617 respondents. They were simply asked, "Which of these types of music do you like to listen to?" (Note: the question did not specify radio listening, concert listening, record listening, etc.—the type of listening was left to the respondent). The possible answers on the survey form were *classical/chamber music, opera, Broadway show tunes, jazz, soul/blues/ rhythm and blues, big band, country-western, bluegrass, rock, mood/easy listening, folk, barbershop, hymns/gospel, other,* and *every type.*

Two dimensions emerged from statistical analysis that allowed each musical type to be placed in space relative to other types. The two dimensions were (a) "formality and complexity" and (b) "ecological or geographical base of the musical style." (Fink, Robinson, & Dowden, 1985, p. 310) The chart reproduced in the published article carried only the labels *Dimension 1* and *Dimension 2*. I have supplied all the additional labels in Fig. 5.1. Dimension 1, *formality and complexity,* runs from high audience formality and performance complexity on the left (-) side, to low audience formality and performance complexity at the right (+) side. Dimension 2, *ecological or*

## 5. FORMATS

[Chart showing music preference items plotted on two dimensions. Dimension 1 (horizontal): High Audience Formality and Performance Complexity (-40) to Low Audience Formality and Performance Complexity (+40). Dimension 2 (vertical): Local or Rural Roots (+40, "Downhome" style) to International or Urban Roots (-40, "Uptown" style). Plotted points: Country (upper right), Bluegrass, Hymns, Barber, Folk, Big Band, Mood, Opera, Musical Show, Classical, Soul, Jazz, Rock.]

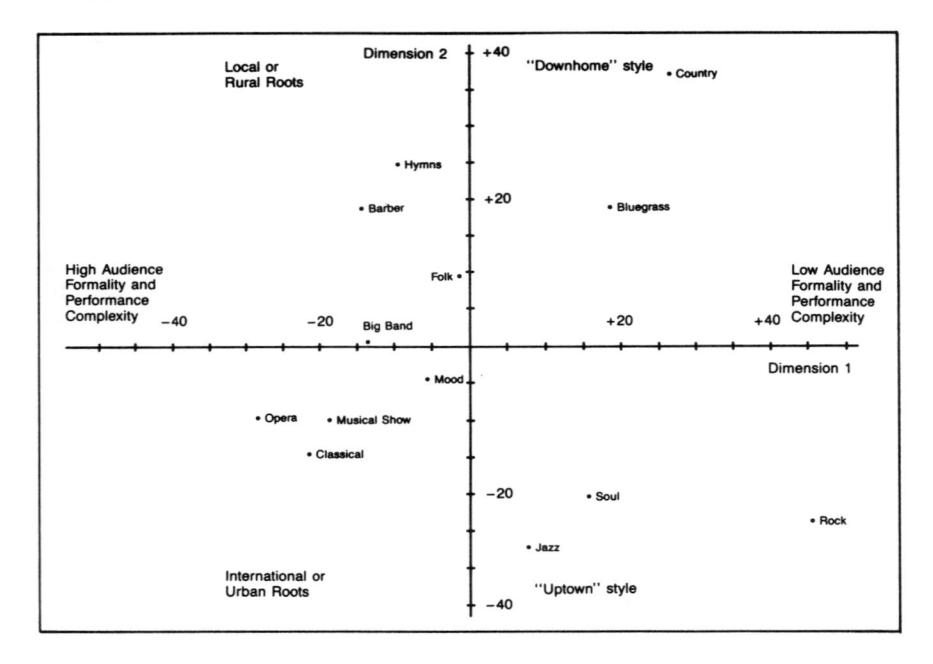

FIG. 5.1. First principal plane for space created from the 13 music preference items. From "The Structure of Music Preference and Attendance" by E. Fink, J. Robinson, and S. Dowden, 1985, *Communication Research,* July, p. 311. Copyright © 1985 by Sage Publications. Reprinted by permission of Sage Publications.

*geographical base of the musical style* was relabeled *International or Urban Roots* at the bottom (-), and as *Local or Rural Roots* at the top (+). I also supplied two shorter labels—*uptown Style* (-) and *downhome Style* (+).

What is remarkable about this chart is that forms that are comprised of widely divergent content and that attract very different audiences may be at about the same point on one or both of the dimensions. Bluegrass, and Soul/Blues/Rhythm and Blues, are both perceived to be in about the same place along the dimension of low audience formality and performance complexity. It is the perception of their roots that separates them. Barbershop tunes and songs from Broadway musicals suffer a similar dissociation on the higher side of the scale of audience formality and performance complexity. Meanwhile, Barbershop and Bluegrass are perceived to be at initially the same place on the Local/Rural/Downhome scale, even though they are separated by differences in familiarity and complexity. And Soul and Rock are thought to be at just about the same level of "Uptown" intensity, although Rock is seen as less formal and complex compared to Soul.

It is interesting to note how music preferences in each of the four quadrants form fairly natural clusters: Hymns, Barbershop, Folk, and Big Band constitute one cluster; Country and Bluegrass is a second; Mood/Beautiful, Musical Shows, Classical, and Opera are a third; and Jazz, Soul, and Rock are a fourth. The natural affinity among the music genres in any given cluster suggests that radio programmers could be bolder in offering formats that purposely encompass more than just one type of music.

Of the 13 musical preference types, Rock and Country are positioned the farthest from the center intersection of the two dimensions, although both share the tendency toward low audience formality and complexity. It is evident that in order for a song to "crossover" from the Country to the Rock charts or vice versa, it has to compromise its sense of roots, sounding neither rural nor urban.

The places where crossovers are most unlikely are from opposite diagonal corners. Barbershop or Hymns do not mix with Rock. Similarly, Country and Classical do not go together. By contrast, Classical and Rock have their "Uptown" roots fairly close together, although the two formats are very different in regard to their complexity and formality. And Country and Hymns are fairly close to each other on the "Downhome" dimension, although quite different in formality/complexity level.

Again, the chart is not specifically about radio listening—it is about music preferences in all kinds of listening situations. But it is based on a good national sample, and its "formality/complexity" and "roots" dimensions are a useful way of visualizing how formats based on these music types may be perceived. Most of all, the chart underscores that certain characteristics are common to what seem to be vastly different musical forms. That concept is important to this book, because one of the main themes of the music selection process to be proposed later is that the traditional labels applied to music genres tend to be used as ways of excluding exposure to certain songs that would likely please the radio listener if he or she were given the chance to hear them.

## The Symbiosis of Format Differentiation and Increased Ratings Detail

Why did the various music formats develop? They may have been generated largely in response to increasingly sophisticated ratings reports that included more detailed demographic information. Top 40 blossomed in a time of very simple "headcount" ratings, when each station's overall market share was the most important attribute to be sold to advertisers. As a result, losing stations began to force the ratings companies to supply audience demographics in order to display subaudiences that the mass-appeal losers were winning. In order to better serve special target audiences, stations began "filtering" music that was on the hit charts, and the music trade magazines responded by developing specialized charts for easy listening, adult contemporary, and so on. The names of the charts coincided with the formats of the stations, and vice versa. The symbiosis between chart names and station formats is important. For example, veteran record producer Jerry Wexler began his music career in the late 1940s writing for *Billboard*. He dropped the term *race music* and instead coined the familiar phrase *rhythm and blues*. We have to wonder if rock and roll would ever have become a national phenomenon in the 1950s if announcers of the day had to use the term *race music* rather than *rhythm and blues*.

Once subaudiences could be more clearly identified, programmers began to develop formats that appealed to those audiences. But at the bottom of it all, every format exists first as a safety net—to prevent being wretched. If there is great entertainment along the way, that is a bonus. Formats do not assure entertainment; they only guarantee that something terrible will not get on the air.

## RECENT TRENDS IN SELECTED FORMATS

According to the Radio Advertising Bureau, 77% of Americans older than 12 years listen to the radio daily. During any given week, 96% listen at some time, for a weekly average of 3 hours and 20 minutes. Eighty-five percent of Americans listen to the radio during morning drive time (6 A.M. to 10 A.M. weekdays), and 80% listen during afternoon drive time (3 P.M. to 7 P.M.; Piirto, 1994). But the radio audience is aging, becoming more middle-aged than the general population. By 1992, the U.S. radio audience had 10% fewer people 12 to 24 years old, compared to the general population, and 10% more people 25 to 54 years old. Only 6 years earlier, radio's audience had been slightly younger than the general population. An analysis by the D'arcy Masius Benton & Bowles (DMB&B) advertising agency pointed to radio's success at retaining aging baby boomers and its failure to recruit new young listeners ("Survey Sees Radio Taking on Middle-Age Bulge," 1993).

What formats were being listened to?

### Country

Nearly 25% of commercial U.S. stations offered some variant of a Country format, among them traditional Country, young Country, and mainstream Country. The majority of those stations were in unrated markets—only about 600 or so Country stations are rated by Arbitron (Schlosberg, 1991), out of the more than 2,600 claiming the format in 1994. About half of the small-market stations and 77% of the medium-market stations derived some part of their program day from a satellite-delivered program service, whereas 20% or less of large and major markets did so (Hollabaugh, 1994).

Programmer Ed Shane (1995–1996) explained the growth in Country formats this way:

> The rise of Country to *a* mainstream format in the 80s, then to *the* mainstream format in the early 90s, was driven by three factors. The appeal of basic values, a backlash to the free-spending 80s, and the casualization of American culture. Country provided a "safe" image when compared to pop music's excursions to the ghetto for rap or the leather bands for grunge rock. Americans faced no fear when confronted with kids in cowboy hats.
>
> Country's rise in popularity paralleled other trends: Poblano peppers and Southwest cuisine; Southwest motifs and decor; denims; Birkenstock™ sandals; "dress down" days at work. They were all indicators of a longing for a simpler life, a search for basics—and, yes—"values." (pp. 3–4)

To Shane's list of reasons for Country's success, I would add two more: Country is the most consistently *melodic* format on the radio and the only one that has a sense of humor in some of its lyrics.

As of the end of 1995, Country was ranked number one nationwide among adults 18 to 34, a demographic that had generally belonged to pop rock stations. But weekly time spent listening (TSL) had hit a 10-year low among certain male demographics, and among all but one of the female demographics. For example, national average TSL among women aged 25 to 35 was down to just 8 minutes and 37 seconds per week (Helton, 1995a). *Radio & Records'* Country format reporter, Lon Helton, pointed out that there were only 39 female program directors or music directors among the trade paper's 214 reporting stations and speculated that men and women might hear Country music quite differently. In spite of dropping TSL figures, female listenership still accounted for 53% of the national Country audience, so Helton (1995d) found such lack of input from women surprising. Indeed, Country's decreasing female TSL figures might be remedied simply by slowing the tempo of some of the music. Legendary guitarist and RCA country producer Chet Atkins was quoted as saying that part of the genre's success came by default, because older listeners were alienated by rock. "If you want to hear a love ballad, where do you hear it? Maybe Whitney Houston and a couple of people like that, but you *can* hear it in some of the country artists" ("I Got Fired Everywhere," 1995). *R&R*'s Helton (1995b), underscored that point in an end-of-year review when he wrote about Country listeners' waning passion levels for the music:

> Today's audience is being fed a musical diet high on up-tempo records. How can radio expect high passion levels, but not play records that evoke passion? Haven't this format's biggest, longest-lasting, best-testing records historically been ballads? (p. 42)

The growth in Country formats was partly at the expense of Top 40 and Adult Contemporary, both of which have seen recent declines.

## Top 40/CHR

Top 40 passed a negative milestone in 1990 when for the first time ever, the Arbitron rating service reported that fewer than 50% of teens listened to some type of Top 40/CHR station (Kabrich, 1993). The number of Top 40 stations fell from 951 in 1989 to 358 in 1994, a precipitous drop.

Top 40/CHR's troubles stemmed from the format's historic mandate to play the hits. But almost every music-format station was playing hits already, be it a Country station or some kind of Adult Contemporary outlet. Ed Shane believed that Top 40/CHR declined because it lost its focus and vitality. There were too many types of music to play, much of which seemed to belong on some competing station programming to a narrower niche. And the hits were available from many sources beside broadcast radio (Shane, 1995–1996). Even in the Rock category, which had become the most closely identified with Top 40/CHR in recent years, there was bewildering diversity: pop hits, dance hits, rap hits, hard rock hits, and new rock hits. Some of those subgenres could not exist gracefully side by side on the same station (Kassoff, 1993).

Sean Ross (1993), associate editor of *M Street Journal,* a radio industry newsletter, put it this way in an article titled "Music Radio—The Fickleness of Fragmentation":

> Of the stations that still consider themselves Top 40, few fit the old definition of playing all the hits, regardless of genre . . . Many are, essentially, R&B stations that hope they can avoid the advertiser bias that plagues the format by insisting that they're something else . . . But it's more accurate to say that they're what listeners are choosing in Top 40's absence. Top 40 is, by definition, a broad-based format. It has withered. It could even die. But it cannot be redefined—Top 40 that sounds like urban or adult contemporary or album-oriented-rock (AOR) is not Top 40. (pp. 95–96)

Ross also pointed out that WCAU-FM—a station that had led a Top 40 rejuvenation in the early 1980s by screaming, playing lots of jingles, and repeating the hits once an hour—was both obnoxious and attention-getting. "Top 40 could do that again. In fact, with the adults too busy to spend much time with the radio and the kids too distracted by TV and video games, showmanship improves the chances of drawing a crowd" (Ross, 1993, p. 101).

To try to attract more adult listeners, some CHRs had gotten more mellow, more like hot Adult Contemporary signals. As pointed out by radio consultant Mark Kassoff, CHR's energy has always been one of its biggest attractions for adults. "Successful CHR has always been an up, fun, exciting format. CHR needs high production values, 'showbiz,' and intensity to satisfy listeners' expectations" (Kassoff, 1993, p. 28). By becoming more mellow, CHR stations may have lost the one thing that set them apart. The success of several of the CHRs owned by Emmis Broadcasting seemed to prove the point. Rather than trying to program for people 25 to 54 years old, or even 18 to 34, Emmis' strategy was to target 18 to 24, and sometimes not over 21 (Novia, 1995c). In other words, the stations were programmed for the same teen-plus audience that the original Top 40 stations discovered—and that many later Top 40s abandoned.

## Alternative/Modern Rock/New Rock

The Alternative/Modern Rock/New Rock format began to grow strongly in 1994. It was heralded by one programmer as the Top 40 of the 1990s (Petrozzello, 1994), and it was natural for dance-oriented Top 40/CHRs to convert to Alternative Rock. A study by Shane Media Services showed that about 80% of the targeted 18- to 29-year-olds were users of music radio, that 73% initially tuned their favorite station to begin their radio listening but 68% would switch if their favorite was not doing what they wanted, and that almost half listened to four or more stations on an average day. That fickleness might be explained by the finding that Alternative Rock listeners were just as likely to listen to rock as to alternative music. Furthermore, females were more likely to listen to alternative music than were males (Alexander, 1993).

## Adult Contemporary

Adult Contemporary (AC) remained the next most popular U.S. radio format after Country, in part because the mainstream format typically targeted females aged 25 to 35—a prime audience to deliver to advertisers. But AC also suffered defections in the first half of the 1990s, dropping from 2,058 stations in 1989 to 1,784 in 1994 (Petrozzello, 1994). In addition, a substantial number of the survivors converted into a subformat such as Hot AC, Urban AC, Smooth Jazz/New Adult Contemporary, or Adult Album Alternative. Some former ACs that opted for the Hot AC subformat began to identify themselves more as rock stations, again stealing thunder from the Top 40/CHRs. AC stations struggled harder to find unique ways to describe their sound using words like *hot, soft, lite, bright, mix or variety.* They also continued to use positioning statement liners such as "continuous soft rock favorites of yesterday and today," in spite of the fact that such phrases are too long to be recalled by the public, provide no entertainment value, and consist almost entirely of abstractions rather than strong images. Some "lite/soft" ACs agonized over whether or not to play instrumentals, worried that they might sound too much like the "elevator" music on now-defunct Beautiful/Easy Listening stations, which had often been used as background music. Thus, many soft/lite ACs continued to shun instrumentals—except for familiar songs by familiar artists such as Kenny G. Typical stations defined themselves (both internally and in promotion) by lauding a few core recording artists, most of whom were vocalists who would supposedly appeal to the targeted female listener.

AC stations also persisted in worrying about how many stopsets (commercial clusters) they should run each hour, how many spots should appear in each, and how long their music sweeps should be. At mid-decade, many were adhering to two breaks per hour, with a limit of four or five units (spots) per cluster, and anywhere from 20- to 28-minute music sweeps. In all the debate about how many spots per break, there was very little talk among programmers of how much less efficient a sales tool the fourth or fifth spot in a cluster might be as a result of inevitable tuneout. Like other formats that tried to deliver "the most music" by playing long music sweeps, AC stations did not want to admit that one inescapable side effect was the creation of end-of-stopset commercial availabilities that would never be heard by as many people as the first spot in the set. In effect, every time a commercial rotated into the last position in a stopset, the advertiser was paying money for audience that was not there. But the practice persisted, because long music sweeps were assumed to be the best way to increase average quarter hour (AQH) audiences, and TSL.

## AOR/Progressive/Adult Alternative

On the other end of the age continuum from Alternative Rock/New Rock were older formats such as AOR, and new formats like Adult Album Alternative and Americana. All of these formats were variations of the Progressive stations that first appeared in the late 1960s. Progressive was never really a format—in fact, the whole idea originally was to avoid the musical constraints of a format and the hype of Top 40. Progressive, however, was challenging to listeners because of its very eclecticism and unpredictability. It appealed most to those who craved novelty and surprise in the music played.

For those who sought musical familiarity and certainty, the AOR format was offered instead. The name soon became a misnomer because many stations actually played only a single track from a given album, not the album as a whole. Because it was easier to program songs with a playlist history, and a focused core demographic such as 18- to 34-year-old males was easier to obtain, AOR became the more dominant form. In the mid- to late-1980s, Classic Rock became an important subformat. Classic Rock

AORs initially expanded their playlists to more than 1,000 titles as former vinyl LP albums became available on CD. But then many Classic Rockers pared their playlists back to only 300 to 400 of the highest-testing songs, with the result that a typical Classic Rock station played the same songs every 1½ days. Obviously, that tended to burn out both the songs and the listeners very quickly (Kelly, 1994). But according to Simmons Market Research Bureau, more than two thirds of Classic Rock listeners were between the ages of 18 and 34. Many were listening to a "nostalgia" format for music that they had not experienced before (Piirto, 1994).

By the winter of 1993, not a single AOR station was rated number one by Arbitron (Maxwell, 1993b). But then Progressive AORs and Album Adult Alternative (AAA) stations began to appear. The latter played both mellow and up-tempo artists, and the music aired could have its roots in a wide variety of styles: rock, blues, bluegrass, folk, and new country (Jepsen, 1995). Announcers on such stations needed to be knowledgable about and respectful of a wide spectrum of music, which meant that golden-voiced slogan-readers could not make the format work.

In January 1994, *M Street Journal* established a separate category for Adult Album Alternative. In April 1994, *Radio & Records* reintroduced its Progressive format charts, listing hot albums rather than tracks (Maxwell, 1994c). In early September of that year, the trade paper profiled KOTR, a Progressive station in San Luis Obispo, CA, that had achieved a number one rating in many key demographics. Even though the station had 10,000 titles in its own library, the jocks also brought in their own music and programmed it entirely themselves. Station owner Bruce Howard said:

> We're taking a giant leap backward about 30 years to where FM was new and not overprogrammed. . . . There's more pressure on the DJs than a normal programmed station. It's something that has to be in their blood or it won't work. The humanness of the deejays is a critical part of the sound of this station. (Alexander, 1994b, p. 28)

In late September 1994, *Radio & Records* changed its newly reinstituted Progressive section to Adult Alternative (Maxwell, 1994b). By the end of the year, the Adult Alternative format had made a major market splash in Los Angeles on KSCA, a former Lite AC, thus proving that the concept did not work only in college towns and smaller markets. Although KSCA eagerly played new artists, they also played the old reliables of AOR such as the Rolling Stones (131 times in 1 month) and Neil Young (129 times). The difference was, they played 30 different songs by the Stones, and 24 different songs by Neil Young, instead of only the top 3 or 4 megahits (Sharkey, 1994). About a year later, leading Adult Alternative stations were being congratulated by record company promotions people for playing more blues music. One commented that it was never a problem of audiences accepting and enjoying the blues—the problem was convincing programmers that it was okay to play that type of music (Wonsiewicz, 1995).

## New Adult Contemporary/Lite Jazz

The name New Adult Contemporary (NAC) was coined by the originator of the format, veteran programmer John Sebastian. As early as 1982, he sensed that there was a significant gap between what formats were offering and what much of the adult audience aged 25 to 54 wanted to hear, some of whom had given up listening to the radio. His original format might be described as a blend of Adult Alternative artists, classic rock songs, New Age music, and smooth jazz. Regardless of Sebastian's strong programming credentials, major stations would not try the format. Nevertheless, a little group of seven stations in tiny markets like Ft. Pierce, FL, and Casper, WY, tried it and were responsible for "breaking" (introducing) such artists as Bruce Hornsby, Sade, Yanni, Tracy Chapman, Enya, Kenny G, David Lanz, and Suzanne Vega. What Sebastian sought in the music he programmed was feeling, passion, and spirituality—music that, in his words, was able to touch people (Archer, 1994a). But one of the reasons that major and large-market stations did not immediately adopt the format is that Sebastian was introducing vast amounts of new, unfamiliar music—music that lacked a playlist history, performed by then-unknowns, and much of it was instrumental. Without a history to base music research on, and because of a habit of assuming that "unfamiliar" music is automatically "unpopular" music, the format struggled in the late 1980s.

By 1990, versions of NAC were being aired in Los Angeles, Chicago, and New York. Some stations had replaced the acoustic-backed vocalists with more soulful, electric-backed singers, and had substituted vibrant, rhythmic songs for the original more ethereal instrumentals. Focus groups had revealed that listeners referred to the sound as "smooth jazz," so that is how many NACs began identifying themselves (Archer, 1994b). But in all cases, a strong, even elegant melody was essential—as it had been in the earliest versions of the format. The CEO of Broadcast Architecture, the most important music consulting firm to the NAC format, suggested that those doubting the importance of a strong melody reread old issues of *Radio & Records* "to see what music *really* lasts—it's the melodic tracks" (Archer, 1995b, p. 67). John Gehron, who had been General Manager of the first Chicago station to air NAC back in 1989 said that one of his greatest joys was finding

> that the audience was willing to be challenged by new and interesting things. While it's true that the format is used to relax and affect emotions, it still has a lot of passion. The people who use this format listen because they

want to know what's going on. They are moving forward musically. They aren't musically dead like many Oldies listeners are. These are people who have never stopped liking new music. They may have been fans of Progressive music in the '70s, and although their tastes have changed, this format is a way to find new things. (Archer, 1995d, p. 78)

By the end of 1995, New Age music had been abandoned by many NACs, and some were changing the typical 70%–30% mix of instrumentals/vocals to feature more singers (Archer, 1995). The format typically gathered a balanced mix of male and female adults between the ages of 25 and 44, with the majority being 25 to 34. Qualitatively, it seemed to be an audience that did not watch a lot of TV and that led an active, outdoor lifestyle. Ironically, NAC was finally a hot format in the major markets, with stations usually ranking in the top five (Gronau, 1995). John Sebastian had not be wrong at all. He was just ahead of his time, and perhaps a little too generous in his belief that fellow programmers would be able to understand his vision and relax their usual overcautiousness.

## Urban

If NAC was in a state of flux at mid-decade, the Urban format was even more so. Nationally, a little more than half of the Urban audience came from the 18-to-34 age group. Much of that audience was concentrated in the major and large markets. But as with most other formats, "mainstream" Urban was not the only flavor available. There was also Urban Gold, Urban Adult Contemporary, Rhythmic Contemporary/Hip-Hop, and CHR-Urban or "Churban." Urban Adult Contemporary stations struggled with how much Rap music to play, if any, whereas stations already airing Rap grappled with controversies over lyrics. Curiously, even the Urban Gold stations did not play much of the great Rhythm and Blues heritage music that was first aired in the 1950s. A listener typically had to turn to an Oldies station to hear those tunes.

## Oldies

The Oldies format continued to grow in the mid-1990s, with nearly 200 additional stations adopting the format between 1989 and 1993. More than three fourths of Oldies listeners were between the ages of 25 to 54, but the core audience was 35 and older (Piirto, 1994). Fifty percent of Oldies listeners fell into the Baby-Boomer category of ages 35 to 44, and represented nearly $1 trillion in income. More than 50% were heavy users of radio and relatively light users of other media, and they were about equally split male–female. One reason for the continued success of the format—beside its ability to attract an audience advertisers were eager to pay for—was that the music offered what one commentator called "a behavioral comfort zone" (DeLuca, 1995, p. 53). However, the future for the Oldies format does not look bright. Because of the declining influence of Top 40/CHR stations in the late 1980s and early 1990s, a common base of pop music from the last decade or so may be impossible to identify.

Indeed, the result of the fragmentation taking place in *all* formats is that there are no longer songs that are universal hits. Russell Shaw (1993) proposed a pop quiz in his article on format fragmentation in *Mediaweek*. He suggested that the reader ask colleagues to hum at least 16 bars of "Informer" by Snow, "Freak Me" by Shai, or "I Have Nothing" by Whitney Houston. He suspected that most would not be able to repeat even a single verse from these songs, each of which had been a number one hit in their categories in spring of 1993, shortly before the article appeared. Shaw opined,

> Just a few years ago, a Number One record, or even a top 10 record, was a timepiece in the making, a universally acknowledged musical bed for our days at the shore, at the party, driving to and from work, picnicking in the park. Now . . . pop culture's music is being fragmented in such a way that large portions of it are totally unknown by very substantial chunks of otherwise extremely culturally aware people. (p. 24)

### Nostalgia/Hispanic/Christian/News-Talk

The growth of four other formats underscored the further fragmentation of radio's "mass music" audience. Nostalgia/Big Band played the music of the 1940s and early 1950s, and as a consequence garnered an audience that was primarily aged 50 and older. The format succeeded because older people were living longer, and some had considerable disposable income. But even more than Oldies listeners, the Nostalgia audience was avoiding hearing new music.

Hispanic and Christian formats both spread strongly in the late 1980s and early 1990s period, and in a way, both were serving specialized populations. The Hispanic population sector, which was growing faster than any other subgroup of the U.S. population, was eager to hear radio in the Spanish language, even as many attempted to assimilate into U.S. society by learning English. It was an especially strong format in major markets, in towns along the Mexican border, and in Miami. Some Hispanic stations were music-oriented, others were news-talk; in effect, Hispanic broadcasting was a microcosm of mainstream U.S. broadcasting, but in Spanish. In many ways, it was the same with Christian stations. Some aired music exclusively, some ran a mix of music and spoken word programming, some transmitted mostly evangelical preaching, and some offered a version of news-talk. But music-formatted Christian stations drew from their own specialized pool of recording artists, just as Hispanic stations did. Neither would be future contributors to a pop-based mainstream Oldies format.

News-Talk showed enormous growth, especially among AM stations. Between 1989 and 1993, *M Street Journal* calculated that the format increased by over 500 stations, a growth of 173% (Piirto, 1994). Talk shows like Rush Lumbaugh's and Dr. Laura Schlesinger's appeared on so-called "full-service" stations that also aired some music. What else, beside strong personalities and high-quality network delivery, spurred the growth of talk? It might have been a yearning among listeners for a sense of community that was missing from modern-day work and neighborhoods. Or perhaps the talk restrictions placed on many disc jockeys prevented them from engaging the listener in dialogue the way successful talk show hosts did.

Programming consultant Ed Shane (1991) predicted that Talk is a format ready to splinter. He foresaw three distinct styles: probing, intellectual talk (like National Public Radio); opinion-flaunting talk (like Rush Limbaugh), and "Boomer-oriented lifestyle triggers" (like Howard Stern but cleaned up). Shane believed that "Rock radio morning shows are talk radio of the future," but he also lamented the fact that the format's production values and content are not relating to younger listeners (pp. 161–162).

Although chapter 8 has more to say about the attributes of a successful air personality, the remainder of this book concentrates on music programming rather than Talk-News stations. The current variety and complexity of all the versions of Talk-News demands a separate and more elaborate treatment than can be provided here.

## MAJOR POINTS

1. All current music-based radio formats are an elaboration of the music-and-news style and countdown shows that eventually became the Top 40 formula.

2. Since the advent of Top 40, stations have sought to differentiate themselves on the basis of their oldies mix, presentational style, station ID jingles and image packages, slogans and liners.

3. "Hot clocks" were devised as a means of rotating the presentation of certain kinds of music in a systematic way. Popularity has been a major component of every post-Top-40 format, but if popularity is necessary, it is no longer sufficient.

4. Some formats have higher "selectivity" rankings than others; that is, their listeners reflect a desire to spend time with media over which they could exercise more choice about content.

5. Among recent overall format trends are: the aging of the radio audience, which is now older than the average age of the general population; Country's number one ranking among adults aged 18 to 34 (a category that had belonged to pop rock stations; Top 40/CHR's continued decline, and seeming inability to mix diverse music genres; the splintering of Adult Contemporary into nearly a half dozen subformats; the rising popularity of Progressive/Adult Alternative stations with a more eclectic music selection, sometimes at the expense of AOR station popularity; the long-awaited large-market success of NAC/Lite Jazz stations, many of which dropped New Age titles and pared their playlists; the splintering of Urban into several subtypes, much as had happened to AC; the rising popularity of 1970s music on Oldies stations, which are faced with future problems because of the decline in current Top 40/CHR listenership; and the strong growth in Nostalgia, Hispanic, Christian, and News-Talk formats.

# CHAPTER 6

# *Format Innovation and Management*

## INNOVATION OF FORMAT ELEMENTS

**Format Clocks**

The format clock is *not* the machinery that makes a music station's programming run, although it sometimes seems that way. The radio trade press reflects the sense among programmers that the development of the perfect format clock is radio programming's Holy Grail, bringing with it the promise of eternal Time Spent Listening (TSL) and heavenly cumes. It follows that once a station anoints a given format clock, the execution of it is expected to proceed with a fierce devotion to consistency. Nonsense. Ideally, a format clock should be merely a suggested route on a road map, not a set of steel rails that forces the same stops in an unchanging landscape.

It is unpopular to say it, but format clocks can be a refuge for the lazy, who do not want to put the resources or the time into continuously developing new entertainment materials. The pioneers who developed the original format, Top 40, did not come up with *the* format clock; they developed new ones more or less continuously, as they discovered more about what their audiences liked. That continuous refinement and tinkering is one of the things that made early Top 40 exciting for the listener, and the lack of it may be one of the factors contributing to the recent decline of the Top 40/CHR format.

Today, too many stations adopt a format clock that worked elsewhere and then relax into an "autopilot" mode, expecting that all of the entertainment value will flow from the clock. In actuality, none will. A format clock is only a structure, a framework, and there is no entertainment value in structure per se. The only thing a format provides is an itinerary of events that will eliminate the dead air that might result from indecision, that will reduce the chance of two conflicting events from accidentally being programmed back-to-back, and that will prevent random choices on the part of the air staff. The audience does not care about any of these attributes, because none of them guarantees entertainment. Remember, radio audiences listen *to* formats because that is what they are offered, but nobody listens *for* formats. I am convinced, however, that many listeners are able to perceive formats being followed, and for some, the sense that their station is following a rigid formula is a turn-off. When the skeleton is showing through, it means there is little meat on the bones. The best formats are mostly undetectable. There may be points within in an hour when a listener's expectations for consistency are satisfied, such as traffic reports every 10 minutes, or news on the hour. But the rest of the time, what happens should feel spontaneous, even unpredictable. It should feel like life, not like a computer.

Here is an example of "clock-thinking" that is correct from a professional programming point-of-view, and almost completely irrelevant from the perspective of a listener: "Clocks should be designed to carry audience from one quarter-hour to the next by strategically placing the strongest songs at the most critical points in each hour" (Love, 1993, p. 27). The prime consideration here is how to maximize audience from one quarter hour to the next for ratings purposes. The question should be, is that what the audience most desires? If that seems a naive, non-business-oriented question, consider this analogous situation. A midwest grocery store chain that serves my town recently began to interrupt their background music service with recorded announcements for specific products. There were at least three things wrong with this, from a shopper's viewpoint. For one, they interrupted singers in the middle of well-known songs to do so. For a second, they were adding to the long list of visual and physical distractions the shopper already had to put up with. For a third, they were reducing themselves to the same low plane as a discount competitor, where shoppers endured the audio assault in exchange for lower prices. But the most important point is this: Management was not thinking like a grocery shopper. If they had asked 100 shoppers if they *wanted* the music to be interrupted by commercials, 100% of them would have said no. But nobody asked, because the shopper really did not come first: Bettering the bottom line did. I can only imagine that short-term gains in selling the featured items will eventually be canceled out by dissatisfaction with the shopping experience. In my town, there is little grocery store competition to turn to. But in radio today, that is almost never the case. Formats that serve the listener first and foremost will win in the long run. It will take a change in thinking about format clocks: from *manipulating* the listener in order to serve the station's need, to *serving* the listener's needs and thereby also benefitting the station.

## Positioning Statements and Liners

In that context, let us consider positioning liners, those phrases that supposedly help the listener to remember the function, the personality, or the uniqueness of the station. Here is a liner that an Atlanta Country outlet was using in 1992: "52 minutes of continuous country music with the right mix of today's hot new country hits and all-time favorites" (Helton, 1995c, p. 44). As I stated before, such a liner is too long and too abstract to be remembered by the listener as a slogan, and it has no entertainment value. But virtually every music station has a format clock that drops in phrases like this several times an hour. To that practice, I apply these two questions:

1. How many times can you stand to hear a kid in the backseat of a car ask "Are we there yet?" before you tell him or her to shut up?
2. If burnout is a factor with records, why would you assume that it is not also a factor with liners or any other heavily repeated element?

The repetition of liners is, like the commercial announcements in the supermarket, a turn-off to those who have to hear them. Further, consultant George Harris (1994) said that it is a myth that if a radio station repeats a claim often enough, the audience will believe it. "Repeated use of a slogan or positioning statement will enable the audience to consider it, but not necessarily believe it.... Because there's been so much hype on the radio, convincing listeners of legitimate claims has become increasingly difficult" (p. 15). And Program Director Sue Wilson objected to claims that make decisions for listeners because radio people assume listeners are too stupid to know what their favorite songs are.

> It's unreasonable to keep saying you're the best. A station couldn't possibly read into a listener's personal music tastes. We aren't giving listeners enough credit. Let *them* determinine if you're playing the most variety. I don't want someone telling me what the best thing is—it depends on what you like. (Kinosian, 1995c, p 34)

But liners and positioning statements persist. The argument goes, "The other stations do them. They've been doing them for years. They must be okay." Wrong. They annoy listeners. If a station cannot find alternative and more interesting ways to get the point across, then at least they can reduce the number of times the same tired phrase is uttered. "Repeating them less often will hurt recall for ratings purposes." Maybe, but that listener is not tuning in so that he or she can be a pawn in your struggle to maximize ratings. When listeners figure out that they are being used by a station for its own ratings and sales purposes rather than to satisfy audience needs, they become ripe for appropriation by another frequency. Or another medium.

## Stopsets

Commercials, as opposed to liners and drop-ins, are indispensable. The only way to reduce the number of commercials is to raise rates, and in a competitive environment, that is often not easy. So the presentation of commercials has become a crucial element in the format clock, as programmers struggle to keep audiences listening while also maximizing the number of spots that can be run.

A cluster of commercials is known in the business as a *stopset*, a term that refers to the fact that the music has to stop in order to play them. How many commercial minutes there should be in an hour, and how many stopsets are optimal, are questions that have been endlessly debated in the trade journals. A 1993 survey of 176 of the Top 40/CHR stations reporting to *Radio & Records* found that stations in the largest markets ran between 8 and 15 minutes of spots per hour for an average of 9 minutes, clustered into an average of two stopsets. Medium-market stations had just about the same range of extremes in spots per hour, but averaged 11 spots per hour in three stopsets. Small-market stations ran between 5 and 21 minutes of spots per hour, but also averaged 11 spots per hour, and these were also clustered into an average of three stopsets (Denver, 1993).

When I worked at a Florida AM station in the heyday of Top 40, we played at least 2 minutes of commercials between every record and were still easily number one in the market. A successful station in North Carolina today runs more than 22 minutes of spots in drivetimes, broken into six units each in four stopsets. But it is much more common, as the *Radio & Records* survey showed, to run only three (or two) stopsets per hour.

What do listeners want in this case? According to Paragon Research ("Why Listeners Switch From One Radio Station to Another," 1994), if they are music listeners, 72% will change to another music station if the original station breaks from music to talk, or begins a commercial cluster, and 54% will also change if they are confronted with news or nonmusic features. Clearly, listeners want lots of music and no commercials at all—but that is not feasible in commercial radio. In response, stations have programmed long music sweeps and clustered about 4½ minutes of spots into two stopsets at large market stations, or about 3½ minutes of spots into three stopsets at medium- and small-market stations—those are national averages for CHRs, based on the *Radio & Records* survey. So then the question becomes the following: Would listeners rather sit through long stopsets as are presented now or more but shorter stopsets?

Paragon Research provided much of the answer in an investigation that was reported in 1994 ("In-car Listeners More Impatient With Radio Spots," 1994). They surveyed 402 adults who listened to radio and found that:

1. 66% of in-car listeners would tune out some time during a stopset. Thirty-three percent would do so at the start of the set, 51% would stay through one or two spots, 12% would listen through four commercials, and only 4% would listen through six spots. Only 30% of the in-car audience would continue listening. Push-button tuning on most car radios, and the fact that the radio was at arm's length made tuning out or changing stations much more likely for the in-car listener. In all categories, men were slightly more likely to tune out than women.

2. 39% of at-home listeners would tune out during a stopset, while 55% would continue listening. The radio in the home is not as handy as the one in the car, and listening might be an accompaniment to a more demanding activity than driving, making retuning more of a hassle.

3. Only 15% of at-work listeners would tune out during a commercial set, whereas 37% would continue listening. About 48% of the sample said the question did not apply to them in their work situation—they did not use radio at work. The low tuneout figures for the workplace may reflect the fact that the radio at work may be rather inaccessible, and the station might have been chosen by consensus.

The in-car listening results are the most important because they reflect how listeners react when they have the most control over the radio. The push-button car radio is the closest analogue to the way the TV remote control empowers the user to make choices. If radios at home were equipped with push-button tuning or remote controls, it is probable that the in-home results would more closely resemble those of the in-car listener.

The survey results imply that even the first spot in a cluster will be ignored by fully one third of in-car listeners, because it signals the start of an advertising marathon and they will bail out. About half would make it through one or two spots, but that means that even a client who occupies the first or second position in the set has only a 50–50 chance of being heard. The fact that only 16% would stay around to hear four or more commercials means that airing more than two spots in a stopset just about guarantees tuneout for the majority of the audience.

The advertising community is not unaware of the consequences of long stopsets. David Robinson (1991), a vice president and group media director for the W. B. Doner & Co. agency made the case this way:

> The problem emanated from our side of the negotiating table. We need ratings to quantify (and justify) our media buying decisions. We want to know that a lot of listeners . . . are hearing our brilliant commercials.
>
> Therefore, the stations have had to learn how to increase their ratings. Unfortunately, many of the programming methods utilized to spike ratings often include making a commercial occasion less than desirable to listeners. The result, of course, is a station that has higher ratings, with an audience which has been trained to tune out commercials. . . . Why not one and two minute commercial breaks integrated into an interesting array of music and features? Too logical? (p. 30)

As Robinson made clear, in addition to forcing listeners away from your station, long stopsets assure that later commercials in the cluster will be almost completely inneffective for the advertiser. When their cash registers do not ring after they bought your airtime, they eventually stop buying your airtime. Yet the phenomenon of the long stopset persists so that megamusic sweeps can demonstrate stronger average quarter-hour ratings. Incredibly, it is imitated even in markets that are so small that ratings are not a factor in the buy. Science, logic, and even hard-headed bottom-line thinking seem unable to exterminate the long stopset. "The other station does it, so we must follow suit." But in the radio business, that other station is probably taking its cues from still another station, and it all becomes very circular. It is not unlike one lemming following another, with the result that the whole flock goes over the cliff together. For too many programmers and managers, it is safer to imitate what doesn't work than to attempt to innovate something that does.

## A Very Slow "Shazzam!"

Although the day-to-day program content of a station may be highly innovative (jock chatter, guests, contest ideas, etc.), innovation is in short supply when it comes to major format changes. And that is not because radio lacks enough "geniuses" to create new inventions. The true radio programming genius was, and still is, an endangered species. But format innovation does not require geniuses, just thinkers. Was it a "Eureka!" lightbulb-turning-on-over-the head experience that Todd Storz and Bill Stewart had that night in an Omaha tavern when they invented the limited playlist? Probably not. It is fair to say that the "Eureka!" event is a rarity in radio. What there usually is instead is a group of people (not just one), working over relatively long periods of time (not overnight), making evolutionary (not revolutionary) changes in programming that (over the long term, and seen in the widest context) alter the content and presentation of radio programming. There is support for this less glamorous but more realistic viewpoint even in the limited playlist story. Storz was quoted in 1957 as saying that he "became convinced that people demand their favorites over and over while [he was] in the army during the Second World War" (Land, 1957, p. 3) When I interviewed Bill Stewart (personal communication, November 4, 1971), he rebutted that idea, saying

> I think that is a little early. Maybe he originally got the idea at that time, but I don't think he ever put it into practice. I think that it was reinforced maybe by several things like this (the tavern experience). It was put into practice long after World War II.

**Keep Fixing What Isn't Broken**

In the limited playlist invention example, one of the crucial elements of the development of new radio format elements is apparent—a gestation period, during which an initial idea receives tangible, observable reinforcement. And although it is not apparent from the earlier quotes, a "Let's try it!" attitude on the part of station management is also essential if new ideas are to succeed. It would not be stretching the facts too far to say that the program directors and station managers who made a success of Top 40 at a time when television seemed to be killing radio tried things in desperation that they would not have tried had their stations been even moderately successful. It just may be today, when most stations can find a significant demographic to target for, and when most FM stations can make money, success may be stifling format innovation more than any other factor. A maxim to describe the situation might be this: With format success comes the narrow repetition of a formula; with format failure comes the wide exploration of alternatives. The term *format failure* can be only a relative one. It cannot mean that absolutely nobody is listening and never has; what is more likely is that some of the people who used to be listening have left, and those who used to listen a lot are now listening less. But today, mere "slippage" can be viewed as failure, because time-buyers at the national level want to see a growth trend, not shrinkage, in audience. So the challenge in radio today is to find ways to keep the format fresh and continue fine-tuning it. FM programmers may feel that radical notions can wait for the future, when technological innovations, economic problems, or shifts in audience behavior provide a greater threat to FM's current health. But just as it is hard for the frontrunner in a footrace to pace himself when there is nobody to catch up to, so is it difficult for FM programmers today to foster the sense of desperation that results in creative flux, and out of which comes really new radio. The prevalent atitude of FM stations today, which parallels that of an immortal but nameless engineer, is "Don't fix it if it ain't broke." AM's that are still succeeding today never quit "fixing" things.

## The Product Life-Cycle Model

If the flux of technological, economic, and social change is the primordial mud out of which comes radio, and if in that mud there are occasional sparks of insight that can—if the environment is hospitable—change old forms and grow new ones, then it seems useful to trace the development of a programming element from its inception through its maturation and decline. Richard J. Lutz (1978) adapted a life-cycle concept for consumer goods to the life cycle of a record on a station's playlist. He used the standard stages in the life cycle of a consumer product to describe the introduction, growth, maturity, saturation, and decline of a record. But the same concept can be applied to radio formats, as shown here:

### Lutz's Programming Idea Life Cycle

*Introduction.* The programming idea is new, and only a few listeners are likely to have heard it.
*Growth.* The programming idea begins to gain acceptance, and there is rapid growth in the number of people who have heard it and like it.
*Maturity.* The number of listeners continues to increase, but not as quickly as in the previous growth stage. The station might be getting better ratings by now.
*Saturation.* The station featuring the new program idea enjoys its peak popularity at this stage.
*Decline.* The program idea begins to wear out as people begin to grow tired of it.

One of the thrusts of Lutz's article was to warn music directors about a pitfall of call-out music research—namely, that for a record to be recognizable when only a 10- to 15-second clip of it is played to the called party over the telephone, the record would have to be roughly in the maturity stage already. If that is so, Lutz points out, then the station is giving up the possibility of introducing new records to its listeners, and eventually the station will be left with outmoded music. "Most consumer goods manufacturers believe that they must have products in *all* stages of the life cycle in order to ensure long-run success," said Lutz. "Therefore, innovation is the necessary lifeblood for the future" (Lutz, 1978, p. 12).

The statement seems true for programming ideas as well as for records, especially when so much of the program "innovation" on many stations is actually mere borrowing of ideas from stations in other markets. Just as most stations hold back on many new records to see which "opinion leader" stations add the song to their playlists, so do many program directors take their cues on programming ideas from stations in other markets, rather than developing their own ideas. The problem with "borrowing" an idea from another market is that the idea may already be "mature" or even in the "saturation" stage by the time it gets on local air. And the idea might even have been an old one when it went on the distant station!

### Burns' Five-Stage Model of Format Innovation

Veteran radio programmer and consultant George Burns would likely agree with the notion of *always* fixing things. Burns offered his own five-stage model of format innovation in an article in *Radio & Records*. Burns identified the five stages as *experimentation, circumstance, technique, fulfillment,* and *decline*.

Burns said that in the first stage, "Someone is generally in the position where they can't make anything out of what they're doing. They get a creative bug and try something weird" (Archer, 1995c, p. 87). Although the experimenters intuitively sense that there is a niche to be filled, they "have no idea what they're doing—they are making it up as they go along" (p. 87).

In the second stage, circumstances that are beyond the experimenters' control become important. They can be advantages or restrictions that can either propel the process forward or hinder it. By way of example, Burns pointed to the technical advantages of FM stereo over AM—he used that advantage when put some of the earliest Top 40 FMs on the air. But he also included the problems other formats are having as circumstances:

> What you're looking for in the evolution of any format is listeners' dissatisfaction with previously-established formats. Any new formats grow when they are fed by what's pissing people off with other formats. Just look at how boring AC is today—it's so disgusting someone should take it out and shoot it!—or how angry Top 40 is making listeners. (Archer, 1995c, p. 87)

*Technique* is the third phase identified by Burns. At this stage, a person of good judgment "takes what's good from the wild experimenter and makes critical long-term choices" (p. 87). The choices made by these persons will influence the long-term viability of the format. If they succeed, the format goes on to the fulfillment stage, where it is "fully developed and making an incredibly rich contribution to the radio scene" (p. 87).

Asked if a format must inevitably go into the fifth stage (decline), Burns answered that as with humans, there are things that can be done to prolong life, such as exercise.

The corollary in programming is to stretch—you must always be stretching. . . . Stations need to be gregarious—get out there with listeners. Staying in touch is a process of inclusion, not exclusion. . . . We're wrong to think of a format as a chess board on which we're moving pieces around: It has a life of its own. It fills a need in a community. People live with it and nurture it, just like they do a human being or a pet. (Archer, 1995c, p. 87)

## Because of What You Aired Yesterday, Today Has to Be a Little Different

Not enough people in radio programming are convinced that what worked literally only yesterday may not work literally tomorrow. They are not enough concerned with a long view that asks "How am I going to take very familiar elements and mix them with enough novel ones to make the sequels original in their own right?" or "How am I going to acknowledge that *because* of what I did for them yesterday on my radio station, my listeners have every reason to expect something a little bit different today?"

The very format elements that a program director has become inured to (because he or she has heard them so many times before that he or she really does not "hear" them anymore) are the format elements that will become—or already are—tuneout factors for the listener. A station should have some audio consistency, but not to the point where it becomes predictable.

John Leader (1980, p. 18) wrote in his "Programmer's Notebook" column in *Radio & Records* about a conversation he had had with a PD who was worried about slipping ratings:

> Seems his station, which used to be considered "the hot newcomer," was now perceived as "the old-line rocker" since a newer station had recently blossomed in the ratings. We talked about a lot of things but finally settled on the fact that the new station sounded a lot "less professional" (his words) than his did and that puzzled him. I pointed out that maybe that was why listeners were leaving his station for the new one . . . not because it sounded "less professional" but because it sounded "less predictable" (my words).

## Clones

Often, a successful station in one market (be it AM or FM) is analyzed, and then an attempt is made to clone it for another market. The transplant fails a surprising number of times. Why?

When he was younger, one of my sons wondered why second movies rarely equaled the original in impact. By "second movies" he meant the films with a Roman numeral II (or III, or more) in their title. We mused over that for a while, and then we considered the first three Star Wars films. We agreed that all three of them are good. It was one of my sons who pointed out that "George Lucas wanted to make more than one movie from the beginning. The first one is called Episode Four right in the titles."

## Don't Just Imitate the Form—Understand the Function

Is that a clue? If you think you're only going to make one show—and then you discover that it is successful—maybe you feel compelled to make another that has the same success factors as the first. Only what are those success factors? The copying of formats and program ideas aside, the very nature of radio programming is repetitive—partly because the listener's routines are. But the listener is often turning to radio to provide entertainment and information that lifts him or her out of that routine. Because station operations also exist on a strict daily rhythm, it is possible to begin to believe that providing something that has a very familiar *form* (such as a simple, fairly rigid format) is the same thing as fulfilling the *function* of a radio station. Sometimes it is, but all too often, it is not. The very term *format* tends to deny the question of what function is being filled—the assumption is that if you play a certain format, the function is being fulfilled.

Programming consultant Lee Abrams was interviewed by *Radio & Records* in 1988 (Kojan, 1988) about the state of the AOR format:

> *Lee Abrams:* AOR is in what I call a mid-life crisis. All the passion is gone. We're "waltzing"—just going through the motions. No one is listening to records. The format is unbelievably boring.
>
> *R&R:* But it all comes down to ratings, and they're still good.
>
> *Lee Abrams:* That's right. Ratings equal money, and money is the ultimate tranquilizer. The attitude becomes, "We're making lots of money. Everything's cool." Of course, GE said that when they made lots of TV sets in the 60s. All of a sudden the Japanese came along and look what happened. (p. 44)

## Editors and Inventors

The point has already been made that most of the people who say they are doing radio programming are acting more as editors than as inventors. The great majority have adopted or adapted a format, a style, and a music rotation that has worked for some other station, and they then conceive of their job as one of fine-tuning rather than real innovation. The small minority of people who are actually involved in trying out new kinds of radio programming are attempting to find or invent the programming equivalent of the Holy Grail. They are trying to invent the one format, the one music rotation, the one presentational style that will be good forever, once they find the key.

The problem with that concept is that it suffers from the same maladies as successful one-shot movies that then go into the cloning business. The very idea that you can "finally" get it right, once and for all, misses the point about originality completely. Nothing is ever "finally right" in radio. It is only right for today. Tomorrow the ideas will be a day older, and the world will have moved on, leaving the audience expecting something new.

## SPECIAL PROBLEMS OF AUTOMATED AND SYNDICATED STATIONS

An automated radio station, or one that airs a syndicated service delivered by satellite, is—by its nature—one that operates from the premise that there *is* one formula or format that works pretty much the same way hour after hour. Only if the station positions itself as a "music utility" can that be true. The more the listener seeks other entertainment values, the more *automated* and *syndicated* become pejorative terms. It has already been mentioned that savvier radio listeners not only can identify an automated station as such, but some even think of *automated* as synonymous with a type of format. And they are right. Because many automated stations run the simplest of formats to minimize equipment expense and programming time, *automated* often equals *simplicity of presentation* in the listener's mind. This is less the case with syndicated music programming delivered live via satellite by such providers as Unistar and Satellite Music Network, but I have heard listeners say dismissively "Oh, that's just a station that plugs into a satellite."

### Serving the Machine

Years ago, IBM had a slogan that dealt with a lot more than just computers in this mechanized age. It went, "Machines should work. People should think." It applies beautifully to computers, which are essentially "dumb" until people tell them to do something. But it also applies to a radio station, which is an assemblage of highly technical equipment, all of which exists only to extend the human creations of a small number of producers to a large number of consumers. Recall that in radio's earliest days, the announcer's job was to introduce the songs played by a live band in the studio. The announcer was present as the music was being created. Radio airplay of phonograph records began to diminish the announcer's relationship to music making. Today, at an automated station or one connected to a satellite service, surrounded with machines that give the weather, tell the time, switch the network news on and off, and play the commercials, it is easy for the staff to get the feeling that they are serving the machine, rather than it serving them. But the IBM slogan still applies: "Machines should work. People should think." What they should think of is ways to communicate more effectively—as entertainers and as program producers.

## Machines as Scapegoats

Automation often becomes the scapegoat for difficulties in management and programming policies—and especially for failures in communication—that would have been present in a live station, although the larger staff and the generally more complex hierarchy at a live station tend to conceal them. Automation may make it feasible to run a station with fewer on-air talent, but if anything, it heightens the need for strong communication with and among the smaller staff.

## The Typist as Program Director

So far as the local programming is concerned, many automated stations in smaller markets are actually programmed by the person who types up the logs and not a true PD. It is the log typist/traffic person who determines spot rotations, where to fit in promos, and so forth. A discouraging number of these people have little or no concern with the station's sound—they simply need to get $X$ number of spots played between 3 P.M. and 6 P.M. tomorrow. Yet, by generating the prelog, they are the individuals most directly in charge of the order of presentation on that radio station.

## Going Live

Some automated stations operate live during certain dayparts. One reason is to handle heavy spot loads or complicated network joins and news feeds. Just as often, the reason revolves around a morning "team" or format that presumably can happen only live. But the question, then, is this: If the programming on the morning daypart seems more effective, why not use it all day long? ("It's 9 A.M. and back to automation. Do you know where your entertainment values have gone?")

## Syndicated Production Collides With Local Production

The audience successes enjoyed by automated and satellite-delivered stations up to now have almost always been attributable to matching the right syndicated service with the music format voids to be filled in the given market. But with ever more stations on the air vying for increasingly distracted listeners, the right music mix alone is not going to make the difference. Today, with satellite-fed music that includes live jocks, there is the possibility of much more timeliness and topicality on the part of syndicated air personalities. A jock in Los Angeles or Chicago can work comments about today's world and national news, music stars, and so on into his or her show and convince us that this is happening live in the studio of our local station. The listener stands to be convinced, that is, until the station plays a local spot or promo. Then the illusion crashes in flames. In too many cases, the disparity between network production quality and local production quality is ridiculous. The automated station, plugged into a satellite-fed network, sometimes sounds like the Jekyll and Hyde of the airwaves: great, then terrible. ("It's 9:14. Time for a network spot break. Do you know where all your production values have gone?")

**Lack of Vocal Variety**

Automated stations often also suffer from a lack of vocal variety, which tends to sound more severe than the same deficiency on a live station does. There are two reasons for this dearth of voices: small staffs mean fewer voices to do spot production, and many of the popular syndicated formats deemphasize host chatter. There are a couple of possible answers, beside the best solution—hiring an additional production person. For one, salespeople could be more aggressive in getting clients' voices on the air. (The same is true for whoever handles local PSAs and bulletin board items.) It takes more work and time to get a good reading, then still more to edit it for timing and cohesion, but making local people sound good wins lots of friends, some of whom have money to spend. A second answer is for the automated station to buy the services of a good voice in another market. Most syndicators can make available announcers to do time, temperature, IDs, promos, and so on. Unfortunately, they often want to sell the *same* voice that is heard on the music service they already are providing to you. Do not buy the same voice unless the station has a very sophisticated automation system and somebody who can really program it so you can be assured that a "bumper" of some other material will be aired between the two different voice cuts. Because, after a lack of vocal variety, the next most prominent sign of poorly run automation is "matching voices" that do not really match.

**Staying Fresh**

Then there is the question of how often a locally recorded element should be freshened. Again, this is a problem for both live and automated stations, where the attitude often is "One good version is enough." But the problem is exacerbated on automated stations because there is less live announcing.

The trouble is, the media on which spots, PSAs, and promos are recorded deteriorate very little with repeated use. Back in early Top 40 when spots and program elements were dubbed to acetate discs for playback, the day when the disc became too scratchy for the air was also the day the content got recut. Carts can be played hundreds of times with little degradation of sound; with digital playback systems, there is no deterioration at all. Such playback perfection would be desirable if the people in charge usually did not stop hearing the elements that listeners hear all the time. Management and the production staff need to pay at least as much attention to the "mortar" as to the "bricks."

## THE PRIMARY TASKS

Management's primary task is to make it easy for a station's air and production staff to make the best possible programming. In the introduction to an earlier chapter, Top 40 innovator Gordon McLendon was quoted as saying that programming was the only thing that ever mattered to him. Todd Storz, the other great Top 40 pioneer, shared the philosophy that building audience through careful programming was an important managerial role—in fact, he put it ahead of boosting sales.

### Trying Things

McLendon and Storz deserve admiration because they were willing to "take a shot," to try things. In Thomas J. Peters' and Robert H. Waterman's classic management book, *In Search of Excellence* (1982; which begat the NAB's *Radio in Search of Excellence (1985)*, also a fine effort), the number one point in their list of eight attributes of excellent companies (ones that are "continuously innovative"—and therefore adaptable to new situations) was "a bias for action." In the early days of the Top 40 format, McLendon and Storz were frankly experimenting with the limits of radio. They did it in part—at least at the outset—because they did not have much to lose: Radio was thought by many to be a dying medium, killed by the onslaught of television. Just as a surgeon can take more risks on a cadaver than on a live patient, so were Storz and McLendon able to feel free to gamble a little. There was a prevailing attitude of "Gee, we've never done that before—let's try it!" More than any era since the beginning of radio broadcasting itself, the early Top 40 period was a time of rich experimentation and change. "Leaving well enough alone" would simply have been a foreign idea to Storz and McLendon. And because they encouraged program experimentation, between them and their staffs they came up with the Top 40 format that many people believe "saved" the radio industry.

It is not that way today, as PD Michael St. John lamented in a CHR-format column in *Radio & Records* (Novia, 1995b):

> We as an industry, driven by creative endeavor, have fallen prey to "reasoning principals" expounded by the scientific study of an art form. And radio programming, when successfully created and executed, is an *art form!* Over the past decade, most of this art form has been lost, or replaced by "audience research". . . . Yet the more information we gather, the lower the Top 40 market share has dropped over the past decade in almost every market. . . . Top 40 must remain a stalwart of fun, creativity, and variety. . . . We must remember we're competing for the attention and retention of those subjects who've so disastrously been prejudged by the numbers. Our new research must center on emotions, fun, and the creation not only of a sound, but an *aura,* just like it was when Top 40 was on top. (p. 34)

Jeremy Schlosberg (1991) writing in *Mediaweek,* made similar points about all FM formats:

> Today, there are very few important major-market stations that develop and implement their formats without one or more outside consultants. . . . When there wasn't a whole lot of money at stake, FM radio formats emerged out of a combination of marketplace dynamics, management insight, common sense and gut feeling (not necessarily in that order.) Today's formats arise from three things: research, research and research. Songs have to be "tested" before they can get airplay; formats have to have "worked" in other major markets before being considered. Radio, like Hollywood, has long since convinced itself that the surest way to avoid failure is to not do anything that hasn't already been done successfully somewhere else. (p. 9)

**The Staff as Source of Ideas and Productivity**

At the stations he owned, McLendon had a system for regularly collecting new ideas from staff and then redistributing those ideas back out to other staff members via a newsletter. He did not for a minute believe that all the good ideas came from top management in his office. McLendon certainly subscribed to another of Peters' and Waterman's (1982) eight attributes from *In Search of Excellence,* called "Productivity Through People." The main idea here is that "The excellent companies treat the rank and file as the root source of quality and productivity gain" p.14). At a substantial number of radio stations, the air staff and office personnel are considered necessary evils. (I know of a station that was designed with two floors: All of the programming and engineering staff are in a mostly windowless basement, whereas all of the sales and management staff are on the light, airy top floor with windows in every office.) These tend to be the stations in which sales come before programming, rather than the other way around. In those places, the sales people are part of the elite, and their status tends to be resented by the balance of the staff.

## If Programming Is the "Product," Then Invention Must Be the Norm

It is too bad that in the past few years, broadcasters have begun talking about their programming using the word *product*. The consumerist viewpoint that is behind such a term deserves applause, but it unfortunately tends to mask the fact that broadcasting is a service business. (*Products* are tangible goods you can hold in your hand—*services* are not.) By extension, the people involved in radio are involved in a service industry, not a product business. More specifically, they are being called upon to make entertainment that is amusing and relaxing and fun, and informational programming that makes a complex world understandable. People involved in such endeavors *cannot* just be cranking out the same standardized product every day. For entertainment to be fun, and for information to be useful, all kinds of creativity, novel approaches, and invention are necessary. Those are the last things you want if your people are supposed to be bolting together Buicks, where you want them all to look like Buicks when they roll off the line. But nobody is going to tune in a news show for the same news they heard yesterday, and no entertainment program or format can exist for long by repeating a limited set of elements. Yes, you do want some uniformity and consistency on your station: You want people to be able to recognize its sound as distinctive from all the competing signals, whenever they tune in. But you do not want that listener to get the feeling he or she has heard most of it before, that this is a repeat. To avoid that, your station must encourage the inventive ideas, the stabs at novelty, the flourishes of freshness. The people at your station must be seen by management as its most important asset—as important as the FCC license to broadcast. The entire staff needs to understand that management does view them "as the root source of quality and productivity gain."

Another of Peters' and Waterman's eight attributes is "Autonomy and Entrepreneurship." They said, "The innovative companies foster many leaders and many innovators through the organization." And again: "They don't try to hold everyone on so short a rein that he can't be creative. They encourage practical risk-taking, and support good tries" (Peters & Waterman, 1982, p. 14).

## Toward Another Meaning for "Productivity" in Radio

When a radio station becomes "productive" in a time sales sense (which means that it is productive from a commonly held management perspective), then the radio station may become less appealing to the people who work there, which, in turn, might bring a decrease in worker productivity. The reasons are these: (a) The more spots that are sold, the greater is the production load. The greater the production load (without an increase in staff help), the poorer the production job each sponsor receives on their commercial. All other things being equal, a spot with poorer production values will be less productive of sales results for the client. (b) Higher spot loads (should) cut down the amount of time that a jock can talk between records, so that when he or she is on the air, he or she sounds less creative and more like an automaton playing records. Thus, productivity increases (in the traditional sense) provide disincentives for typical air personnel to do their best work. What is needed is nothing less than a redefinition of *station productivity*—one that does not sacrifice quality and self-esteem for profits; one that instead finds a way to generate increases both in spot loads and in on-air staff involvement.

It is crucial to have strong people—and enough of them—in production. When the spot load goes up, the first person hired should be an additional production person. What should not happen, but does all too often, is for one or several of the jocks to assume responsibility for an additional part of the production load. This is a no-win situation. Either the station has a jock who puts his or her best into spot production and then is tired when he or she gets on the air, or a jock who puts his or her best into an air shift and is tired when he or she does the spots. The answer is to hire someone to do only production, but that typically happens only in major markets. In the case of the Country format, a survey showed that at small-, medium-, and large-market stations alike, no less than 85% of the time the production director also pulled an air shift ("CRB Survey Says," 1994, p. 52).

By hiring an off-air production person, in addition to getting dependably top-notch commercial work, the station gets a very important bonus: Never need a jock's voice appear in a taped commercial while that jock is doing a live show. More variety in voices means less monotony for the listener. And it saves the impact of the live jock's voice for live announcements. If your station has an announcer who can speak well, can ad lib, can be creative, and keep it all in good taste, then it is a waste of talent to confine that person to canned announcements, time, temperature, and titles. The idea of taping something in production is to do a better job of it than you can hope to do live. The production should presumably require such precision, such care, that only one "take" in a dozen might be good enough to air. The model should be the jingle companies, which spend thousands of dollars an hour to get an orchestra on tape, to make the perfect beds for later vocal overdubs. The instrumental track has to have enormous integrity, because it will be heard repeatedly. The same should be true with the production your station does: Do you want 'em good, or do you want 'em by sign-off tonight? Which kind of spot has the better chance of keeping the listener tuned, and getting the client to renew? The answer is obvious.

### The Full-Time, Off-Air Program Director

This chapter must conclude with an argument for that endangered species, the full-time, off-air program director. According to a survey by the Country Radio Broadcasters, the PD is on the air at 99% of small-market stations, 85% of stations in medium markets, 50% of stations in large markets, and at 25% of major market stations ("CRB Survey Says," 1994, p. 57). In the Adult Contemporary format, about 90% of small-market stations, 75% of stations in medium markets, 52% of stations in large markets, and 19% of major market stations had their PDs on-air (Kinosian, 1994). Some of the PDs who did have air shifts wanted to get a better sense of how all the elements worked from the air staff's point of view, and obviously, there are strong staff-expense factors that require most smaller stations to put their PD on the air. But try out these four scenarios to see why an off-air PD makes sense at almost any station that can possibly afford it:

1. If your station is automated, you listen for the transitions.
2. If you are the typical GM or sales manager, you listen for what your advertisers would hear.
3. If you are a jock, you listen to other stations, because you are sick of the music on yours.
4. If you are a newsperson, you are too busy to listen to anything but the police scanner.

In each of those four cases, who listens like the listener? Nobody, unless the PD specifically has that job responsibility. The PD probably does listen to check the music and to monitor what the jocks say, but unless management has specifically asked the PD to be the listener's surrogate, that task tends to "slip through the cracks." And unless management keeps the PD's air work and production load light, he or she will get too bogged down in daily work to ever get around to listening like a listener. Oddly, the radio station can still go on sounding very professional, but it may be out of touch with its audience.

## MAJOR POINTS

1. Format clocks assure only that blatant errors probably will not happen. The audience does not listen *for* formats, although they listen *to* them because that is what is offered. But none of the components of a format

clock guarantees entertainment; that has to come from other elements in the programming that have the feel of spontaneity. Really good formats are undetectable by the public.

2. Positioning statements and liners are often too long and too abstract to be remembered, and few of them have any entertainment value. Burnout of liners should be considered right along with burnout of music, to avoid annoying listeners.

3. Long uninterrupted music sweeps may keep listeners tuned, but long stopsets are a clear cause of tuneout. Among in-car listeners (those with the most chance to change the dial), 66% would tune out sometime during a commercial cluster, with only 12% listening through four or more spots. Airing more than two commercials in a stopset causes more than half the audience in all listening locations to tune away. Only the advertisers who are featured early in the cluster receive much benefit from running the spot.

4. Format innovation is usually evolutionary, not revolutionary. With format success comes the narrow repetition of a formula; with format failure comes the wide exploration of alternatives. The successful station "pretends" that failure is ahead, and keeps fixing what isn't broken.

5. The product life cycle, applied to radio programming, suggests that programming ideas should follow the same progression (introduction, growth, maturity, saturation, and decline) as popular music. A station probably needs to have ideas in all stages of the life cycle. Borrowing an already-mature idea can be dangerous.

6. Because of what you put on the air today, the listener expects that tomorrow's programming should be a little bit different.

7. When one station clones the sound of another, too often the clone tries to imitate the form without understanding the function.

8. The special problems of automated stations include: making machinery the scapegoat for difficulties in management policy and communication, allowing the person who schedules the spots to actually program the station, the disparity between the sound of syndicated and local production, a lack of vocal variety, mismatched voices, and failure to stay fresh.

9. If programming is the "product," then invention must be the norm. For entertainment to be fun, and for information to be useful, all kinds of creativity, novel approaches, and invention are necessary. The programming people must be seen by management as the most important asset in causing those things to happen.

10. Most stations could benefit by hiring an additional person to do production. Commercials would get made with more care and would be more effective, and there would be more vocal variety on the air.

11. The off-air PD can better serve the station as the listener's surrogate, keeping the station in touch with its audience by trying to listen like a listener.

# CHAPTER 7

# *The Structure and Appeal of Acoustic Space*

### THE LISTENING ENVIRONMENT

> The three most revolutionary sound mechanisms of the Electric Revolution were the telephone, the phonograph and the radio. With the telephone and the radio, sound was no longer tied to its original point in space; with the phonograph it was released from its original point in time. The dazzling removal of these restrictions has given modern man an exciting new power which modern technology has continually sought to render more effective. (Schafer, 1977, p. 89)

A chapter that intends to produce greater awareness of the importance of acoustic space must begin with an excerpt from the mind- and ear-opening book by R. Murray Schafer, *The Tuning of the World* (1977). Through the power of his writing, Schafer is able to make us imagine sounds and silences we have never known. Most of his book serves to awaken the reader to the noise pollution of industrialized society, a good part of it the result of mass-mediated sound reproduction. He does not go so far as to say we should shut off all radios and TVs and go back to crickets, but in reminding us of what a *natural* high-fidelity sound environment is like, he provides the historic baseline from which all *electronic* soundmaking has departed. If radio production and performance people desire to attract and entertain listeners in today's soundscape, they must do so cognizant of the natural acoustic environment that mankind has inhabited for all of previous human history. Millenia of experience with that natural sound environment have become a part of our instinctive behaviors. When radio production and performance lack certain of the familiar sound cues of the past, some listeners might react strangely, or might fail to react at all to particular sound stimuli.

## Hi-fi/Lo-fi

What we think of today as high-fidelity sound reproduction might be very different from what Schafer meant by the term. Quite early in *The Tuning of the World,* Schafer introduced the concept of hi-fi and lo-fi soundscapes, which he referred to in his later writings. In a hi-fi soundscape, there is a low ambient noise level, so discrete sounds can be heard clearly and with perspective. By contrast, in a lo-fi soundscape any one sound is likely to be overwhelmed by many others, and perspective is lost. For example, "On a downtown street corner of the modern city there is no distance; there is only presence" (Schafer, 1977, p. 43).

## The Shift From Discrete to Continuous

Schafer also explained the importance of the change from the discrete, interrupted sounds common in preindustrial societies to the continuous, uninterrupted sounds of the industrialized world. Today, the soundscape in an industrialized society is likely to be comprised of much continuous sound that has no beginning or end but that drones on continuously. Examples include the whir of a refrigerator, the buzz of fluorescent lights, the throb of an automobile exhaust, the whoosh of an air conditioner, or the hum of a desktop computer. These devices are so much a part of our lives today that we no longer are much aware of their special aural existence. Today we are subject to

> permanent keynotes and swaths of broad-band noise, possessing little personality or sense of progression. . . . Just as there is no perspective in the lo-fi soundscape (everything is present at once), similarly there is no sense of duration with the flat line in sound. It is suprabiological. . . . The function of the drone has long been known in music. It is an anti-intellectual narcotic. . . . Man listens differently in the presence of drones. . . . (Schafer, 1977, pp. 78–79)

Schafer's words awaken us to the fact that radio content will be heard in a soundscape in which there may be so many different sounds that they blend into indistinctiveness, and where the flat-line drone of machinery is the norm, even in the quiet suburban home. When a radio's volume is turned low, it may be a contributor to that indistinct, lo-fi soundscape; when it is turned higher, radio must compete for attention against an increasing number of aural distractions.

## Signal Processing

Years ago, some radio stations tried adding reverberation to their program line in order to make their air sound seem more distinctive. Most of them have since given it up, because added reverberation disturbs both the space and time of the original sound, leaving the listener with less distinctiveness, not more.

More recently, the audio processing at many hit music stations was set up to deliver a bright, crisp sound, emphasizing upper midrange and treble frequencies. These frequencies have the ability to cut through most background noise well. But depending on the listening space, the bump in high-frequency output could make the overall tonal balance unnatural. In nature, treble frequencies are the ones most easily absorbed, bass frequencies being the hardest to attenuate. At a middle distance, especially against background noise such as that encountered in a car, the frequency balance was okay. But listening up close, as with headphones, resulted in excessive hiss and oversibilance because of the strong upper midrange and treble. Thus, a radio station whose audio processing was "bright" was probably best listened to at intermediate distances in relatively noisy environments.

So-called "brick wall" compression and limiting was also employed by some hit music stations to make them sound louder than other stations on the dial. Usually, one result was that the dynamic range suffered: The quiet sections of the music were louder than the original, and the loud sections were quieter. Compact discs played on stations with such processing sounded quite different from the same CDs played in the home.

Another factor relating to compressed dynamic range has to do with whether the listener plays the radio as a foreground or a background experience. A listener to a foreground service such as an AOR format typically plays the music fairly loud. When that listener encounters a talk segment on a station with considerable compression, the talk turns out to be unnaturally or even excruciatingly loud. An AOR station that marketed itself as a high-fidelity outlet (wide dynamic range, low or no compression) might try running the music at peak modulation, then purposely backing down the level of talk segments so that they are a little less loud than the music. This heretical idea (having your commercials not quite as loud as your music) has the virtue of retaining your rock music listeners through stopsets, rather than forcing them to reach for the radio to turn the volume down. Once their fingers are at the radio, they might change the dial. Quieter talk segments would give them less reason to do so. The reverse situation might apply to Soft Jazz and New Adult Contemporary formats. Because the music on these stations is often heard at background levels, talk segments would be aired at peak modulation, and the music would be transmitted at a lesser loudness.

I am aware that not fully modulating the signal decreases an FM station's stereo coverage area, and that some listeners choose a station simply on the basis of loudness. However, these disadvantages may be outweighed by the chance to superserve a narrow segment of the audience that currently finds the volume level of talk segments on their favorite station in sharp contrast to how they like to hear their music. When they play cassettes and discs on their home and car stereos, they do not have these problems. Radio's loudness processing should not create any for them.

## Headphone Listening

By 1988, nearly half of all radio listening was taking place outside the home. A growing portion of that out-of-home listening was to small battery-operated portable sets with lightweight headphones. In regard to the increasingly prevalent headphone listener, Schafer said that some sounds seem to come from inside the cranium itself, whereas others are restricted to a small sphere around the listener's head.

> ... when sound is conducted directly through the skull of the headphone listener, he is no longer regarding events on the acoustic horizon; no longer is he surrounded by a sphere of moving elements. He *is* the sphere. He is the universe. (Schafer, 1977, p. 119)

In a way, the wearer of headphones, whether listening to radio or cassettes, is living inside of a small yet ultimate acoustic shell. But even when heard through loudspeakers in a room, radio can act as what Schafer called a "sound wall."

## Radio As a Sound Wall

Schafer pointed out that the castle garden of the Middle Ages was surrounded by a physical wall to enclose the sounds of its birds and fountains and to screen the noises of the hostile world outside. Today, Schafer said, "radio has actually become the bird-song of modern life, the natural soundscape, excluding the inimical forces from outside" (p. 93). People previously built walls to isolate sound, whereas these days sound walls are constructed in order to isolate. The high outdoor level of amplification used by people playing boomboxes and car subwoofers is intended as much as a shield as a social lubricant. Such a sound wall allows the person inside it to be alone, withdrawn, and disengaged from society. The background music that is so common in public places is an example of the omnipresence of sound walls (Schafer, 1977).

Being cognizant of audiences in different environments with different needs for signal clarity and isolation or involvement allows the programmer to be intentional about serving those people. But it is difficult to imagine a level of signal processing that would satisfy both headphone and loudspeaker audiences, or a music-and-talk format that would please both background and foreground listeners. The programmer can *target* listening groups, but *delivering* specific groups is always more iffy. In radio production, audio processing is largely a "set-it-and-forget-it" proposition, affected only occasionally and temporarily by aural effects such as reverberation, echo, and frequency manipulation already recorded into music or commercials.

The case that Schafer made about sound walls almost portrays sound used in this way as a "force field." Sound walls keep unwanted sounds out and isolate the hearer to a limited acoustic environment. Headphones do this in an insistent foreground way; sound walls do it in a persistent background way.

## "Time" and "Force" Sound Parameters

The discussion of the listener's need for signal clarity, isolation, or involvement all have practical application in setting up the radio station's sound. The radio programmer can best manage *time* factors by controlling the rate of presentation of both the spoken and musical elements, both of which are discussed in later chapters. The time sound parameter is really not amenable to adjustment by audio processing equipment, except as it relates to perceived space, discussed later. However, the station might offer programming that works as an appropriate sound wall *force* for its target audience. That programming could range from background "elevator" music to foreground rock heard through speakers, to variations on these themes intended for listening in cars, to still further elaborations designed for headphone wearers.

## Managing Perceived Acoustic "Space"

In radio production, controlling the amount of isolation or involvement is largely a format choice—and the choice of formats is also a long-term, generally unchanging situation. But if the presentation rate time and the isolation/involvement force that a listener perceives are usually a compromise, the space need not be. Perceived acoustic space is a variable that can be under continuous control by the radio programmer. Indeed, perceived acoustic space and the rate of presentation are the two factors that can be most closely directed by programming people. Generally, only rate has gotten much attention.

In my audio classes, populated as they are by students who have used television from their earliest consciousness and who have only in their teen years discovered radio, it has proved helpful to use visual analogies to explain audio effects. They already know the "grammar" of TV as if it had been imprinted in their chromosomes; it is the supposedly simpler audio terms that are more difficult for them. Thus, to understand the importance of controlling perceived acoustic space, some analogies to television camera lens angles are useful.

## A SENSE OF PLACE IN ACOUSTIC SPACE

### TV Gave Up Space Exploration

If controlling the sense of acoustic space has been largely ignored in modern radio, at least it is also true that for about the past 40 years, television has not been working as hard as it might at exploring space either. Probably one of the reasons we still revere the so-called "golden age of television" is because of the early-style lenses that the cameras used until the mid- or late 1950s, when the zoom lens came into widespread use. Prior to that, TV cameras had a turret with three lenses on it—a normal lens, a wide angle, and a telephoto. The camera had to be offline in order to rotate the turret to a different lens. One of the effects of this was that a camera was forced to dolly in or dolly back in order to get closer to—or farther away from—an object. In the process, other objects in the background were concealed or revealed by the relative change in size of the foreground object.

A zoom lens does not change the size of the foreground objects relative to the background ones. When it is zoomed in, they all grow at the same rate; when zoomed out, they all shrink at the same rate. And nothing is concealed or revealed behind them.

So the net effect of using a zoom lens is that it allows the camera to stay stationary and the glassware in the lens does all the moving. Perhaps golden age television was more "three-dimensional" in the sense that the viewer had a greater feeling of moving through space, toward—and away from—an object. When the camera got close to an object, it really loomed large compared to everything around it. And because the in–out camera movements are psychologically the most powerful anyway, the substitution of the zoom may have had something to do with diminishing the impact of later TV. (In 1988, ABC's use of tiny "point-of-view" cameras on skiers and lugers for the first time in the Winter Olympics brought "the ultimate dolly" to sports coverage, although most prime-time shows continued to rely on the zoom lens.)

## The Questions Raised by Zoom Lenses

If this were a book about the effects of television, then some of the next questions might be these: What has 40 years of seeing things with zoom lenses done to our sense of community? Our sense of place? Our sense of being with someone, somewhere? If for the past 40 years television had been presented the way people actually see things (with a three-dimensional quality, with concealments and revelations in physical space), might our society be different compared to 40 years of television in which we get closer but things do not get bigger, and where the spaces behind things are left unexplored?

Because this book is about radio, the questions must be different. Television was enjoying its golden age at just about the same time radio was having its darkest hours in the 1950s. The rise of the Top 40 format happened in part because it was the only programming that seemed to find an audience in the face of the onslaught of TV. The earliest Top 40 disc jockeys were true personalities, and thus enjoyed considerable freedom to talk. Their inevitably less talented imitators survived until programmers discovered that audiences could be increased by shutting up bad disc jockeys and playing more music. Eventually, most nonmusic programming (such as remotes, news, and, of course, commercials) came to be viewed as tuneout factors to be minimized on music stations. That is why today, music format radio gets by with very little "talk" compared to radio as it was prior to Top 40, and very little of that talk happens in other than a studio environment. Thus, the predominant acoustic-space cues of modern radio come not from the announcer, but from the way the records are recorded. And too often, what is around that music on radio is the aural equivalent of a blue cyclorama curtain in TV: limbo.

## Why Radio Sounds Like Limbo

The reason radio studios sound like "limbo" is because traditionally, radio control rooms and studios were designed to be fairly "dead" to dampen the sound of the mechanical switches, solenoids, relays, and motors associated with radio production equipment. But these days, many of those switches are silent electronic ones, not noisy mechanical models. About the only noise still left in some control rooms is the broadcast cartridge player, and those are being replaced by silent digital playback machines. Soon most radio control rooms and announce booths will be dead silent. Why? Is a radio studio supposed to have the hush of a funeral home?

In television's early years, production people went through all kinds of contortions to hide the microphone from view, even on talk and interview shows. Today, microphones are very much an accepted part of the picture.

So why is radio still afraid of the minor sounds its soundmaking equipment makes?

In addition to attenuating unwanted noise, radio control rooms and studios were also designed to be neutral or benign in their effect on the frequency response of voices. The admirable idea has been to try to achieve "flat" (linear) frequency response, which translates to high-fidelity reproduction. But these days, radio studios are virtually the only places where voices are heard that way. The more television has abandoned the studio for remote locations, the more it has gotten us accustomed to hearing announcers in all kinds of novel acoustic spaces. And it is the rare modern recording that seems to have been made in an acoustically dead studio. Many records today use chorus and reverberation effects to broaden or deepen the sound, and the frequency response of the voices on modern recordings is almost never "flat."

### Questions Raised by Control Rooms

If being in acoustic limbo has been the case with radio for the last 40 years or so, then it must be asked, what has 40 years of hearing things from largely the control room perspective done to our sense of involvement in the community? What has the close-miked disc jockey done to our sense of being talked to by someone in an actual environment? If for the past 40 years, radio had instead continued to develop the announcer as a full-fledged actor in "the theater of the mind," or at least as a person at the site where the music was being made (as on the old big-band remotes), might our society be different compared to 40 years of radio in which only the musicians make such acoustic explorations?

Clearly, one challenge for a radio announcer in the MTV era is to create the same sense of *place* that the visuals do on carefully made TV. Instead, the announce-booth or control room mike is usually worked up close or at a middle distance, which precludes hearing much of the room. Working the mike fairly close, along with the acoustic treatment of the room itself, combine to make the announcer sound as if he or she is nowhere in particular.

### The Ambience of a Remote

What is needed is a real acoustic sense of place, and of things that are happening in that place. Maybe more of modern radio should have the ambience of a remote, whether or not the announcer is actually doing one. The trick then would be to keep the atmosphere of the remote without losing the discipline of the studio.

One of the things that happens in a remote is that announcers and guests are sometimes "off-mike." "Off-mike" is often thought of as a negative term, but it can be viewed as a positive effect, too. Because when a person is off-mike, what is heard instead is the missing environment.

ABC television's coverage of the 1988 Winter Olympic Games was notable for more than its revolutionary participant's point-of-view cameras. The network was reported to have used more than 500 microphones overall, to be sure that there would not be any audio "dead spots" on bobsled runs, ski race courses, and so on (Polskin, 1988). ABC was trying hard to capture the total sounds of these wide-ranging events, just as for years football broadcasts had featured pickup of the sounds of scrimmage from a parabolic sideline microphone. In both TV and radio sports coverage, the sound of the competitors is mixed with the sound of the crowd, which is in turn mixed with the sound of the announcer. Notice that two of those three are environmental sounds. But also note that once the sports remote ends and the sportscasters "send it back to the studio," the sense of place in acoustic space largely disappears. That is why radio needs to have the ambience of a remote, even when it is in the studio. If the studio has been designed to sound "dead," it can also be processed to sound more "live." But most of all, many announcers must learn to sometimes work at greater distances from the mike, so that the sense of the space can come across to the listener.

Control of the important influence of the sense of acoustic space in broadcast music is considered in chapters 10 and 12.

## RATE

It was mentioned earlier that the sense of acoustic space and the presentation rate are two factors that are very controllable by radio production people, and that only rate has gotten much attention. Actually, rate has been considered only in its largest, most obvious manifestations. Rate has always been a factor in music rotation systems (and is discussed at length later). Announcers speak at different overall rates and thus suit some formats better than others. And the rate of individual program elements (such as commercials and jingles) has also been considered. In the mid-1960s, nationally-prominent programmers decreed that the longest, least-produced spot should come early in a commercial cluster, while the shortest, most highly produced commercial should come last. The idea was to give the listener the sense of progressively shorter "talk" elements before returning to music, and heightened listener rewards achieved through the enhanced production. At about the same time, station jingles which provided a "tempo buffer" between a slow song transitioning to a faster one, and vice-versa, became available.

Little consideration has been given to the "editing" rate of radio production—that is, how slowly or quickly the program elements are put together with each other. Again, analogies to television seem useful to explain audio events to a generation that understands editing primarily from a visual standpoint.

**Television Editing Applied to Radio**

In television, the major editing effects are the cut, the dissolve, the fade, the wipe, and the key/super.

The *cut* is an instantaneous switch from one picture to another, and is by far the most common transition. The cut is like the segue in radio, except that the segue usually inserts a beat of silence between the full-up end of one element and the full-up beginning of the next.

The TV *dissolve* is very much like radio's crossfade—as the first elements are faded down, the next elements are faded up at the same rate. The replacement rate can be so fast the effect is like a cut (except with a slightly softer edge), all the way to a dreamy, languid transition lasting dozens of seconds.

The *fade* in TV is usually to or from "black" (although it could be any color). "Black" is TV's visual limbo. It is no-place, no-time, although time may be presumed to pass while in black. TV often goes to and from black between scenes, which is like a visual "new paragraph." Occasionally, TV will go to black and stay there for several seconds, often to allow time for what has just transpired to be digested by the viewer (e.g., several seconds of black after an obituary). It is a "moment of silence" for the viewer's eyes and mind. Overall, TV still uses more black than radio uses silence, because there are more dramatic moments on TV that demand such a visual pause. But radio, too, can benefit from pauses, as is pointed out in the next chapter.

*Wipes* and *keys/supers* are not really edits in the traditional sense, but ways of adding new information to the picture so that for a time the viewer's attention is shifted from the original scene.

A *wipe* is just a novel way of shoving one picture off the screen in favor of another. Today, radio counterparts of the wipe are not much in evidence, but back in Top 40's infancy, the playing of the next record would often be preceded by a highly produced intro that would proclaim "WQAM's Number Four-Four-Four" (with echo effect), or "WKKO's Rocket Riser!" Rarely was a song started without at least being announced by the jock, but featured music got the full production treatment. Short station ID jingles that gave the station's call letters just before or just after a song were called *stabs* or *shotguns*, and these names are as good as any to describe the radio version of the wipe.

The *super* is like a dissolve held midway between two pictures, so that we see 50% of one and 50% of the other. The foreground elements in a super are transparent—we can see the background through them, which gives a wispy, dreamlike effect. There is no audio equivalent, because playing two records each at 50% volume is just audio chaos.

The *key* also puts the elements of two pictures together, but in this case, the foreground elements seem opaque and thus they blot out the background elements in the other picture. Graphics of names, scores, and statistics are often keyed over the regular shot. In radio, the corollary to the key is the "drop-in" when it is used over some other element (not between elements). The key and the drop-in do not serve as transitions to something new, as the wipe does. Instead, the key or drop-in briefly adds information to the existing scene or sound, then returns to just that existing scene or sound without the additional information.

## Radio Editing Rates

The previous introduction to the radio "editing" terms *(segue, crossfade, silence, stabs,* and *drop-in)* now allows a consideration of the editing rates that are inherent in certain well-established radio production procedures. Paying closer attention to editing rates could serve a station that wants to vary its editing between elements to achieve random variety, or that wants to control editing rates to build a greater overall sense of rising and falling pace—to name just two examples.

The slowest edit is one where there is talk over a fade of the first element, talk over silence, then talk over the faded-up intro of the next element.

A slightly faster edit occurs when there is a fairly rapid crossfade between two elements (usually instrumental-to-instrumental) without any intervening talk.

Next fastest is an edit that is like the previous one, but where talk occurs over the instrumental portions, usually in order to bridge between a talk or vocal segment in the first element and another talk or vocal segment in the second segment.

Faster still is a segue-with-talk: The first element ends full-up (no fade), followed immediately by talk over the faded-up instrumental beginning of a second element. This can also happen the other way around: The first element fades, with brief bridging talk over the fade until the second element is started full-up.

Fastest of all is the pure segue. One element ends with talk, vocal, or instrumental full-up, and the next element begins the same way, with only (at most) one beat between.

Most of the time, on most stations—even ones with very tightly controlled music presentation systems—the editing together of the various other program elements is left entirely up to the discretion and ingenuity of the disc jockey. At the very least, this results in considerable disparity in the impact of the programming from jock to jock, even though they might play the same elements in the same order. At the worst, the way the program elements are edited together may work counter to the desired effect in controlling the order of the music and the commercials. So it seems worthwhile for stations to consider editing rates in their overall air presentation scheme.

Research by consultant Ed Shane (1991) into the subject of variety relates to the editing rates just described, and especially to *when* and *how often* an announcer talks. Shane has found that enjoying variety is one of the reasons that listeners tune any station, regardless of format. In part, that means they like the way the tempo changes between records, or from current to gold, or from a spare texture to a thick one. But here is the other part:

> In most of our research sessions, we play music tapes for our respondents. A typical tape contains four or five recognizable segments of songs edited together to represent a style of radio. In such a test, the respondent evaluates the tapes by choosing which he or she would listen to "most often, "sometimes," or "not at all. . . ."
>
> During one test, we used the exact same music sequence three times, changing only the announcer pattern in each play. In one, the announcer talked over the intro of every record. In another, two songs played back to back, the announcer talked, then the other two songs played back to back. Yet another played all four songs with no talk, with the announcer only at the end.
>
> We were surprised to find respondents using the word "variety" to tell us what they liked about the all-talkover tape. That tape received twice as many mentions of "variety" as the others. In none of the tapes did the announcer use the word "variety," and respondents were asked only "What did you like most about this tape?" They were not led by any choice of terms. The announcer's approach created variety. (pp. 117–118)

This chapter has tried to develop the concept of the space between a listener's ears as a sound stage—a stage whose space is affected by the content presented, of course, but just as much by such factors as audio processing, the distance of the announcer from the microphone, the distance of the listener from the loudspeaker or headphone, the design of studio spaces, and the rate at which elements are melded together. In the next chapter, the stage receives its actor: the air personality.

## MAJOR POINTS

1. Today we live and produce radio programming for consumption in what R. Murray Schafer called a *lo-fi soundscape,* in which individual sounds are lost in a dense collision of other sounds.

2. According to Schafer, in an earlier time, most sounds were discrete and interrupted. Today, many sounds drone, one note sounding continuously.

3. Audio processing that seeks to overcome the noise problems of the "average" listening environment by increasing upper midrange and treble is probably best listened to at intermediate distances in relatively noisy environments (such as cars), rather than through headphones or loudspeakers in a quiet room.

4. Today, said Schafer, the portable radio (played as a boombox, or through earphones) exists as a sound wall that allows isolation, in the same way that stone walls used to be built to isolate sounds.

5. In radio production, controlling the amount of listener isolation or involvement is largely a format choice, and is thus not easily changed. But perceived acoustic space can be continuously controlled by the programmer.

6. The use of zoom lenses in television replaced camera-dolly movements that used to give a greater sense of exploring visual space. The radio control room/studio has helped radio to sound like "limbo." So has a generation of announcers who tend to work the microphone only at one fixed distance.

7. Television editing terms have audio counterparts: The cut = the segue; the dissolve = the crossfade; the fade-to-black = a silent pause; wipes = produced intros and ID jingles; and keys = drop-ins used over other audio.

8. Audio editing rates range from the slowest (talk over a fade of the first music segment, talk over silence, talk over the intro of the next music segment), to the fastest (pure segue—one element ends full-up, and the next begins the same way immediately).

9. In one test, a simulated station had more perceived variety when the announcer talked between every record than when he spoke only between each pair, or backannounced four songs at one time.

# CHAPTER 8

## *Air Personality: The Structure of Spoken Gesture*

There are lots of terms for the people who comprise the on-air staff of a radio station. Most of those terms leave something to be desired. Many *disc jockeys* never manipulate any physical discs these days, and the term seems inappropriate when applied to nonhit-music formats. The older moniker of *announcer* has its problems too. People speaking over an airport PA system who tell which flights are arriving are announcers in the literal sense of the word, and one would hope that a radio announcer would be more entertaining and engaging than that. Perhaps the best term is the one least used: *host,* in the sense of the person who has invited you to a party. The word is often used in the Talk format, but unfortunately not much in the rest of the business, so in this chapter we settle for *announcer* as if it encompassed all the other terms.

The focus of this chapter is the announcer-as-actor, a performer in the theater of the mind. If that sounds like a throwback to the ancient golden age of radio drama, it should not. Any radio performance still needs to have its roots in theatrical performance. In fact, the more our society becomes a visually oriented one, the more important the announcer-as-actor becomes.

### THE CHALLENGE OF RADIO PERFORMANCE IN A VISUAL ERA

More than 30 years ago, Edmund Carpenter (as cited in Ohlgren & Luhan, 1977) posed the challenge for radio in the present television age, when the visual image has become the dominant one even for the hit music listener:

The gestures of visual man are not intended to convey concepts that can be expressed in words, but inner experiences, nonrational emotions, which would still remain unexpressed when everything that can be told has been told. Such emotions lie in the deepest levels. They cannot be approached by words that are mere reflections of concepts, any more than musical experiences can be expressed in rational concepts. (p. 9)

The question for radio is, how to convey those inner experiences, those nonrational emotions that cannot be put into words. The music does it in large part, and the more a radio music listener has absorbed of MTV-type videos, the more those videos unreel again in the listener's mind as the radio supplies the sound track. Music videos seem almost to be textbook examples of visual gestures that "are not intended to convey concepts that can be expressed in words, but inner experiences, nonrational emotions, which would still remain unexpressed when everything that can be told has been told." Music videos provide the listener a very concrete visual stage for very amorphous, nonrational experiences. The visual stage is reexperienced each time radio replays the video's music. The question is: What happens to that stage when the music stops?

In the previous chapter, I appealed to radio announcers and producers to pay attention to preserving a sense of place in acoustic space—that when the music stops, some place with discernible spacial qualites ought to be discernible by the listener. If an adequate acoustic place for speech can be assumed, then attention can turn to the actors who perform on that stage and what they do and say.

## Radio Performers Are Salespeople

In an earlier section, a case was made that the listener expects radio to be very much in the entertainment business, so the idea of having "actors" on the radio is not a departure from that theme. However, radio is also in the selling business. Specifically, commercial radio is in the business of selling other businesses. Radio programming is entertainment, but it is also a sales vehicle.

Some people seem to think that these dual roles for radio are incompatible; that if you are really good at one aspect, then the other will suffer. These folks believe that a program with truly superior entertainment values will have trouble finding sponsors, or that the very presence of a sales effort alongside the effort to make good programs somehow contaminates the program production effort with "lowest common denominator" thinking. Not so.

The best radio is radio that sells. It sells everything: the music that is played, the people who play it, the news that interrupts it, the commercials that support it, the station itself.

Consider the singers who are popular with the mass audience. Most of them do not merely mouth the words and hit all the notes. They shape the words and the melodies to their own personalities, so that what comes out is a mixture of the song and the singer. They do more than deliver the song. The really fine singers sell it to you by investing themselves completely in the event. Through the force of their personality entwined in the way the song is sung, the great performers make you care about the song, make you need to hear it to conclusion, make you believe in it, persuade you, and suspend your disbelief. It is the ultimate communication: the singer, the song, and the audience merged into a single thinking, feeling entity. The success of the singer and the song becomes important to you—you want them to be great. You stop analyzing what is and is not working and simply get caught up in the moment, wanting it to go on, wanting to hear it again.

Wanting to hear it again; that is, wanting to hear the song again. But what about the commercial that just aired? Does your station's audience want to hear it again, too? Did the announcer make the audience suspend their disbelief and care about the product? Did the audience get caught up in the moment and wish for it to continue, wanting the announcer to go on being great?

If your answer is "No, of course not—these are commercials, not pop songs!" then you probably believe a stop set is an accurate name for what happens on lots of radio stations: Many of the entertainment values inherent in the music screech to a stop when the music ends and the spots begin.

## NEEDING ARTHUR GODFREY AGAIN

In 1931, a young radio announcer named Arthur Godfrey was in a serious auto accident that kept him in a hospital for several months. He listened to the radio a great deal, and made an important realization. Most of the announcers of that day were not talking to an individual but rather to a group. "Ladies and gentlemen of the radio audience" they would begin, visualizing a mass audience of thousands or millions as they spoke. They talked as if they were public speakers in a huge auditorium, exaggerating consonants for clarity, and punching everything out with lots of volume and intonation. They were more like platform orators than what we think of today as announcers.

### Speaking to the Audience Individually

Godfrey realized that even if several people listened together (as families did when they gathered around the radio in the 1930s), an announcer actually was still talking to each person individually. Godfrey decided that he would talk to just one person at a time, even though he knew he would be reaching many others at the same instant. (Note that much commercial copy today uses "you" statements or implicit "you" statements. Godfrey used "I" because it is a personal testimonial, like "word of mouth." The nameless announcer on the typical production spot usually is making "you" statements.)

Once he had determined that radio listening was a solitary experience, even if done in a small group, Godfrey went on to develop a speaking style that would be congruent with this intimacy. He dropped his volume to a conversational level. He stopped intoning like a platform speaker. He did not exaggerate consonants for clarity—in fact, he dropped consonants and spoke like normal people do (e.g.: *goin'* instead of *going*). His natural vocal timbre—rich and warm and resonant—made him sound like he was confiding in you. He talked like a neighbor, a companion. He was somebody you could trust. He did not talk down to you. He talked a lot like you did. This was no snake oil salesman. This was a friend. The public believed him, and they bought the products he talked about. Godfrey was probably the most successful radio network selling voice of his time, just as newscaster Paul Harvey is today.

## Emulate the Analysis, Not Necessarily the Style

The conversational style that Arthur Godfrey invented has waxed and waned over the years (it almost disappeared entirely in the hyperkinetic early days of the Top 40 format.) This is not meant to be a plea for more Godfrey-type, or Paul Harvey-type conversationalists on radio. But the same kind of analysis that Godfrey did can help any announcer to find a style for her or his particular daypart's boardshift, or for the 4 P.M. newscast, or for the spot he or she is going to do for the local shoe store. Among the questions to ask are: Who are your listeners likely to be? Where are they likely to be? What else are they likely to be doing? (Remember, radio is hardly ever given sole attention.) How long are they likely to stay tuned in?

Such audience analysis is bound to improve any speaker's effectiveness in reaching the intended audience in the desired way. But there are techniques to consider from both the field of public speaking and from stage acting that will work for any would-be radio communicator—even if the precise makeup of the audience is not well known. A good radio announcer needs to be a public speaker who brings much of the drama of the stage to his or her utterances, and/or an actor who is especially effective at delivering monologues. Either way, the intent is to solidify the structure and deepen the appeal of his or her spoken gestures.

From public speaking, we are going to borrow the concepts of the four aspects of the speaking voice: *rate, intensity* (volume, loudness), *timbre* (distinctive vocal quality), and *pitch*. And from training in stage movement comes the concept of three distinct patterns that are reflected via the actor's body: a pattern in time, a pattern in space, and a pattern of force. As suggested by Oxenford (1952), when actors move from point A to point B, we can analyze their traverse in terms of (a) how long it takes them (time), (b) the amount of room they take up with their body, gestures, and stride (space), and (c) how much energy they invest in the process, as revealed by their gestures.

*Time.* We begin with time, which we'll stipulate is the same as the rate of delivery. Obviously, an announcer usually has to get through a 30-second spot in 29.5 seconds. Arthur Godfrey was never very concerned with keeping his ad-libbed pitches timed to the second; they often ran over or under. But more important is what he did with time within the commercial. He would often take a very long pause, during which the listener could hear a complete breathing cycle. He was not speaking on a radio announcer's time, which is clock-bound. He was speaking on a listener's time, which is sense-bound. He paused to let things sink in, and he paused before important words to put some "sparkle" around them. Then he would steam through a sentence of mostly unimportant words, dropping consonants by the wayside, until he arrived at the next important idea, pausing before and after it again, to let it stand alone. Godfrey used variations in time (rate of delivery) to put the equivalent of white space around important words. A pause in the delivery made room around an important idea and helped it to stand out. Thus, in Godfrey's delivery, time (rate) also influenced space.

*Pitch.* The breathing space around important words was also influenced by the way Godfrey pitched his voice. He knew when to do a monotone and when to do a roller coaster of different pitches. He often avoided the falling pitch that typically marks the end of a declarative statement, and instead let his voice go up at the end, using the same inflection as when asking a question. Newscaster Paul Harvey uses this technique extensively, and several texts teach this trick to young actors, but not very many young radio announcers use it. That is too bad, because this technique leads the listener to believe there is more yet to be said. It keeps the audience "tuned in" to what is coming next, and adds a sense of expectation and curiosity. Godfrey used pitch to keep an important idea dangling in front of the listener, as if it were a kite in a strong breeze, bobbing and darting, but never coming to earth until the whole flight was complete. He used pitch to focus attention on the important ideas, giving them the space they needed in the listener's mind.

*Timbre and the Distance From the Microphone.* Arthur Godfrey was aware, as most announcers are today, that it is not possible to vary intensity (volume) as much in radio speaking as is possible in public speaking. (Talk too soft or too loud on the radio in the old days and you would either get lost in the hiss or you would blow out the microphone. Today, processing equipment will not *let* you be too loud or too soft.) So, because the radio medium imposes limits on changes in intensity (volume), Godfrey compensated by accentuating changes in vocal timbre (quality). To listen to Godfrey do a spot is to hear someone who can run the gamut from warm, soft, and deep, to icy, hard, and nasal. He had a wonderfully flexible vocal mechanism, but not any better than many today. What was more important than the physical components of his voice was the way he apparently accentuated changes in vocal timbre by changes in his distance from the microphone. Icy, hard, and nasal works best when speaking loudly and at a distance from the mike. Warm, soft, and deep happens as close to the mike as possible without popping Ps and Bs. Godfrey spoke with a close-up, warm, soft, and deep timbre because he invented the style, but he could back off and holler, too. Godfrey used changes in timbre and in distance from the mike to affect the sense of psychological distance from him felt by the listener. Timbre and mike distance affected the sense of space, and substituted for radio's inability to project changes in vocal force.

It is amazing how few of today's announcers know how to change their rate to get more emphasis, know how to vary the pitch to build expectation, and seem unaware of the vastly different psychological impact that talking just 3 or 4 inches closer or farther from the mike can have. In his book *Cutting Through,* Ed Shane (1991) introduced the term *proxemics,* which is defined as "the consideration of distances at which members of various cultures interact" (pp. 42–43). The inventor of proxemics, Edward T. Hall, had measured four distances at which Americans operate in true physical space:

- Intimate distance–0 to 1½ feet. For Americans, only the most personal communication. Family, lovers, and so on.
- Personal distance–1½ to 4 feet. Handshake distance.
- Social or consultative–4 to 10 feet. Offices, meetings, and so on.
- Public distance–10 feet or more. Shopping malls, addressing an audience, and so on.

Microphones are just not as sensitive as the human ear. When a mike is worked at a distance of about 1 to 3 inches, it produces the "intimate" effect. A simple "good morning" said at that distance is the sort of greeting one would only expect to hear from a lover on the next pillow, but many people have gotten used to radio talent talking to us that intimately. The "personal," handshake distance can be portrayed by talking about 8 to 12 inches from the mike. The "social or consultative" distance has the mike about 1 to 3 feet away, and the "public" distance puts the mike about 3 feet or more from the person speaking. "Good morning" said loud and about 3 feet away from the microphone sounds like a greeting to a neighbor in the next driveway.

Shane pointed out—and I concur—that U.S. radio is very intimate, both because of the usual close miking of announcers, and because our playback instruments are also relatively close by. Radio listening is also becoming more "up close and personal," thanks to increasing numbers of headphone-type personal stereos, and to radio-equipped computers that put the tiny speakers only a couple of feet away from the user. As a result, a close-miked style can seem overly intimate, whereas distantly miked voices sound shrunken in both size and volume, rather than far away. In either case, real people do not yell at each other at such close ranges, unless one of them is a drill sergeant.

*Space.* You have noted by now that with Arthur Godfrey's (or any good announcer's) style of speaking, every aspect of the voice affects the component of the actor's arsenal known as *space*. Arthur Godfrey succeeded not just because the listener knew who he was, and what he stood for, but also because the listener always knew *where* Godfrey was in relation to her or him. Godfrey's was not a disembodied mouth anchored forever at some middle distance like many of today's small-market announcers. Godfrey was a whole person, because he could leap over the unimportant stuff and suddenly stop scrambling to admire the important material; he could hang that voice up in the air or land it squarely on earth; he could move himself very far from you or closer than anyone but your bedmate.

Godfrey's voice did not just happen in space—it *used* space, moved around in it, reveled in it, like our own bodies do. Godfrey's voice put his whole body across. He became, without any video to reinforce it, a physical character in people's lives. He had an aura of physical vitality, because he used the actor's tools of time, space, and force so well. A sizzling background instrumental music bed or a well-timed sound effect would have only detracted from the powerful impact his unadorned delivery had with an audience of millions.

Movement theorist Joseph Lange said that certain actions or movements can evoke emotional reactions. For example, the physical act of jumping quickly backward as if to avoid a speeding car can evoke the emotions of fear, shock, and relief associated with the actual event. On a stage, careful blocking (placement and movement of objects and actors) can help the actor to portray his or her character's emotions, because good blocking puts objects and people where the actor can use them to best physical advantage. However, in radio, there are no physical objects and rarely are there other people for the announcer to interact with. The only thing akin to blocking (in the sense of relational placement and movement on the stage) is the announcer's distance from the microphone. And most announcers never vary it.

## Targeting and Selling the Listener

Knowing where the audience is, and knowing what else they are doing, is helpful. But it is not essential. If an announcer assumes, as Godfrey did, that he or she is not talking to homogenized masses but to each audience member individually, then listeners can be targeted one on one. There will always be some listeners who are not where the announcer would like them, or who are not devoting strong attention to the radio. It is up to the announcer to place the listener where the announcer wants him or her to be, and to get the listener to pay foreground attention to what the announcer is saying. That is done the same way a singer sells a song: by letting the singer's personality infuse the lyrics and power the melody. In announcing terms, that means not letting the copy or the clock dictate the effect on the listener, but letting the rapport the announcer wants to have with the listener determine it.

The listener comes to any given moment on the radio with no expectations at all. For the moment, think of the listener as a car, and the show or spot as a trip to be taken. The listener does not begin in any gear—he or she is in neutral. The announcer alone determines the speed to go, the route to take, and how often the car will be slowed to allow sightseeing along the way. It is the listener's car, but the announcer is driving it. And the listener will allow that to happen, so long as he or she cannot do it better for herself or himself. But it takes nothing less than the force of the announcer's personality, entwined around the client's product or the station's format, like a singer wraps a song around her or his own psyche.

## Your Neighbor as Salesperson

One more analogy: Too many radio announcers rank in the listener's mind along with itinerant door-to-door salesmen of the sort that keep pestering Dagwood Bumstead in the middle of a nice bath. They ring the bell insistently to get your attention, they launch into a wild-eyed pitch that will not keep you standing on the porch—dripping wet—any longer than necessary, and they go for the close in a hurry. They have a certain bravado because they expect to be rejected, and they need to sound "bigger than life" at least for their own egos. Why should you buy anything from a guy you do not know, who is here now but will be God-knows-where tomorrow? What reason do you have for believing him? What do you know about him? He can make all sorts of claims, but you have nothing but his breathless word for it. And he will be back someday too soon pitching something else—maybe even a competing product. If Dagwood were really interested in buying the product, he would probably ask his neighbor Herb Woodley for a recommendation. Dagwood's been talking with Herb over the back fence for decades. They have had their disagreements, but Herb is a known quantity. Herb is a companion, a confidante. Herb is who you would want to have selling your product. Herb is who you would want on your radio station playing records. Herb is any radio announcer who is himself or herself first, and a voice second. Herb is Arthur Godfrey.

This needs repeating: It is not that all the world's radio announcers should try to imitate Arthur Godfrey. But radio announcers succeed best when they (a) try to become as much in tune with their audience's needs and expectations as Arthur Godfrey was; (b) become as much of a companion, friend, and trusted spokesperson as Godfrey became; and most important, (c) never let the form of communication become more important than its function.

In the heyday of Top 40, AM hit radio's "bad boy" was Dick Biondi, the quintessential "screamer." Biondi yelled everything he said, which at the time was a revolutionary affront to the close-miked, soft-spoken types on traditional (non-Top-40) stations. When Biondi rared back and hollered, it was the vocal equivalent of a jump into hyperspace. Biondi succeeded on points (a) and (b), but the very act of shouting everything eventually seemed to become a formula. Later, Wolfman Jack succeeded well on point (a). On point (b), he was a companion and friend (*a la* his role in the classic film *American Graffiti*), but he mitigated that trust by being an overenthusiastic spokesperson for almost anything. On point (c), he employed his voice to great effect, using all three vectors of time, space, and force well (especially the last two), but after a while, the vocal razzle-dazzle seemed to settle into a formula and his style began to seem closer to shtick. The form took over. Yet Dick Clark has succeeded for four decades by adhering to the three points. In his case, selling all sorts of things has not seemed to hurt at all, perhaps because he brings the same measured earnestness to the music and performers he describes that he brings to a pitch for acne medicine.

There must be at least 300 people in the country who have a vocal mechanism as good as Dick Clark's. But good announcing only appears on its surface to be about golden, pear-shaped tones, clear diction, superb phrasing, and the like. It really is about engaging another human mind in an efficient and imaginative communion. In that communion of two minds can come the kind of participation where the audience wants the singer to be great, cannot *wait* to applaud, and wishes fervently to hear it all again. Having sold herself or himself, and the client's product, the announcer has gone on to sell you, the listener, on yourself: Yes, you are good enough. Yes, you can be more. Yes, the world is going to go on. And yes, together we can figure out what we're supposed to be doing in it.

## THE ANNOUNCER AS IDEAL MATE

The announcer just described is an idealized human being. So consider Table 8.1 which excerpts the answers to a survey that asked men and women, "What do you look for when selecting the ideal mate?"

The top three responses (warm/loving, sense of humor, and intelligent) got substantially more than one-third of the responses from both men and women. Traits such as honesty, shared interests, and being good company all hovered in the one third area. Traits that got substantially *less* than a third of the votes included being self-confident, enthusiastic, and optimistic. Now, ask yourself: If people do not think it is very important to spend their whole lives with a self-confident, enthusiastic, optimistic person, why

TABLE 8.1
Traits of the Ideal Mate

|  | *Men %* | *Women %* |
| --- | --- | --- |
| Warm/loving | 51 | 66 |
| Sense of humor | 57 | 58 |
| Intelligent | 50 | 37 |
| Honest | 30 | 43 |
| Interested in same things I am | 37 | 31 |
| Good company | 33 | 30 |
| Dependable | 24 | 35 |
| Self-confident | 20 | 17 |
| Sexy | 21 | 6 |
| Enthusiastic | 9 | 10 |
| Optimistic | 6 | 8 |
| Serious | 8 | 6 |

*Note.* Adapted from a survey by D'Arcy Masius Benton & Bowles, Inc., Fears and fantasies of the American male. (1987, August, *Men's Fitness,* p. 49. (Copyright © 1987 by *Men's Fitness* magazine, reprinted by permission.)

is there so much self-confident, enthusiastic optimism among the radio personalities we want them to spend a few minutes with? If what people want in a person they can put up with for more than one night are traits like being warm and loving, having a sense of humor, and being intelligent, why do we not hear more of those? As we comic strip readers perform the voice of that wild-eyed salesman with the new gizmo on Dagwood's porch, we probably have him sounding self-confident, enthusiastic, and optimistic. But we do not believe him—perhaps *because* that is how he sounds about everything. At the bottom of it, self-confidence, enthusiasm, and optimism are all largely self-referential emotions. They mostly reflect the psyche of the speaker. They do not involve the audience in an exchange the way a warm and loving relationship does, the way a sense of humor rewards us with laughter, the way intelligence lifts us up with insight.

### The Public Smile

We have all seen—and have come to suspect—the professional, public smile. We suspect it because we have seen that public smile vanish in an instant when the cameras were thought to be off. A radio voice that is only projecting self-confident enthusiastic optimism is a public smile, and we often do not believe it. (I always believed a classic radio grump like Larry Lujack more than an eternally bright and cheerful fellow like Casey Kasem.) An announcer who is genuinely warm and loving, who has a sense of humor and is intelligent, will likely have a smile in her or his air voice that is generated spontaneously by a sense of interaction with the audience. It is not a pose. It is who the announcer really is at that moment.

## ANNOUNCERS AS ACTORS

### Playing Actions, Not Emotions

The truly effective radio announcer shares the actor's objective of accomplishing a true two-way communications exchange. Notice the word *objective*. Actors play objectives and intentions, not emotions. Playing emotions leads to stereotypes, which merely meet the audience's preconceived notions. That is why trying to convey self-confidence, enthusiasm, or optimism often does not work. Neither will an attempt to portray one or some of the list of appeals in chapter 4. The appeals describe the results of programming decisions, results that audiences can perceive and react to. It is not sensible to ask somebody to *be* more novel or more nostalgic. Portraying nostalgia is a result of the actor *doing* something to achieve that situation, such as, "I'll try to regain a moment in my childhood." An actor cannot get to that moment through some form of the verb *to be*, as in *be more pensive* or *be more moody*. The verb *to be* followed by an adjective simply is not translatable into action by most people. The action itself must be defined, and then the adjective will be the result, the fallout from the action.

Actors following the Stanislavski "method" try to discover the reasons for their actions. They often start by expressing in a single sentence the smallest of their objectives—the ones that apply for just that given moment of the play. They then move on to larger objectives, such as the ones for a scene. Finally, the actor attempts to define his or her total goals—the "super"-objectives in their interaction with others in the entire play.

Radio air personnel could benefit from a discussion with management about the station's aggregate target audience, the average ideal listener, the smallest (moment-by-moment) programming objectives, and the super-objective of the station's total impact on the community. But in all of these, the verb *to be* must be avoided. Instead, there must be a concentration on intentions and objectives—what the actor/announcer *wants*, moment-by-moment on that day for the station as a whole.

### An Exchange of Effort

Part of the communication process is an exchange of effort on the part of both the actor and the audience. Perhaps the audience requires a greater effort from a live actor on a stage than from an actor on TV or radio, simply because the audience has made an effort to go to the theater versus "just" tuning in. The radio audience has done less to hear the announcer, so demands less announcer effort. The whole listening experience, then, is both less demanding and less rewarding.

Although radio announcers could hope that audiences would arrive at their radios fully ready to participate, previous chapters have shown that *in*attention is more likely. Thus, the burden of upgrading the communication exchange must fall on the announcer. And although an objective such as "achieving a communion" may be appropriate, there is one noun connected with the process that is useful to keep in mind: *quality*.

### Quality

Robert M. Pirsig, author of *Zen and the Art of Motorcycle Maintenance* (1975), wrestled with the question of whether the quality of an object or an event resides in the thing itself or in the eyes of the beholder. Eventually, Pirsig came to the conclusion that

Quality couldn't be independently related with either the subject or the object, but could be found *only in the relationship of the two with each other.* It is the point at which subject and object meet.

That sounded warm.

Quality is not a *thing.* It is an *event.*

Warmer.

It is the event at which the subject becomes aware of the object.

And because without objects there can be no subject—because the objects create the subject's awareness of himself—Quality is the event at which awareness of both subjects and objects is made possible. (p. 233)

In other words, quality is an exchange of one person's best effort for the best efforts of another. In radio terms, the best efforts of a producer of a program collide with the best efforts of a listener to appreciate the program, and in that event, quality is realized. Too often, neither the creator, the owner, nor the user (to quote Pirsig's terms) feels a sense of identity with it, and hence it has no quality.

**Intense Concentration**

This kind of awareness is certainly much easier to accomplish in live theater, where the actor and audience can see and hear each other. In live theater, there are moments when the audience so completely "loses the frame" that there is total belief in the reality of the on-stage action. A kind of "tunnel vision" takes over, blotting out the proscenium, the lights, even other audience members. The mind's eye "zooms in" on the action, bringing the actors up close no matter how far back in the house the observer may be. And a hush overtakes the audience in a profound way—no one unwraps a candy, no one coughs, no one even moves. The communion is complete, both visually and aurally. Actors—without ever seeing the audience sitting in the darkness—report feeling "energy" coming from them at such moments. The actors can somehow sense the intensity of the audience's concentration.

It is the radio announcer's job to accomplish such an intensity of concentration by adopting the Godfreyesque stance of talking with only one person at time. It is essential to imagine talking with that idealized listener, and doing it with the same care that you would take in talking with an actual person who mattered to you very much. In such real-life conversations, there can be the same timelessness and sense of being "in flow" that comes from wonderfully carved ski turns or from perfectly played sonatas—because there is an exchange of one person's best efforts for the best efforts of another. In radio, the best efforts of the producer/announcer/actor are perceived by the listener, who then is encouraged to put forth his or her own best efforts to appreciate the program. In that delicious collision, quality is realized.

With an idea of what it is radio announcers should strive to do, we can turn to the question of what they should say.

## WHAT IS THERE TO TALK ABOUT?

### The Wednesday Afternoon Format

Perhaps it is best to begin with the things to avoid. Programming researcher and critic Gary Bond wrote a well-focused essay on the junk phrases that pass for radio personality which he called "The Wednesday Afternoon Format," so named because of all the times he heard one disc jockey telling his afternoon listeners what day of the week it was—and even what year! Bond quoted the same jock delivering this all-too-common banality: "How are you doing today? Hope you're having a nice one. Nice to have you along. . . ." Some of these irrelevancies, said Bond, are the result of infrequent airchecking by program directors:

> Listen to the Wednesday Afternoon jocks and it becomes much easier to understand the number of talk restrictions that have evolved over time. Some programmers who are allegedly anti-personality are simply anti-crap. Restrictions have come about because of some believers in personality who had no personality. Programmers said, "If you're going to say nothing, I'd rather hear it in 4 seconds than in 40." That way, at least the jock is limited in the number of irrelevancies he can speak.

Bond concluded his essay by pointing out how radio programmers' willingness to forgive banal and irrelevant chatter contrasts with TV:

> The useless phrases that are continually repeated on radio throughout the country do not speak well for the medium. We should have the same respect for our medium as the television man who reacted indignantly to 5 seconds of black screen by saying, "I could have sold that time!" That respect calls for saying what is relevant and entertaining and avoiding filler cliches.

### Confirmation/Consistency/Predictability

Some people have read "The Wednesday Afternoon Format" and have reacted by saying, "But people *want* to have information confirmed." This is true, up to a point. Confirmation is okay, but too much time spent telling me what I already know as if it were new information is the sin. Talk radio consultant Bill McMahon said, "A lot of hosts are like football color commentators who tell you things you can see for yourself. If they don't get *ahead* of their audience, they don't provide enough reason for listeners to keep tuning in" (Bloomquist, 1993, p. 23). As Program Director David Isreal said, "We've found people perceive lots of talk when there's little information" (Kinosian, 1988, p. 49).

Gary Bond made the point that many of the mistakes of the Wednesday Afternoon Format could be caught with simple airchecking. But sometimes, even airchecking does not work, perhaps because those in charge of radio programming do not listen to their stations the way listeners do.

I have had a problem for years with college freshman and sophomore broadcasting students imitating what they heard on the radio back home. What they often heard was the Wednesday Afternoon Format. When a student asks what *should* be included in an aircheck, the answer given by longtime Program Director and Unistar executive Gary Taylor seems best. Taylor used to tell announcers looking for work on his stations what he *did not* want in an aircheck: He did not want the tried-and-true time and temperature, he did not want the jock's name over and over, he did not want the obvious title of the record and the name of the familiar artist; he wanted what was left. For too many would-be Wednesday Afternooners, nothing was. Those who still had something succinct and fresh to say might make it.

## Plain Talk

Plain talk should not be confused with the hackneyed blather of the Wednesday Afternoon Format. Plain talk is the avoidance of radioese by sticking to words that everyday people use. Here is an example from WDOK, Cleveland PD Sue Wilson, who said that only radio announcers ever utter phrases like "Currently on the outside, we have 59 degrees on tap."

> If a listener called and asked if it was going to rain, our personality wouldn't say, "The possibility of measurable precipitation is 80%." I don't allow our talent to even use the word precipitation on the air. If it's going to rain or snow, they use those exact words. Take the forecast that was written for a meteorologist and rewrite it for people who aren't meterorologists. (Kinosian, 1995c, p. 34)

## Real Talk

Consultant Mike McVay (1994, p. 54) said that an announcer's preparation for what will be said on the air should ideally happen all day long, by being sensitive to changes in the community that others might take for granted. Talk format consultant Bill McMahon pointed out that even on a conversation station, a host must do much more than make the headline in the morning newspaper the topic of the day's show. He believes that radio people who talk for a living must be true to themselves, and must be encouraged to portray their innermost feelings and thoughts. Like the best soap operas and sitcoms, a radio show host must project an established character, whose typical behavior is known to the audience. The talk show hosts who do the best job of "creating dramatic interest in their shows are those who have strong, defined personalities and a core of beliefs that don't change" (Bloomquist, 1994, p. 35).

## Zero Talk and Commercial-Free Hours

In an effort to be the station that has the most music and the least talk, many "more music" operations have tried playing as much as an hour of segued songs uninterrupted by either disc jockeys or commercials. As pointed out in an earlier chapter, one immediate result of such "zero talk hours" is the lengthening of stopsets when one finally occurs. If multiple spots are clustered together, a stopset becomes aptly named, for the entertainment generally does screech to a halt. However, one of the consequences of also muzzling the disc jockey is that virtually all of the entertainment value must then be derived from the music, making music selection and rotation extremely critical. And because—as is demonstrated in later chapters—current systems of music selection and rotation are fundamentally flawed, it is not surprising that listeners tend not to feel much passion for these stations.

Some stations have promoted their music sweeps by calling them "commercial-free" hours, but W. R. Sabo, Inc. (1988, p. 29), a radio marketing and programming advisory company, upbraided the industry for such phraseology in a trade ad. The bold headline read "DIRTIEST WORDS ON RADIO: 'Commercial Free'." The copy continued, "You can win big ratings without saying those dirty words. Great programmers get ratings with full spot loads. Profitable sales promotions. And with personalities who can bring customers to your retail advertisers."

## Selling the Music

Another result of "zero talk hours" and long music sweeps without announcing is that a great many casual listeners have no idea of how to ask for music that they have heard on the radio. The record industry tried to fight this trend in the late 1980s with a "Play It and Say It" campaign aimed at programmers and announcers. Veteran programmer Bill Drake (1988) commented on this situation in a *Radio & Records* interview:

Nobody should have to be told it's unwise for your audience not to know what the music is. Radio may say it's not in the business of selling records, but it *is* in the business of selling music. Stations must realize that by not selling the music there will be very little enthusiasm for it by the listener, which can translate to little enthusiasm for the station playing that music. (p. 28)

## Why Talk About the Music?

For many students, and lots of practicing announcers, the mainstay of disc jockey chatter that attempts to go beyond mere song title and artist identification has always been deeper information or further comment about the music being played. But depending too much on airplay music to provide grist for the conversational mill can be a trap. The trap has to do with the relative familiarity of the music. If a song is quite new, it is likely to provoke a strong listener response, as the melody and lyric begin the progression from being completely novel to being totally familiar. It is ironic that disc jockeys are *most* likely to have something to say about a song at this early stage of acceptance, just when the listener has plenty of responses of his or her own. To make matters worse, the jock is *least* likely to have anything to say about a song when it is older, just when the listener is also running out of responses. Thus, new songs can "speak for themselves" to listeners, whereas older ones would benefit the most from amusing interpretation by the disc jockey.

It goes against human nature for a disc jockey not to be more excited by a new song than an old one, and not to have more things to say about it early in its life span than later. That is why the good announcers are actors: They can portray interest and excitement even when the music is very familiar. But the easiest way to avoid this problem is not to talk about just the music in the first place.

## Two Audience Expectation Guidelines

These observations can be summarized as two "audience expectation" guidelines for disc jockeys: (a) help me when I need it, not when I don't; and (b) don't tell me what I already know. Too much predictability is tantamount to telling me what I already know.

If the same liners make the station too predictable, and talking about the music leads the jock into the trap of helping the listener when he or she does not need it (thus telling the listener what is already known), then what *does* the announcer talk about?

Almost two decades ago, the Associated Press Broadcast Services division (1988, p. 13) ran ads in radio trade magazines with the headline "After 10 in a row, play today's hit single." A photo showed a disc jockey holding a singular piece of wire copy. The text of the ad continued, "Think of AP as an exclamation point at the end of a 27-minute music statement. A way to focus your audience's ear and brain; a way to set up a commercial break, a station promo, or a new addition to your playlist." The remarkable thing about this ad is that it had to explain how disc jockeys might find uses for radio wire copy.

## TALK ABOUT THE COMMUNITY'S STORIES

Ideally, the jock talks about what the community is talking about. The really great announcers seem to know everything that is going on in their cities. But not only do they have the facts, they also have the feelings, the mood. And they convert those facts, focused through the lens of the community's moods, into stories.

The radio announcer who wants to become a true communicator needs to consider the behavior of ordinary people who are in an entertainment-seeking mood in public places—a mood that is similar to the one they are in when they hear a radio station in private. Announcers need to observe people at picnics, at bars, on the beach or in the park, and try to hear what they talk with each other about. Once they get past the opening pleasantries, people are likely to begin to tell stories. Funny stories, lightly amusing stories, surprising stories, and simple narratives recounting the events of their lives. People do not generally engage neighbors in furious debate over "controversial issues of public importance," to quote an FCC programming guideline. It is usually impolite, indelicate, or dangerous to a friendship to do that. So people stick to telling stories for each other's gentle amusement.

The 1996 Summer Olympics in Atlanta were obviously a sports event of international importance. But they were covered by NBC television with the same technique that Roone Arledge of ABC TV's "Wide World of Sports" had used for several previous decades—telling stories about individual athletes "up close and personal." According to Frank Deford (1996, p. 53), writing in *Newsweek,* NBC Sports President Dick Ebersol was emulating Arledge's concept of making the Olympics "an athletic Scheherazade, a succession of folk tales about characters mostly unknown." Deford quoted Ebersol as saying "With storytelling, Roone Arledge saw that he could provide viewers with an investment in an event they knew nothing about. . . . That especially appealed to women. Women come at it for the story, the men for the results." Bob Costas, who was the primary host for the Atlanta coverage, underscored the point by saying that what television did best was to capture decidedly human moments: "It's at its best when it's just kind of eavesdropping on something that would be essentially the same if TV weren't there. And when you get those moments, you get touched" (Starr, 1996, p. 51).

Some people tune in the radio primarily for stories. Garrison Keillor's enormously popular "News from Lake Wobegon" segment on Public Radio International's "A Prairie Home Companion" is an obvious example. The cassettes of only the stories from the radio show have become big sellers. Or if you have listened to the legendary Wally Phillips on WGN, Chicago, you have heard someone who is both a conversationalist himself and someone who attracts other storytellers to speak on his program. We are back to that moment of communion—the ultimate radio communication: two people sharing their minds and hearts freely while thousands listen in. Almost every station has someone capable of holding up his or her end of a telephone conversation. It makes sense to put more of those actual two-way conversations on the air, if the announcer cannot achieve good listener rapport without it. But be sure he or she is not just doing "The Wednesday Afternoon Format" with added call-in banalities. Calls with listeners still need to be topical, current, fast-moving, and involving.

Larger market stations often assign a producer to screen and edit actual calls to be used by the host of a morning show. Only a handful of stations continue the practice throughout the day, perhaps because the rarity of air talent with good two-way communication skills makes them expensive, or because paying an additional producer just to edit calls when the station is already paying an announcer seems inefficient. But Program Director Roger Gaither at Charleston, South Carolina station WKQB encouraged his airstaff to put many listeners on the air all day long: "They don't have to be contest winners, either. . . . They've learned that if they have something to contribute, they can be a part of the on-air activity at Q107. It makes Q107 feel like someone's friend instead of just another radio station" (Denver, 1989, p. 41). A station not willing or able to make a commitment to all-day call-in communion could still move closer to the ideal of being a two-way conversationalist and storyteller by changing its "comment line" telephone call recorder to a line that takes calls from listeners who have any kind of a story to tell. It could be a joke, an amusing anecdote, a believe-it-or-not, or merely a slice of life. The PD could screen the taped calls, then sprinkle them throughout the day, formatting them in some cases, or otherwise just dropping them in. The result is likely to be a radio station that sounds more like a neighbor—a station with genuine community involvement at the deepest level: real people.

## The Need for Feedback

Even though feedback in a mass medium such as radio is delayed as compared to live theater, it is still an essential part of the communication process. It literally closes the loop. Every second they are on the air, announcers send out the equivalent of verbal Frisbies™, and they do not get tossed back until minutes, even hours later—if then. In the meantime, the announcer has had to depend on training or ability as an actor in order to imagine the audience, approximate the timing, and assume the response. For the radio announcer, the "flow" experience is all imaginary, because he or she must provide his or her own feedback at the time he or she speaks. The delayed reaction from listeners, if any, is all just gravy.

Two-person annnouncing teams and "zoo" crews have been one useful method for announcers to have an audience, know the timing, and discern the response. These have sometimes led to excesses, where chatter or shtick goes on too long, or where there are too many "inside" jokes (because the "audience" in the station is not the same as the actual audience). And what works for Wally Phillips in AM drive may not work in other dayparts when a more "background" service is desired.

There is good evidence that laughter—even "canned" laughter—can increase the enjoyment of comedy and humor, because the supplied laughter is a cue that tells the listener how much he or she should laugh (Zillmann & Bryant, 1986). And as Andrew Crisell (1986) pointed out in his book *Understanding Radio,* laughter from a live audience influences the timing and delivery of the speaker's material for the best. But Crisell cautioned that a studio audience can also be counterproductive when the listening audience feels the show is being addressed to the *studio* audience instead of the radio listener. This is especially true in the case of visual jokes—things seen in the studio that the listener cannot see. The listening audience in this case feels excluded rather than included—which is just the opposite of the desired effect.

## Reality Therapy

So the answer is to be in touch with the actual audience. Ideally, that could happen via an air personality's show being performed in a public place. Not every standard-issue disc jockey would like that, and there is still plenty to be said for the control the studio allows. But if the show does not originate in public, at least it should be based *on* the public—what the people are thinking and feeling. The radio studio must not be the monk's cell. It must be a haven only for a while. The announcer who would be great must get out of the station and stay in touch with the real characters of the world, observing them as actors do in preparing for a role. Because, the irony is, only by really knowing who he or she is in relation to the world outside can that person be portrayed by the actor on the air.

Stanislavski said that an actor should answer these four questions: Who am I? Why am I here? What do I want? Where am I going? Maybe the secret of the best air personalities is that when they are on the air, they continuously answer those four questions for themselves, and for their listeners.

## MAJOR POINTS

1. The best radio is radio that sells everything—the music played, the people who play it, the news that interrupts it, and the commercials that support it.

2. Many of the entertainment values that listeners find in pop songs— especially the sense of interaction with the artist—needlessly disappear in commercial stopsets.

3. Arthur Godfrey adapted his announcing style to his new conception of the audience as millions of *individual* listeners. Today's announcers do not necessarily need to emulate Godfrey's style but rather his analysis of the audience.

4. The stage movement concepts of time, force, and space are useful in analyzing an announcer's technique. *Time* (rate) is the easiest to control, but often announcers let copy or clock considerations take over. *Force* (volume) is limited by audio processing and transmission technology, but *timbre* (quality) changes are possible. *Space* (a sense of physical closeness or distance) is easily controlled but is largely ignored as a tool by most announcers, who tend to work at one microphone distance exclusively. Usually, that distance is quite close, which makes most U.S. radio sound very intimate.

5. The best radio salespersons come across as neighbors, not carnival barkers. They do not overstate vocally.

6. When seeking an ideal mate, people look for personalities who are warm and loving, have a sense of humor, and are intelligent, far more than they seek people who are self-confident, enthusiastic, or optimistic. Yet the latter qualities are heard more on the radio than the former ones.

7. Good announcers sound that way because they are (in acting terms) playing actions and objectives rather than portraying stereotypical emotions. It is for that reason that management needs to help the announcing staff understand the listener-oriented actions and objectives of the radio station.

8. The radio announcer bears the burden of upgrading the communication exchange from one of possible listener inattention to one of fairly intense concentration. This is done by imagining the "flow" of a real-life conversation in which an exchange of efforts occurs.

9. The Wednesday Afternoon Format (a term coined by Gary Bond) is comprised largely of irrelevanciess and filler clichés. It is too highly predictable. It probably talks most about music that is already familiar. And it violates two audience expectations: help me when I need it, not when I don't; and don't tell me what I already know.

10. Plain talk is not the same as hackneyed talk. Plain talk uses the everyday language of the people, (e.g., *rain* rather than *precipitation.)* Real

talk is conversation with and about the community that allows the host's personality and core beliefs to be glimpsed as well.

11. The great radio communicators help to elicit and to retell the community's stories. They are not self-referential. They feel secure out of the studio, observing and staying in touch with the real characters in the real world outside.

12. One of the consequences of zero talk music sweeps is that all of the entertainment value must then by derived from the music, which is not always strong enough to provide it.

# PART III

## *Music Programming*

The first part of this volume examined the makeup of the radio listening audience, attempting to expand the usual list of psychographic terms to offer new ways to think about attracting target demographics. The second section looked at formats, at radio's soundstage, and at the voices on it. This section builds on that background in considering music programming, the major ingredient in many stations' recipes for success. A case is made here that most music format categories are too rigid and exclusive for today's audiences, and a different scheme for selecting music is explained.

In the second chapter of his very readable book *The Psychology of Music,* John Booth Davies (1978) wrote:

> Music is something of a mystery. Most people spend considerable amounts of time listening to music of one sort or another, and some people dedicate the major part of their lives to musical pursuits. Yet, unlike other activities such as reading, talking, or watching television, where the transmission of a more or less unambiguous message is readily apparent, music does not appear to pass on any message we can readily identify. Music does not really satisfy the requirements that would completely justify its being called a "language", since we tend to use the word "meaning" rather differently in the context of music than in the context of language. In addition, music seems to have something in common with simple forms of sensory experience like warmth, taste, or the smell of jacket-baked potatoes. For example, one can, in a sense, appreciate the taste of a good steak, although the question "What does it *mean?*" is hard to answer. By the same token one can ask "What does Beethoven's Fifth Symphony *mean?*" and again be at a loss for a satisfactory reply. Any answer we might attempt would be couched in terms of our own

reactions and feeling, and these are not identical with another person's responses to the same piece of music. By contrast, the message "The cat sat on the mat" is fairly precise in its meaning, and relatively unambiguous. However, it is not the kind of message that most of us would become excited about. (p. 25)

When Davies said that "music is something of a mystery," he said a mouthful. How music works its special magic on a listener is indeed one of the most mysterious phenomena in aesthetics, psychology, and physiology, and this brief look at the area by a nonmusician does not do justice to the complexity of the problem.[1] However, the ideas presented in this section about how music affects us will later be combined to develop a mood-evoking music presentation system. The arguments and viewpoints in each succeeding chapter depend on the cumulative effect of the material presented previously, so the reader is urged to read through this section consecutively rather than skipping ahead.

---

[1]For more complete coverage of research on the psychology of music, see Deutsch (1982).

# CHAPTER 9

## *Choosing Radio Music—Today*

This chapter explores how listeners choose a music radio station and how radio stations currently select music for airplay. There is a discussion of the prevalence of music research in modern radio programming, and a look at some of the methods that are used to produce a playlist. All of the research material in this chapter is presented as a foundation for the music moods research that is offered later.

### HOW LISTENERS CHOOSE A MUSIC RADIO STATION

A few years ago, I had many opportunities to observe my teenage sons and their friends choosing the stations they listened to for music on the car radio. That radio had push-buttons (to access preset stations), and also signal-scanning (which jumped to the next strong signal each time a button was pushed). The more each teenager made listening choices, the more it became apparent that neither the popularity of the song or artist, nor the prestige or reputation of the station were the primary reasons for punching a button. When asked why the listener had changed the station, the answer was almost always some variation of the idea that the hearer just did not like the song being played. Sometimes factors linked to popularity were important: The song or artist was unfamiliar or too novel, or on the opposite end of the scale, the song was too well-known/burned out. (Occasionally, the song was okay but the artist was held in derision—often because he or she had become too popular with the mass audience. It seems that, at least with some teenagers, achieving mass popularity leads almost inevitably to a next stage where that very popularity places the artist in contempt.)

Pressed harder to explain why they liked a song, the teenagers usually said something like, "I don't know, I just like it. Bug off!" But persistently asking *"Why* do you like it?" would sometimes elicit an answer that ran something like this: "I just like how it makes me feel." It turns out that "I just like how it makes me feel" is a far more cogent answer than it appears to be. How a song makes a listener feel is the root cause of whatever eventual popularity the song might enjoy.

The kind of ad hoc, moment-by-moment station selection that the teenage listeners used is not just confined to that fickle age group. Dolf Zillmann and Jennings Bryant (1986) found that deliberate choices about program content are the exception—that

> the choice of entertainment is usually made "on impulse." The program that holds the greatest appeal at a given time and under given circumstances, for whatever particular reasons, is likely to be picked. The factors that determine this appeal tend to be unclear to the respondents. It would be the rare exception for respondents to engage in formal and explict evaluative comparisons of the choices before them. It is more likely that they make these choices rather "mindlessly," without using reliable and never-changing criteria in their appeal assessments and ultimately in their choices. (p. 306)

On the other hand, research by Zillmann and Bryant (1986) found that people form mood-specific preferences—that is, they behaved as if they sort of "understood" what kind of programming they needed given the particular mood they were in.

## Uses of Music By Teens

Traditionally, people are in their early teens before they do much radio listening. Once they find "their" music on the dial, listenership increases dramatically. Because teenagers will eventually become the audience for all succeeding formats, it is helpful to know more about how teens use music on the radio.

A study by Carroll et al. (1993) found that 14- to 15-year-olds reported the highest level of "interactive" radio listening—in other words, this age group was the one most likely to call the station to request songs or to take part in contests, and so on. They are the people Top 40 stations are likely to hear from the most. When stations report "phones" activity to music trade publications, it is 14- to 15-year-olds who are likeliest to be making those calls to ask for their favorites to be played.

Research by Panzarella (1980) demonstrated how for some listeners music was a "peak" or ecstatic experience, whereas Larson and Kubey (1983) explored the possible mood reactions to music depending on the adolescent's social milieu. A study by Alan Wells and Ernest Hakanen (1991) titled "The Emotional Use of Popular Music by Adolescents" asked high school students to identify the emotions they felt when they listened to their favorite type of music (choices included rock, classical, reggae, easy listening, heavy metal, jazz, R&B/Soul, country, pop, and new wave). Excitement, happiness, and love were the most frequently associated. Emotion ratings were found to vary signficantly by gender, with women tending to associate emotions with music more than men, except for the emotions of confidence, anger, and pride (Wells & Hakanen, 1991).

Wells and Hakanen also asked the high school students to rate five ways they used music to manage their emotions:

> Getting "pumped up" is the most frequent use. This energizing is followed in popularity by "mood strengthening" and also "lifting spirits." All three may be seen as mood enhancing using music as a stimulant. Less frequent, but clearly established, is the use of music as a tranquilizer. Thus about a third of the respondents use music a great deal to "calm down" and "mellow out." (Wells & Hakanen, 1991, p. 453)

Wells also cited his own research with college students concerning the emotions that both genders most associate with their favorite songs. He found a strong congruence of the frequency of selections of emotions among both men and women, and that gender differences were not great.

> Women chose songs that express hope, happiness, passion and grief slightly more than men. Men were more likely to choose excitement, delight, anger and hate. While popular music exposes the listener to a broad range of emotional feelings, the most frequently chosen were happiness, excitement, love, hope, confidence, delight, and passion. (Wells & Hakanen, 1991, pp. 447–448)

## Station Search Patterns

If we assume for the moment that listeners of all ages are searching for a certain set of appeals, or something to fit, extend, or change a certain mood, then these two questions arise: How do radio listeners search among stations, and how do they choose the one they ultimately settle on? Carrie Heeter and Bradley Greenberg (1985) identified three different "orienting search pattern attributes" that apply to the way people search through cable TV channels to discover a suitable program. These are worth a closer look because of the implications they hold for radio station selection. The three different search pattern attributes are *processing mode, search repertoire,* and *evaluation orientation.*

One of the processing modes Heeter and Greenberg identified was *automatic processing.* In this mode, TV channels are searched in numerical order by the receiving device. In both radio and TV sets with electronic tuning, that kind of search would usually be accomplished by an "up/down" or "scan" button.

The *elaborated search repertoire* is one that includes all or most TV channels. In radio, this would be the equivalent of "twirling the dial" from one end of the scale to the other, or manually pushing the up/down tuning button multiple times to access every possible frequency. In this kind of searching, the *listener* decides to make the size of the "repertoire" of possible stations all-inclusive. In contrast, a *restricted search repertoire* would include only a limited number of channels, such as might be the case in tuning a push-button radio or a receiver with a limited number of presets. In this case, the listener's earlier choices about which stations to preset are the only ones readily available. The repertoire of possible stations is thus restricted.

Then there is the crucial question of evaluation of the choices offered. Heeter and Greenberg defined *exhaustive evaluation* as searching *all* the channels in a given search repertoire before returning to the best choice. By contrast, in a *terminating evaluation,* channels in a given search repertoire are searched in order only until the first acceptable choice is found.

In radio, the exhaustive evaluation would mean that *every* available/preset station would be briefly sampled, and only after that would the listener return to the best choice. In the terminating evaluation, the listener would stop an orderly search when the first acceptable option was found.

Especially among music listeners, the terminating evaluation is very common: The listener searches only until a desirable song is heard and stops on that frequency. The exhaustive evaluation is likely only when no desirable music is heard on the normal repertoire of stations, and the listener seeks to expand the range of choice.

## A Program Choice Model

Dolf Zillmann and Jennings Bryant (1985) have developed a choice model that explains a certain set of operations that people tend to follow in selecting among offered entertainment programs. The description of what people do in this choice model may seem to be "just good common sense" but Zillmann and Bryant did us a service by writing it down very precisely. Their focus was more toward TV programming, but a shortened version of their choice model is still very useful for radio. Because music listeners are searching for certain song types rather than complete programs, substitute the word *song* for the word *program* in the following text:

1. An arbitrary selection is made. A particular program is encountered by chance or by mindless probing.
2. If the encountered program is pleasing, it is accepted. If it is displeasing, it is rejected. Being pleased or displeased is considered an immediatate affective [emotional] reaction that does not rely on elaborate cognitive deliberation. It is, so to speak, a gut reaction. The program either "feels good," or it doesn't. The affective response to an encountered program is a function of prevailing moods and emotions.
3. If the encountered program is accepted, respondents refrain from further program sampling. Should dissatisfaction set in, acceptance is withdrawn, and the inclination to reject will grow to the point where the program is abandoned and program sampling recurs. If the encountered program is rejected, program sampling continues.
4. Rejected available programs are entered into short-term memory. In continued program sampling, the sampled program is compared with those in memory. Essentially, this comparison is between the affective reactions that were evoked by the compared programs, and it takes the form of *better* or *worse*. Respondents will return to recalled programs that are deemed better than present ones. This return to better offerings can be applied successively until the program deemed best is reached. More likely, however, respondents will cease making comparisons (i.e., they will discontinue the sampling process) once a satisfying program has been found.
5. If programs or program components are known (i.e., stored in long-term memory), the anticipation of pleasure or displeasure that is based on prior responding to the programs (e.g., episodes of a series) or program components (e.g., actors with particular roles) enters into the comparison process. It expedites this process in the sense that little exposure to sampled programs is needed to render a verdict of accept–reject or better–worse. (p. 157)

In the fifth point just listed, the "program components" in the radio analogy are likely to be other songs from the same album or by the same artist. They might also be the remembered points of pop songs—that is, the "hooks." Perhaps the listener recognizes enough of a song to know that other pleasurable or unpleasurable elements are coming up.

The fourth point suggests that the procedure of holding rejected programming in short-term memory with *better* or *worse* labels attached is the means a listener might use to settle on the "least objectionable programming" when he or she just cannot bear to turn off the radio.

## Factors Intrinsic to the Song

After punching around the buttons, quite oblivious to all of the research just mentioned, the author's teenagers usually settled on a song that they liked because of how it made them feel. Tied up in their phrase "I just like how it makes me feel" are plenty of popularity factors (peer acceptance of the song and the artist, participation in current fads or trends, etc.). But there is also the sense that "how it makes me feel" might have a lot to do with things that are intrinsic to the music rather than the song's "hit" ranking, or the social milieu in which it is heard.

The question then becomes, are there certain factors in the music itself that cause people to have characteristic patterns of reactions to it? Because, if there are, and if it were possible to predict what those reactions might be from playing a certain song or set of songs, a new way of programming popular music on the radio could be developed. Ultimately, it might even be possible to program music in such a way that a station's listeners would arrive at a commercial cluster or stopset primed to receive the messages more readily because the preceding music would have gotten them into the desired mood. But even if a programmer only became adept at evoking moods through the careful selection of the music to be played, the time spent listening to that station should theoretically increase. And time spent listening (TSL) needs to increase. My kids are not the only ones who carry cassettes into the car if they are going to be on a trip longer than 10 minutes. They plug the cassettes into the AM/FM/cassette player because that way they can *guarantee* the mood that the known music on the tape is going to evoke. What they currently get on the radio is haphazard. As concerns the establishment or the extension of a certain mood, even the number one hit music stations offer no more than a pig in a poke.

A system for selecting music based on the moods it evokes in listeners is explained in succeeding chapters.

## HOW MUSIC STATIONS CURRENTLY CHOOSE THEIR MUSIC

Most commercial music formats have one factor in common: They are all based on some measure of popularity. As every modern format had its basis in the market-oriented Top 40 hits format, that is not surprising. And because no commercial station wants to play music that is unpopular and thus drive listeners away, popularity with some core or target audience is almost always a key factor in developing a music format. At the heart of the original Top 40 station's music policy was the then-radical notion that what the station should play was what the general public wanted to hear (what was currently most popular). From that concept came the idea of the limited playlist, in which the most popular songs are played more often than the less popular tunes, again in an effort to minimize mistakes.[1] Because various trade publications reported the relative popularity of current music, it was possible to devise music "clocks" that prescribed which title to play when. Over the years, programmers have also experimented with categorizing by such things as the tempo of the song and the sex of the artist, but the one constant consideration has always been the record's popularity. That is why measurements of popularity (or favorability or liking) have been a major factor in every format that has evolved out of Top 40 in the last three decades.

## Measuring Popularity Via Record Sales and Airplay by Other Stations

In the early days of Top 40, record sales were measured by calling local record stores and asking for a verbal report of what was selling fastest. In spite of the strong possibility for "hyping" the report to favor certain artists or records, this verbal/recall approach continued for almost 30 years. It has now been replaced by a system that tracks actual sales at barcode-scanning cash registers in major record store chains. Now, at least if the record company wants to hype a song, they have to send people out to buy a lot of their own records to do so.

"Music monitors"—tape recordings of the music being played by other radio stations—can be ordered by a station willing to pay the fee. But most radio stations are content to find out what music other stations are playing by reading about it in such trade papers as *Radio & Records, The Gavin Report,* and *Billboard.*

Stations that report to the trades typically must meet certain market size criteria, and are usually among the dominant stations in their format. The presumption is that stations that appear to be hyping a certain record or favoring particular companies will be dropped from the list of reporters.

Until 1994, record promoters were interested in getting their records played in as high a rotation (exposure category) as possible. To avoid having to give bad news to a record rep, radio people would sometimes lie and say that the song in question had moved to a better rotation, although subsequent music monitors would prove that the record was getting much less exposure. Now, instead of reporting "light, medium, or heavy" rota-

---

[1] John Kluge, who in 1959 was chairman of the board and president of what was then known as Metropolitan Broadcasting Corporation (later Metromedia), was quoted as being skeptical of top-singles lists: "When I see one of those lists . . . I'm always reminded of the fact that man is on top of animal kingdom charts because he makes out the list" (Metropolitan Soars With Kluge at Helm, 1959).

tions, stations report the number of plays per week that they expect the song to have, which at least provides a little more accuracy than the loose rotation terminology (Maxwell, 1994a).

## The Importance of Trade Paper Music Charts

The "charts" produced by the major radio and music trade paper publishers are especially important in music decision making at stations in smaller markets that cannot afford to do their own research. There are charts for every major format and some subformats, and breakouts that show which records are the most added, most active, and more. From the industry point of view, the charts perform a useful service by narrowing the focus to 100 or fewer songs, so that programmers do not have to deal with the many hundreds of albums that are released each week (Parker, 1991). But the charts are a disservice, too. Much good music never makes it onto the charts and thus dies an untimely death commercially. The implicit message is that the more sales/adds/high rotation moves that a record has, the better it is artistically (Parker, 1991).

The use that is made of the charts is also a concern; as music critic Greil Marcus (1987) pointed out about the *Billboard List of Number One Hits,* Bob Dylan does not exist because he has never had a number one record, but Rick Dees and His Cast of Idiots ("Disco Duck Part 1") does exist because he did.

## Measuring Popularity Via Call-Out and Auditorium Music Tests

Stations in medium-sized and larger markets are likely to be able to afford to do their own testing of music, rather than rely on trade newspaper information that necessarily reflects a regional trend or a national average. In call-out research, very short segments of songs are played over the telephone to get the respondent's reaction. Because of the poor fidelity of the phone line, and the fact that the respondent is surrounded by the distractions of the household, call-out research can test relatively few songs per call. But because most hit-oriented formats do not add many new songs each week, call-out works well for testing new music.

On the other hand, auditorium music tests are often used to test libraries of familiar music. In an auditorium test, a large room is rented in a conveniently located, neutral, pleasant location (such as a hotel), where short segments of music can be played in comfortable, nondistracting surroundings. The participants are sometimes known to be listeners to the station doing the research; in other tests, respondents may be recruited by target demographic group rather than by station listenership. An incentive, usually ranging from $25 to $50 per session, encourages people to spend several hours giving responses to anywhere from 350 to as many as 700 songs.

## Factors in Airplay Decision Making—
## Eric Rothenbuhler—1981

With all of these methods for determining what music the public wants to hear, why do people still say they cannot find what they want to hear on the radio? A research report by Eric Rothenbuhler (1985) titled "Programming Decision-Making in Popular Music Radio" offers important answers. His report reflects 9 months of firsthand study of the decision making at an AOR station in one of the top 50 markets in 1981. My reading of radio and music trade publications today shows that most of the practices he chronicled are still very much in effect.

Rothenbuhler's report listed five ways in which the station he studied operated more as a local outlet for the music being distributed and promoted by the record industry than as an entity making decisions based on the local audience's expressed needs and desires. First, the record distributors determined which records would be sent to programmers across the country, and when they would be advertised and promoted. That practice alone drastically narrowed the field of choice if the station was going to be in step with national trends. Second, the pitches of record promoters, and data and opinion from industry tradesheets, were influential in determining which records would be considered. As a result, records by unknown artists that did not have such backing were rarely listened to. Third, station programmers felt compelled to play the "consensus cut"—one particular song from a new album being promoted unanimously by record reps and/or in the trades, or the cut that other stations were playing. Unless there was either strong promotion or strong airplay for a particular cut, many stations hesistated to play the record at all.

Rothenbuhler's fourth and fifth points are linked to the "gatekeepers" in the radio music business. His fourth point was that people in programming positions tended to be hired not for their knowledge of the local community's tastes and needs, but for their knowledge of the format and the industry. The fifth point was the strong influence—and sometimes absolute veto power—of the outside programming consultant.

Rothenbuhler concluded that it was rare for local tastes and needs to be considered as decisions were made about which records to play. Information in the trades, from other programmers, and from program consultants were all felt to be more reliable and objective than the expressed desires of the local audience.

Rothenbuhler's findings from his 1981 study are congruent with my belief that in the 40-plus years since the Top 40 pioneers decided that their stations would play the music that the public wanted to hear (rather than the songs the station owner or the announcer liked), there has been a gradual abandonment of that apparently "populist" principle. It appears that if one were to survey the entire potential audience of a station, what the average listener really liked hearing would not be a good predictor of which songs would become hits. A much better predictor would be what record companies and key radio stations were saying about the records.

## Rothenbuhler and McCourt—1992

A decade later, Rothenbuhler and Tom McCourt (1992) published an article that expanded on Rothenbuhler's earlier study. It made important new points about the "gatekeeping" process that determines which songs become hits. It really is a process of *preselection*—a system by which choices are made in the public's behalf without the public's direct participation.

> Preselection involves a sequential, staged filtering of over-abundant products in anticipation of an uncertain demand. . . . Decision makers try to anticipate what will be successful at later points in the system by using feedback on recent successes.
>
> Radio stations try to operate efficiently in order to produce maximum revenues. The preoccupation with efficiency limits the variety of music that is transmitted to the public because commercial radio stations believe that they benefit economically by making predictable choices about what music to play. The incorporation of computers into radio station operations . . . has increased the speed with which an "aberrant" song can be eliminated from the playlist, which in turn contributes to the standardization of music that is played. . . . As a result, radio concentrates on airing familiar and "least objectionable" material in hopes of avoiding audience "tuneout." (pp. 103–105)

Rothenbuhler and McCourt went on to describe how those involved with selecting music participated in two basic decision-making processes: *sensing* and *valuation*. In sensing, the decision-makers select the records that are the least problematic and most promising. In valuation, those records are then judged in comparison both to other new records, and in terms of what adding the record would do to the overall balance of tunes in the existing playlist. The authors reported that of the 467 albums that were available for selection during the 10-week period of the original study, "only 81 (17%) were seriously considered for addition to the playlist. Of these 81 albums, 35 (43%) actually received airplay" (p. 109). In the conclusion to their second article, Rothenbuhler and McCourt stated:

> The result of all this is that a very small proportion of music that is recorded receives massive broadcast exposure while the rest goes nowhere commercially. Because the music industry seeks to capitalize on hit songs, today's hit inevitably will affect what record companies offer tomorrow. . . .
>
> The industry's reliance on formats, trade journals, music industry promoters, and consultants tends to reproduce the choices at station after station . . . this means that, as a rule, contemporary commercial radio actively discourages significant stylistic innovation in popular music and the communicative potential that such creative endeavors would produce. (pp. 113–114)

## Other Opinions About the Music Selection Process

Some stations might feel that Rothenbuhler's research would not have come to the same conclusions if he had studied *their* selection methods, but the inescapable truth is that for most music-format stations, the selection process for hit music remains highly self-referential, with one of the main points of reference being what other programmers are doing.

Still others might point out that Rothenbuhler's complaints stemmed from observations he carried out back in 1981. But consider the following criticism from George Lang (1995), whose piece appeared more recently in the *Oklahoma Gazette:*

> Because of the overweening influence of record companies on radio playlists, a conflict of interest has been festering for more than 30 years.
>
> It's not difficult to spot the problem. Artists who shouldn't have been let within 50 yards of a recording studio regularly appear on radio playlists.
>
> And if the radio plays it, a frighteningly large percentage of the listening audience will buy it. A vicious circle ensues, with record companies signing unlistenable acts such as SWV, fully knowing that radio stations will slap that hunk of plastic in the machine and churn out dollars. (p.4)

Here is more proof that what Rothenbuhler found is still happening. The Country Radio Broadcasters' 1994 "state of the industry" survey reported that music research was performed by 33% of stations in small markets, 46% in medium markets, 75% in large markets, and 95% in major markets. But the survey also revealed that about 45% of both small- and medium-market stations depended on industry trade papers to make decisions about which records to add and to drop, whereas only 10% of major-market stations did so. Independent, in-house research was used by small market stations only about 14% of the time ("CRB Survey Says," 1994). Because small- and medium-market stations comprise the bulk of the Country outlets serving the nation, the fact that they tend to depend on the trade papers rather than their own research means that the Country format is tied to copying what other stations are playing in much the same way as the AOR stations studied by Rothenbuhler.

The rise of MTV and music videos since Rothenbuhler's study have made the "consensus cut" even more influential. Because music videos are expensive to produce, a new album's promotional strategies must be centered on a single cut. As one music critic put it, "perhaps the most significant development in which music video participated was the institution of the single-song as the crucial factor in the marketing of an album" (Straw, 1988, pp. 251–252). In effect, music videos brought the "single" record back to importance. The promotion provided to the album by airing of the video results in sales of the album; strong album sales are reported by the trade magazines and the record promoters as signs of success, and thus radio stations that pay attention to the trade papers wind up playing music from an album that may have been bought primarily because of the appeal of the video produced for a single cut. Television exposure of the record company's consensus cut becomes the tail that wags the very large dog known as radio.

It should now be clear that relative to the 11,000-plus U.S. radio stations, just a handful of people are determining what becomes hit airplay music. I would not criticize this concentration of control if it really seemed to be in the best *long-term* interests of the radio industry, the music industry, and the public, but that is not necessarily the case. Take, for example, the several Grammy Awards won by Bonnie Raitt and the Travelling Wilburys in 1990, even though their records got very little airplay on CHR/Top 40 hit-oriented stations ("Mix Stations Target Growing Adult Audiences," 1990, p. 28). In the final analysis, the public is less cautious about embracing good new music than are record promoters or radio programmers. The public has no stake in preserving the symbiotic copromotion practiced by radio and the record industry. That may be one reason why the public's true, broad-ranging musical taste is not very much considered in choosing music for airplay.

Figuring out what a station's core audience really wants to hear is difficult, but settling merely for measures of popularity as the controlling factor in choosing music for airplay is too easy. As the 1990 Grammy Awards example demonstrated, records that have received very limited airplay can still be deeply appreciated by the public when it gets a chance to hear them via some other medium, and conversely, a record can become "popular" as evidenced by sales and heavy play at other stations, and yet it can have a neutral or even negative impact on your station's listeners. Requests for the record are notoriously unreliable indicators of a record's real popularity, because only a fractional part of a station's cumulative audience ever calls to request a song. Moreover, the callers are unlikely to represent the station's core audience (Harris, 1994). Yet the music trades continue to report which songs are "getting strong phones." The ringing of the phones at your station and the cash registers at the record stores may be hard to ignore, but paying too much attention to them will divert you from discovering what your core audience really wants to hear.

## THE STANDARD COMPONENTS OF RECORD POPULARITY

For the past 40 years, a record's popularity has been the chief factor determining how often it is played, or whether it is played at all. Among the terms that the radio industry uses to describe a song's popularity are *favorability* and *liking*. Familiarity of the song is another positive factor—up to a point. When the song becomes overexposed, it suffers from the opposite of *liking*, which radio people call *burnout* or sometimes simply *burn*.

### Liking and Popularity

It is important to note that *liking* and *popularity* are not the same thing. Consider the oldie, or some obscure jazz tune, or a dusty piano sonata. None is currently "popular" in the traditional meaning of the word. And yet there is high "liking" for these forms among certain listeners, quite apart from the question of how big a hit they were (if they were a hit at all).

The amount of liking for a song will obviously be one of the factors affecting the song's overall popularity. But some listeners will express *liking* for a song primarily as a result of its "hit-ness"—it is the cool new thing. For such listeners, the fact that the record is popular with somebody else is enough; among these trend followers, popularity begets more popularity. They like it *because* it is popular, not necessarily for the music itself.

### Popularity Versus Familiarity

*Popularity* should also be distinguished from familiarity. Familiarity can be a strong and desirable component in the attraction of any song—perhaps not the song *en toto*, but at least the familiarity of the elements that make it up. In defining categories of familiar music in *Music and Program Research*, James E. Fletcher (1987) said of "current" songs:

> It is not always correct to characterize a "current" as new music, since popularity is based on resemblance to music already familiar to the targeted audience. Actually, fans expect only about fifteen percent of a song labelled

"new" to be really new. If a familiar and beloved performing group releases a recording in another musical style, old fans often issue a strong negative reaction. (p. 17)

It is good to keep in mind that originality—the flipside of familiarity—can be as appealing to some audiences as familiarity. However, radio music programmers across the format spectrum seem nearly obsessed with playing only familiar music. In fact, some programmers will not even test unfamiliar music. Here are the comments of an AOR PD: "I don't think you can test new music. . . . The only way you're going to find out if a song is successful is by playing it and letting the audience decide. You make hits by finding good songs and then playing them a lot. Repetition makes them familiar, and familiarity breeds either discontent or likability" (Maxwell, 1993a, p. 28) The assumption here is that a person can neither like nor dislike a record until he or she has heard it several times. That is clearly not the case. Those of us who have heard a song once and rushed to a record store to buy it can attest to a song's instant likability, and those of us who have heard a song that made us quickly change the dial have affirmed that a song can be instantly unlikable, too.

Familiarity takes a long time to achieve, because most radio listeners don't listen for hours at a time. One record promotion person said, "The research I've seen shows that when a station plays a record one or two times a day, it's usually six weeks before even its core listeners hear it" (Maxwell, 1995, p. 74). A PD in the Alternative format said, "We don't test a record until it plays over 100 times—although we find hitting something hard early can be 80%–90% familiar in about a week and a half" (Alexander, 1994a, p. 22). A researcher working in the AOR format said, "I've seen music tests from dozens of stations in various formats showing it takes a year or more for a song to reach high familiarity" (Maxwell, 1994d, p. 32). But another AOR music researcher pointed to the real problem: "For most stations (except those with high TSL), you have to play a song at least 15–20 times a week for three to four weeks before you can even begin to get a measure of familiarity. It's a waste of time to start music testing until it's been significantly exposed" (p. 28).

That quote points to one cause of the programmer's quest for familiarity. It is true that until a record has been played quite a few times, not enough of the audience will have heard it to be useful for purposes of music testing, where small samples tend to invalidate the findings. But that kind of mindset again puts the station's needs ahead of the listener's. If the record is right, the listener can enjoy it on the very first hearing. Familiarity is not a prerequisite for liking a record—familiarity is only necessary for *testing* a record employing the usual procedures.

Influence from the music industry is another reason that radio programmers believe that familiarity is essential to liking a record. A rock music promoter for a major record company said:

> If TSL is the name of the game in the 90s, you can't afford to play multiple tracks from new artists, because the audience won't listen to a record they can't identify with. You can play multiple tracks without a tuneout problem only once a single track has become familiar and develops into a hit." (Maxwell, 1994d, p. 32)

The statement that "the audience won't listen to a record they can't identify with" is nonsense on its face. If it were true, how would anybody ever hear a new song for the first time?

Another music-industry-oriented view came from a spokesman for a radio research company: "The record industry wants a focused effort to help drive sales of a CD. They know repetition breeds familiarity which breeds preference. . . . The repetitive approach is also accepted by most programmers as the best way to build song preference" (Maxwell, 1994d, p. 32). An Adult Alternative PD has stated, "The idea is to create hits, and you can't really create a hit unless you force-feed it to listeners" (Maxwell, 1995, p. 74). Those statements beg the question "Why are PDs trying to build song preference?" That clearly is the job of the record promoters, but shouldn't the program director's job be to *reflect* audience tastes rather than to create them?

## Familiarity, Variety, and TSL

It has already been noted that familiarity is a factor that varies depending on the length of exposure to the radio. With increased radio listening, familiarity with all musical elements also increases. Today, radio ratings depend more on high TSL figures than on a big cumulative audience. And there are researchers, programmers, and consultants who understand that playing a record in heavy rotation to increase its familiarity may hurt TSL. Lou Patrick of Bolton Research said:

> You don't play songs over and over—that's counter to the whole TSL philosophy. High repetition only serves to grate on the core audience's TSL tolerance. . . . In focus groups all over the country, people are asking why radio plays just one song at a time. They know there are many good songs on an album, because they've bought it. (Maxwell, 1994d, p. 32)

Patrick said that Progressive AORs could successfully play several cuts at once from a new album, and thereby develop the image of being the station that plays "all the good music from artists that listeners like most" (p. 32). Some programmers in the New Adult Contemporary format saw ratings increase by playing only one cut per new album, but others adhered to the format's early practice of playing any tracks that fit the target audience. Some even felt that doing so helped, rather than hurt, album sales. Program director Steve Huntington said, "If they hear multiple tracks that they love as we love, it becomes a 'must have' CD and that benefits the label. If you trickle tracks out one at a time, as they do in other formats, that level of excitement isn't achieved right away" (Archer, 1995a, p. 82). Even a national director of promotion for a record company—GRP's Beth Lewis—concurred. "One track at a time is boring. When I listen to the radio, I don't want to hear the same song by an artist over and over. I'm not going to buy a record unless I've been exposed to three or four cuts" (p. 82).

## "Turnoff"—Early-Stage Burnout

Eventually, the continued repetition of a record leads to burnout, which radio people associate with the mature stages of a hit record's life cycle. But a record can become a "turnoff" much earlier in that progression. A recent experimental study by Brentar, Neuendorf, and Armstrong (1994) showed that the point at which continued exposure to a popular song stopped having a positive affect (emotional impact) and turned into a negative affect was between 8 and 16 plays. That is much lower than most radio people assume. The authors' findings also suggested that novelty as well as repetition affected liking for a song; among their participants, the perceived innovativeness or newness of a record was positively associated with preference. They concluded:

> Radio decision makers often select songs that best reflect current audience familiarity, rather than anything that sounds new or different. . . . This conservatism of rock and pop music programming has been heavily criticized for not reflecting audiences' interests . . . and for strangling creativity in the music industry . . . rock and top-40 radio stations using such a programming philosophy may not be as successful as they could be. Overexposure of songs and homogeneity of music played may be causing potential listeners to tune out. (p. 176)

If hit songs are to be put into the typical sort of "heavy" rotation, then the following caution should be kept in mind: A likely time for adult tuneout that results from music repetition is when the listener hears a *second* song for the second time. The listener will accept a repeat of one song in a mix of music that otherwise has not been heard during that listening period. But when he or she hears a *second* song that has been played before (the second song heard for the second time), the listener is cued that the music rotation has indeed started over. At that point, many adults will tune away, because your station is playing something they already heard. For adults, that can be almost as bad as telling them something they already know.

## Recurrents

*Recurrent* records are ones that have stopped being current hits, are too new to be considered "gold" (oldies), and are not yet "burned" enough to be "rested" (not played for a while). Most stations only play recurrents that have the chance to be played later as gold—something that has staying power. Beyond that, there seems to be less unanimity in the handling of recurrents than any other radio music category. For example, there is little agreement on how old a recurrent can be before it becomes gold, whether a current should be rested before it reappears as a recurrent, what percentage of hits in various rotation levels should become recurrents and at what rotations, and so on.

*Radio & Records* surveyed a panel of CHR programmers about their practices in airing recurrents. The lead-in to the article stated:

> no records have the potential for more familiarity and popularity than recurrents, even though powers are the hottest of your currents. That's the up side of recurrents. The down side: recurrents also have the potential to bore listeners and make them punch out, especially if the record in question has been played too much. (Denver, 1988a, p. 40)

The article reported the programmers agreed that a recurrent had to be a former power song, but not a novelty, and be familiar, but not be burned out. From that point on, the panelists disagreed. One programmer tended to move a power song into the recurrent category when 12- to 17-year-olds stopped calling for it and adults *started* calling for it. (This person apparently chose to ignore the strong research that shows how remarkably different callers are from the typical listener.) Another programmer said he tried to get maximum benefit from recurrents without sacrificing familiarity by resting the currents for *a week or so* before putting them in the recurrent category. (He apparently believed that a week of not airing a song is actually enough time for the majority audience of casual listeners to notice that the song is missing from the playlist.) Probably this person relies on recurrents so heavily because of his stated beliefs that recurrents are the records that keep the passive listeners tuned in while the station plays newer music appealing to active listeners.

One of the reasons why recurrents are handled with such variability relates to the volatility of records that are in the late stages of their life cycle as hits. Heavy listeners will have heard them far too many times, whereas light listeners will just be getting to know the tunes. The trick is to play a fading hit just enough to please light listeners without burning out the heavy listeners. Recurrents are thus some of the most dangerous records a station can play, if audience attitudes toward them are not carefully and continually researched. As a source of potential tuneout, they should seem much scarier than new music. But some radio people, convinced of the need for familiarity above all, do not see it that way. One Alternative station manager said:

> If a current song is showing high burn, we might just decide to rest it. But three weeks later, I might put it back after a good test. When a song isn't working, rather than adding something with no familiarity, we might bring something back for a week or two until something [current] is ready to move up. (Alexander, 1994a, p. 22)

## Favorability, Familiarity, and Burnout as Music Research Reveals Them—An Abbreviated Example

In the spring of 1995, Rantel Research conducted extensive auditorium music testing of songs for the CHR/pop format. The respondents were 1,200 women aged 15 to 34 who were either CHR listeners or CHR/pop music fans. The results for 303 records were published by *Radio & Records* in the September 8, 1995 issue (Novia, 1995a, pp. 66, 68). I have selected only eight songs, to illustrate how widely favorability, familiarity, and burnout can vary. In Table 9.1, the term *favorability* refers to the record's mean favorability rating, with the scale ranging from 1 (strong dislike) to 5 (strong liking). Thus, a score of 3 would indicate a song that was disliked as much as it was liked. I have listed the eight records from highest to lowest favorability. The term *familiarity* refers to the percentage of respondents who were familiar with the song. The term *burnout* refers to the percentage of respondents who were tired of hearing the song. It was possible to express liking for the song yet still be tired of hearing it.

The Beatles song had the second highest favorability ranking of the 303 records listed (the highest was 4.08), and "Twist and Shout" was familiar to all but .4 of the CHR-oriented respondents. Yet only 7.5% were burned out on the tune, in spite of the fact that it had first been a hit in 1964 and charted again in 1986 thanks to exposure in two movies. Would these positive numbers cause CHRs to play the song again? Probably not. "Twist and Shout" would have been deemed too old to be a "good fit" for most CHR stations' sound in 1995; besides, the song was available on Oldies and some Classic Rock stations.

## TABLE 9.1
### Favorability, Familiarity, and Burnout

| Artist/Title | Favorability | Familiarity | Burnout | Year |
|---|---|---|---|---|
| The Beatles/"Twist and Shout" | 4.07 | 99.6 | 7.5 | 1964/1986 |
| Van Morrison/"Brown Eyed Girl" | 4.01 | 99.9 | 9.7 | 1976 |
| Whitney Houston/"I Will Always . . ." | 3.94 | 96.1 | 35.5 | 1992 |
| Billy Joel/"Scenes from an Italian . . ." | 3.83 | 83.3 | .9 | 1978 |
| Pat Benatar/"Love Is a Battlefield" | 3.78 | 96.5 | 1.4 | 1983 |
| Alice in Chains/"Man in the Box" | 3.57 | 41.6 | 1.9 | 1993 |
| Tom Petty/"You Don't Know How . . ." | 3.49 | 98.6 | 48.7 | 1995 |
| Rob Base & DJ EZ Rock/"Joy and Pain" | 3.48 | 81.1 | 0. | 1989 |

From "A CHR/Pop National Auditorium Test" by T. Novia, 1995a, September 8, *Radio & Records*, pp. 66, 68. Copyright © 1996 by *Radio & Records*, Inc. Reprinted by permission.

Only four other records were ranked at 4.0 or higher on favorability; one of those was Van Morrison's 1976 hit "Brown Eyed Girl." It was one of only three listed records that scored a 99.9% familiarity rating. In spite of that nearly universal exposure, less than 10% of respondents were tired of it. Given such good numbers, would CHRs play "Brown Eyed Girl"? Probably not. It was already overplayed on Classic Rock stations, and some ACs. And not only did the sound not fit with 1995, but the song had been a hit before some of the CHR's target demographic was born. The fact that these songs and artists continue to connect with listeners—even CHR listeners—was probably rationalized away using one of the scenarios I suggested earlier.

Now consider the Tom Petty song, which was a recent record when the testing was done. It, too, had a very high familiarity ranking, but in this case, it garnered the highest burnout score among the published titles, which may have contributed to its relatively low favorability at the time. Temporarily, at least, overfamiliarity had bred contempt. Might it have been considered more favorably by listeners if it had not suffered the fate of being put into a high rotation?

The 1992 Whitney Houston hit was near the top of the 3.0s, just below the Beatles and Van Morrison, and yet more than a third of the respondents were tired of hearing her song 3 years after it had charted. That shows that current hits are not the only "burned" songs. Interestingly, the 3.83 favorability score achieved by Billy Joel's 1978 hit "Scenes from an Italian Restaurant" was also a high mark. The very low .9 burn score means 99% of the respondents were not tired of hearing it, and since most CHRs had left such nonrock "story" songs to Soft AC stations, it certainly had not been overplayed on CHRs. But the relatively low familiarity score also derives from the fact that some of the 15-year-olds in the test had not been born when the song was a hit. Remember, though, that familiarity is *not* a prerequisite for liking a song. Familiarity may enhance favorability, but a record can be liked on first hearing, as this one no doubt was by some of its youngest hearers.

The much more recent (1989) song by Rob Base and DJ EZ Rock achieved one of only two 0.0 burn scores among the tested records, but it was toward the bottom of the pack so far as favorability was concerned. That shows that low-burnout alone does not assure high favorability.

The very low 41.6% familiarity score of the Alice in Chains record—by far the lowest in the test—did not push the song to the bottom of the pack. Songs by Steve Winwood ("Roll With It") and Tina Turner ("What's Love Got to Do With It") both were ranked lower in favorability at 3.47, even though they both scored 99.3% on familiarity. So familiarity does not guarantee success, either.

There is no denying that popularity of the song (and perhaps even moreso of the artist who recorded it) is an important factor in choosing music for mass appeal radio airplay. But popularity, as important as it is, must finally be viewed not as an answer in itself, but as merely one of the most visible symptoms of many other factors that cause the audience to listen to and enjoy that song. It is sensible to ask "How popular is this song, and with whom?" but that does not go far enough. The question begging to be asked is *"Why* is this song popular, and with whom?" or *"What factors* make a song popular in the first place?"

What does guarantee success? The same thing that causes you to stop punching the buttons on your car radio and settle in to listen to a song. You probably do not care how big a hit it is, or was. You probably do not care how old or new it is. You probably do not care how familiar it is, unless it is *too* familiar. What you care about is "how it makes you feel"— the mood that it helps to create, sustain, or change. How a song makes you feel has to do with factors intrinsic to the music itself, and those factors are generally ignored by standard radio music research. They are explored in the next chapter.

## MAJOR POINTS

1. Listeners choose a hit music station by how it makes them feel at the moment they tune in. How a song makes the listener feel is the root cause of whatever popularity the song might enjoy.

2. There are several search strategies that a music seeker might use to settle on a station, but the "terminating evaluation" is very common: The listener searches only until a desirable song is heard and stops on that frequency.

3. Measures of hit music popularity do not go far enough. The question to be asked should be *"Why* is this song popular, and with whom?" Beyond

that, what factors intrinsic to the song make it popular? What are the elements that cause someone to say "I like how it makes me feel"? If there are characteristic patterns of reactions to a song, then discovering those reactions can be an important element in music research.

4. Over the years, record popularity has been tracked by sales, requests, music monitors of other radio stations, call-out, and auditorium music testing. In almost all cases, the factors considered to be of most importance were limited to familiarity with—and liking for—the record being tested.

5. "Liking" and "popularity" are different concepts. The public's attitude toward a popular song changes with each hearing over the course of that tune's advent, ascendency, zenith, and decline. Oldies are "liked" even though they are no longer "popular," for example. Many popular songs are largely based on familiar musical ideas.

6. A study by Rothenbuhler showed that airplay decision making by music stations is often more tied to record industry needs and the practices of other stations than to the tastes of the local audience. One result is that only a very small percentage of all records get massive amounts of airplay, whereas the great majority remains unexposed.

7. MTV and other music video services have made the "consensus cut" more important that ever—in effect, bringing the single record back into prominence. Because of the influence of video exposure on record sales, some radio stations wind up playing music that may have been bought primarily because of the appeal of the video produced for a single cut, rather than any real musical appeals.

8. Some music directors appear to believe that it is their job to aid the record companies in making new songs into hits. That is one of the reasons that music rotation systems exist—to give a record strong exposure so that it will *become* a hit, rather than because the public has already made it one. Music directors also believe that they cannot properly test a record until heavy exposure gives it a good familiarity score. The assumption is that the audience will not listen to a song they cannot instantly identify.

9. A study reported in 1994 showed that the point at which listeners stopped having a positive response to a record, and instead began to be "turned off" by repeated hearing of it, was between 8 and 16 plays. That figure is much lower than most radio people assume.

10. Recurrent records are some of the most dangerous records a station can play if audience attitudes toward them are not carefully and continually researched. As a source of potential tuneout, they should seem scarier than new music. But some radio people, convinced of the need for familiarity above all, do not see it that way.

# CHAPTER 10

## Choosing Radio Music Tomorrow— By "How it Makes You Feel"

We listen to music—from whatever source—because it moves us. Researcher Avram Goldstein of Stanford University found that 96% of a test group of more than 250 people reported being "thrilled" by certain musical selections, which put music a full 26% ahead of sexual activity as a thrill-supplier. Goldstein's subjects described thrills in terms of such physical sensations as goosebumps, chills, shudders, tickling, tingling, a lump in the throat, or crying (Rosenfeld, 1985). The same research showed that although the intensity of response was different between one listening session and another, people tended to have the same pattern of thrills every time they heard a particular piece of music.

In an earlier chapter, the listener's desire for not just "feeling" but actual physical reactions to what he or she hears was outlined. Of course, the wish to experience kinaesthetic responses also applies to the music listener. According to Otto Ortman (1968), music performers often experience "motor" responses to the music they hear: the pianist feeling a phrase in the fingers, the horn player in the lips, and so on. Rhythm is one obvious source of these responses, but not the only one. Kinaesthetic responses are also a result of

> the outline described by melodic motion, and the strain and relaxation involved in dissonance and consonance, as well as in *crescendo* and *diminuendo* . . . kinaesthetic sensations are . . . far more usual than is generally admitted, and form the true basis of many responses that are daily traced to auditory sources. (p. 254)

Moreover, one does not have to be a performer of music to have such responses. As is shown later in this chapter, considerable research suggests that physical responses to certain rhythmic patterns and melodic lines may be virtually universal. But it is probably the rare instance in which broadcast music alone can cause a listener to laugh, cry, get goosebumps, and so on. It is more likely to do so in a context, as when songs with similar (or perhaps contrasting) themes are played consecutively. Or when the song itself provides a strong context, telling a complete story with vivid images. Or when the listener provides from memory a nostalgic context for the song.

As has already been stated, the job of evoking kinaesthetic responses, of making radio participatory, is that of the total format, and should not fall primarily to the music played. It is the format as a whole, including commercials and all the elements that do *not* involve the announcer or the music, that provides the total experience of the radio station in the listener's mind. But when music is the primary stimulus, and sometimes the only entertainment content of a radio station, the specific kinaesthetic effects it has on listeners are worth studying closely. That is the focus of this chapter.

# RESEARCH ON HOW AND WHY MUSIC AFFECTS US

## Expectancies and Novelties

Musicologist Leonard Meyer said that we bring with us a set of expectations about how things will likely proceed when we listen to music. If the music is congruent with what we expected, then we are in a relaxed state; if it is not what we expected, then we grow tense. Meyer said that the gratification we derive from listening is from the alternation of tension and relaxation that comes from our expectations being frustrated and then fulfilled (Rosenfeld, 1985, p. 50). This is a classic psychological explanation of a gratification deriving from the release of tension, and its roots go back to Aristotle's *Poetics*.

Music both satisfies our expectancies and suprises us with novelty. Whether or not the listener expects something, or is surprised by something else, relates to two variables: how well organized the music seems to be, and how much knowledge or experience the listener has about the ways the music could be organized (Davies, 1978). Psychologist John Booth Davies and others pointed out that differences among listeners in the level of their previous musical experience would certainly cause them to experience any given piece of music as having different levels of complexity. But

Davies predicted that, in general, people would prefer music that provided them with enough "information" to reduce their uncertainty about upcoming events in the music. Conversely, he believed that people would not like music that failed to reduce such uncertainty, either because it did not provide enough information (there was too much novelty), or because it provided too much information (there was too little novelty). Most people, Davies predicted, would like music that contained an intermediate amount of information: music that was both novel and predictable at the same time. Recall James E. Fletcher's statement in the previous chapter that popularity of a new song "is based on resemblance to music already familiar to the targeted audience. Actually, fans expect only about fifteen percent of a song labelled 'new' to be really new."

**Complexity Elicits More Attention**

Davies (1978) also predicted that listeners would pay more *attention* to music that is slightly more complex than the music they would listen to just for pleasure. Put in terms of pop music played on the radio, this seems to say that we pay closer attention to music for which we have to work a bit to appreciate, but we tend to enjoy music that is a little simpler. On the other hand, each time a piece is repeated, the listener is likely to find it less complex. If the initial complexity seemed to be too high, the listener may well find that the music becomes more enjoyable. But where the initial complexity was too low, repeated exposure will make the music seem unchallenging and not worthy of attention, presumably because too little new information is available. Davies also said that a period of "intense exposure" to a tune may well cause us to be "fed up" with it, but that if the song is put away for awhile, the next time it is heard it is stimulating again. He probably would question the wisdom of radio music presentation systems that play current songs in a heavy rotation to the point where the public is "burned" on the record, and he might take exception to the practice of putting late-stage hits immediately into the "recurrent" category without resting them for awhile.

**Familiarity and Novelty**

A study by June E. Downey and George E. Knapp (1968) reported on the relationship of familiarity and novelty to the listener's response. They pointed out that certain individuals have such a strong need for familiarity that everything strange is viewed as unpleasant, whereas others are obsessive about experiencing the new or the bizarre and cannot abide the familiar. But for most people:

Familiarity is in itself a pleasant feeling; it involves the *recognitive thrill* which is in part a feeling of safety, of being *at home*. . . . With too great acquaintance, however, familiarity lapses into triteness and pleasingness washes out. The only protection against such waning in value is a very rich content in the object.

Novelty is a second factor which forces attention and brings in train the joy of adventure. In order that the *familiar* may not pass over into the *trite,* its contents must be so rich, so complex, as to insure continued discovery of new beauties, or subtleties not to be grasped from one presentation. (pp. 238–239)

## The Appeal of Complex, Original Music

The quote just cited explains how the basic program appeals of familiarity and novelty apply specifically to music listening. The colorful language of the phrase "With too great acquaintance, however, familiarity lapses into triteness and pleasingness washes out" is about the best description we will ever get for what we would today call *record burnout*. And the proposed cure is also worth noting: "In order that the *familiar* may not pass over into the *trite,* its content must be so rich, so complex, as to insure continued discovery of new beauties, or subleties not to be grasped from one presentation." That seems to be a call for music that is not necessarily assimilable in just one hearing. Instead, for many listeners, music should be "dense." In fact, what Downey and Knapp said about music might well be said about audio production and everything else in radio programming: If it is going to be heard more than once, it should be rich enough with detail and nuance that it can stand up to repetition.

## The Appeal of Obvious, Familiar Music

On the other hand, it is important to also take into account—as Downey and Knapp did—the fact that certain listeners will find anything out of the ordinary to be disagreeable. Often, younger teenage listeners fall under this description, because they are struggling to make statements about their individuality before they are really clear about who they are. Music that is too novel can be threatening to teens because it probably lacks peer approval. The form, the presentational style, even the names of Heavy Metal and Rap groups are cases in point. In spite of the high level of musicianship often displayed, it can be argued that Heavy Metal and Rap are very narrowly defined genres, that allow little leeway for true experimentation. The lyrics of many rappers suggest a surface alienation, and the vocal style of many Heavy Metal groups suggest a certain recklessness, whereas for both genres the form of the melodic lines, instrumentation, and performances tend to be comfortably familiar to teens. Thus, teenage listeners who adopt such music can, in effect, cloak themselves in a verbal aura of aloofness, angst, or danger while the other musical elements stay safely grounded in familiar, peer-approved territory. The result is often music that is remarkably strict in its adherence to form, while fulfilling the function of saying something like "Kiss off!" or the impolite equivalent. Like the ballet, it is a form where all the possible moves have apparently already been invented; now the appreciation comes not from innovation but from the virtuosity of technical accomplishment in the way the moves are presented.

Those who remember the Disco format will recall that the emphasis on a narrow range of rhythms tended to make one song sound like another, just as some people feel Rap music does today. And if most Heavy Metal music seems to take its cues from other Heavy Metal music, the same is also true of the pop love ballad. In any pop song, there is likely to be far more that is familiar than is novel.

### Reliability

Percy Tannenbaum (1985) made the point that certainty is related to familiarity, in the sense that what is certain is preferred to what is uncertain. Certainty, when paired with familiarity, begets reliability, a very positive attribute. Bedtime stories repeated endlessly to satisfy a child have great familiarity. Because they are the same every time, they also have certainty. The resulting reliability is why they soothe a child to sleep.

Perhaps instead of concentrating on the familiarity of airplay music, we should be looking at its reliability. Reliability carries with it the notion that the same result will be produced for the listener upon each rehearing, much as a bedtime story once did. The question to be asked then is different. It is no longer "Is this song familiar?" Rather it should be "Does this song make you feel roughly the same way it did when it was new to you?" Reliability does not mean that a given song is good forever. On the contrary: Because reliability takes *continued effectiveness* into account, songs that are very familiar to the point of being overplayed might not be reliable ones.

### Novel Versus Familiar "Hooks"

The term *hook* is widely used in describing a certain short melodic passage in a popular recording that is thought to be the novel element that sets this song apart from others in the listeners' minds, and thus augments the record's popularity. In both auditorium music testing and call-out research, it is often the *hook* of the song that is played for the listener. The novel elements may be of any sort: production effects, vocal inflection, rhythmic change, unexpected timbres, and so on. For example, the 1984 hit record "Jump" by Van Halen began with a synthesizer timbre that was then new to the public. That quality came to be known as the "fat synth" sound because it was perceived as richer and bigger than previously recorded synthesizers.

Clearly, some of the record's success was a result of that then-unique sound—nothing quite like it had been heard before. Soon, the sound became commonplace. Although a listener could easily recognize the "fat synth" hook, it no longer worked as novelty, but rather as familiarity. That is what happens to pop music hooks. Because they generally are different in only one way, they do not offer the denseness and richness of more elaborate music. The *novel* pop music hook becomes *familiar* and eventually passes over into being *trite*.

## Pitch of Music Helps to Determine the Emotional Reaction

Years ago, psychologist Kate Hevner found that listeners fairly consistently judged the same short musical excerpts similarly, basing their judgments on particular elements in the music itself. One of her discoveries was that people tended to describe music that was high-pitched as being playful and happy; low-pitched music was judged to be serious and sad. And although pitch was important in determining the mood, Hevner found *tempo* to be the single most important factor (Table 10.1; Rosenfeld, 1985, p. 51).

## Pleasantness and Activation Reactions

Earlier findings reported that listeners' reactions to music could be ranged on a "pleasantness" continuum from happiness and amusement, on the one hand, to disgust and sadness on the other; and on an "activation" continuum from tension and excitement, at one side, to relaxation and sadness on the other (see Table 10.2; Rosenfeld, 1985, p. 51). Thayer, Tanaka, and Winborne found that listeners' reactions were consistently related to the music's pitch and tempo. Specifically, pitch affected the pleasantness rating, whereas tempo affected the activation rating. Note how this corroborates Hevner's findings about pitch.

TABLE 10.1
Pitch a Factor in Determining Emotional Reaction

| *High-Pitched Music* | *Low-Pitched Music* |
|---|---|
| Playful | Serious |
| Happy | Sad |

TABLE 10.2
Pleasantness and Activation Continua

| *Pleasantness Continuum – Most Affected by Pitch* |
| --- |
| Happiness, Amusement <- - - - - - - - - - - - - - - - - - - - - -> Disgust, Sadness |

| *Activation Continuum – Most Affected by Tempo* |
| --- |
| Tension, Excitement <- - - - - - - - - - - - - - - - - - - - - -> Relaxation, Sadness |

## Either Very Exciting or Very Quieting Songs Preferred

As concerned the relation of pleasantness to exciting and quieting effects, Washburn and Dickinson (1968) found that listeners enjoyed music the most that moved them away from whatever their median state was, and that music that was either much more exciting than usual or much more relaxing and soothing than usual was appreciated more than music that straddled the middle ground. This has links directly to the findings presented in chapter 4 showing that most people desire to be either aroused or satiated, rather than live in a median state between the two extremes.

## Desire for Mood Maintenance or Change

Research by Max Schoen and Esther Gatewood (1968) supplied some early answers to the question of consistency; that is, how many people desire music like their present mood each time, and how many desire music that is different each time? Although cautioning that there were only two trials with 32 people, the invesigators nevertheless found high consistency.

> If they chose music like the existing mood on one occasion they also did the second time. If, on the other hand, they chose music unlike the existing mood they again chose music unlike the existing mood. It therefore seems to be an individual variation which is consistent with the individual. (p. 154)

## Music Mood Novelty/Stability Seekers

This is an important concept. It says that music listeners can be classified two ways: as what we might call "music mood stability seekers" and as "music mood novelty seekers."[1] Neither the format nor the music can expect to change this basic predisposition. There is some evidence that

---

[1] Ed Shane (1991) wrote of three classes of listeners: Loyals, who call in for requests and listen closely; seekers, who keep tuning until they find the kind of song they want; and passives, who use the radio as aural wallpaper and thus generally leave it on the same station.

emotionally intense people seek novelty, complexity, and variety, but that the average level of intensity drops during each decade of life. The greatest drop in intensity is between the 20s and the 40s ("Studies Portray the Passionate, the Impassive," 1987, pp. B-4, B-6). In terms of current format radio listening, it would mean that certain listeners are going to be dial-hoppers no matter what; some of them (the mood stability seekers) going elsewhere because the station is not supplying a consistent enough mood, and others (the mood novelty seekers) going elsewhere because the station seems to be supplying too much of the same mood. No format (unless it makes music mood its first consideration) could hope to keep such listeners long term.

It is important not to confuse the seeking of a novel mood with the seeking of novel music, or the seeking of a stable mood with the seeking of familiar music. Hearing *either* familiar *or* novel music could satisfy either the music mood stability seeker or the music mood novelty seeker. For example, a music mood stability seeker could seek to achieve that mood stability through hearing either familiar or novel music. The same is true of the music mood novelty seeker.

### How Does a Station Match a New Listener's Mood?

The short answer to the question above is that it probably cannot. If the song that is currently playing appeals sufficiently to the listener, he or she will continue to listen to it. If the current song is not appealing, that listener will keep changing the dial until something more satisfying is found, and there is little a station can do to keep that from happening. But the *continuation* of listening is another matter. Research by Schoen and Gatewood suggested that the majority of listeners—whether in an active or passive mood—prefer *succeeding* music to fit their existing mood (Schoen & Gatewood, 1968). The mood that made them stop on your station and continue listening to that initial record is one that you should try to continue (with variations) into the song that follows. It is much more important for a station to sustain, develop, and subtly modify a mood from song to song than to worry about the preexisting mood of new tuners-in.

## MENDELSOHN'S MUSIC MOODS RESEARCH

If you are still skeptical of the importance of mood in determining which records and which radio stations a listener chooses to hear, the classic music moods research conducted in 1961 by social scientist Harold Mendelsohn (1966) should convince you. Mendelsohn studied radio listeners in New York City for radio station WMCA, which at that time was running a Top

40-type pop music format. Mendelsohn conducted intensive personal interviews with 150 teenage and adult radio listeners in the New York metro area. Note that the emphasis supplied to the quotes from Mendelsohn's study all came from him; the headings are mine.

## Pop Music Listeners Accept Many Diverse Music Forms

A major finding of Mendelsohn's research was that people did not seem to have a taste for just one type of music to the exclusion of every other type. The one exception was

> a general distaste for strictly classical music. For the most part, every possible combination of nonclassical music received some acceptance from someone.... In other words, popular musical tastes seem to be highly individualized, and form no clear-cut pattern of persistent choice. It would be mistaken to visualize the listener to popular music as enjoying *only* rock and roll, or enjoying only "cool jazz," or enjoying only "show tunes." (p. 121)

## Individual Mood Needs Are More Important Than Taste Predispositions

Mendelsohn's research more than 35 years ago made a key discovery that shows the link between (a) a lack of exclusive preferences and (b) the element in music that gives pleasure.

> The key to understanding why there is a lack of exclusive preference where taste for popular music is concerned also helps unlock the mystery of what it is about popular music that is found to be pleasurable. The data in the New York radio audience study, and later on in the Colorado study, indicated that taste for a specific kind of music is generally more dependent upon the immediate *mood* of the individual than upon any immutable "taste predisposition." This is to say that popular music is enjoyed primarily because it either serves to *create* a desired mood; or to change an undesirable mood; or, to *sustain* and accompany an already established desirable mood. Where these mood needs are satisfied, pleasure is derived from a wide variety of musical forms. (pp. 121–122)

It would be hard to overemphasize the importance of this long-overlooked finding. The reason people do not have strong taste preferences for one kind of music to the exclusion of all other types is because the music is chosen to create, change, or sustain a *mood*. This finding was further underscored by Zillmann and Bryant (1985), who said:

> The suggestion that entertainment preferences might vary with affects, moods, and emotions generally evokes considerable skepticism. It seems to be counterintuitive because people tend to believe that, if they are free to choose, they usually select whatever best meets their seemingly never changing taste. (p. 157)

To be fair, radio format consultants have sometimes acknowledged the audience's desire for musical variety. But the typical response is often akin to this one, which appeared in a radio trade publication:

> Because variety is so much in demand, it might seem like the perfect time to alter our philosophies of targeting specific demos and increase variety in our music and programming mix, right? *Absolutely not!!!* The audience wants to sample different styles of music *but not on one station.* This common misconception springs from hearing listeners talk about their favorite music. They do want variety from their favorite station—a perceived variety—but only in the confines of a specific music genre.
>
> Listeners who want to hear a variety of musical styles don't want it at the expense of altering their favorite station's sound. . . . With all the available options, they will tune in a station that superserves their desire to listen to a specific form of music. (Pollack, 1988, p. 36)

The standard radio industry solutions just quoted make sense in large markets where there are many "niche" signals to choose from, but the smaller the market, the less practical it becomes to superserve a narrow target demo. Perhaps the programmer was thinking most about the desires of the youngest radio listeners, who tend to have a high tolerance for song repetition and who develop strong affinities for certain peer-approved stations. He was not thinking about the type of listener for whom inconsistency of presentation and lack of song repetition are a drawing card.

Mendelsohn's crucial discovery decades ago was that people were not listening exclusively to certain musical genres. The style of the music was not nearly so important as the mood it created, changed, or sustained. Mendelsohn's research went on to explain why radio listeners might feel compelled to tune around the dial to find the song they wanted:

> It appears that two basic "mood needs" dominate the tastes and preferences of popular music devotees. . . . the need for active mood accompaniment and the need for release from psychological tension. If the popular music fan seeks active mood accompaniment he will turn to music that in his words is "lively and peppy." On the other hand, if the popular music enthusiast's mood becomes fraught with psychological tensions, he will seek out the

psychologically releasing music that he considers to be "relaxing." Curiously, "relaxing" music can be either pacifying such as waltzes or stimulating such as rock and roll. (Mendelsohn, 1966, p. 122)

As we saw earlier in the work on "activation" there is a continuum—most influenced by a song's tempo—that runs from the pacific relaxation of waltzes to the exciting stimulation of rock and roll. Thus, the fact that relaxation from psychological tension can result from both quiet and exciting music is not so curious after all.

## The Moods Questions That Need Asking

Keep in mind that two different studies by Mendelsohn "indicated that taste for a specific kind of music is generally more dependent upon the immediate *mood* of the individual than upon any immutable 'taste predisposition.'" The word *popularity* does not appear anywhere in that sentence. Nor do any of the nouns or adjectives that describe contemporary radio music formats. Nowhere did listeners say that they primarily wanted music that was played softly and had a slow beat, or music that came from African or Caribbean sources, or that did or did not include synthesizers programmed to sound like pan flutes. Yet for the most part, music research at radio stations continues to ask questions that deal mainly with the respondents' knowledge of the music ("Do you recognize this song?") or liking for the music ("How much do you like this song?"). Mendelsohn's research tells us that the real questions ought to be "How does this music make you feel?"

A study by Alan Wells in the late 1980s extended his inquiries about the way young people use music to manage their emotions. Two groups of New England and east coast college students with a median age of 19.6 years were asked to indicate their favorite type of music and to name their favorite songs. Most were able to identify at least three favorites. Some songs were the big records of the day, but there were multiple votes for tunes by Pink Floyd, Led Zeppelin, Billy Joel, Elton John and the Beatles. Some of the latter records were nearly 20 years old.

The 234 participants were then presented with a list of emotions, and were asked to select those that they felt were expressed in their favorite songs. The menu of choices came from a list of the most frequently cited emotion terms developed by Joel Davitz, a specialist in the communication of emotional meaning. Wells did not offer definitions of the terms, but allowed respondents to make choices by "common sense." The available emotions were fear, hope, love, surprise, anger, confidence, delight, happiness, hate, passion, pity, pride, relief, shame, grief, and excitement. According to Wells, few respondents had any difficulty making a choice. He found seven emotions that appeared to be the most common: *happiness, excitement, love, hope, confidence, delight,* and *passion.*

Wells (1990) reported that gender differences did not appear to be great among the 119 female and 115 male respondents. He said that men were "a little more swayed by excitement, delight, anger and hate" (p. 112) whereas women "chose songs that express hope, happiness, passion and grief slightly more than men" (p. 112). However, with certain emotions, there *were* interesting differences in the number of mentions by each gender. In regard to their favorite songs, men were only two-thirds as likely to mention happiness as were women (88 male mentions vs. 131 female mentions). The same ratio applied to excitement, but in the opposite direction, with that emotion receiving only 86 mentions by females versus 121 mentions by males. Men were only five-sevenths as likely as women to mention love, but they were twice as likely to mention pride or relief, five times more likely to mention anger, and nine times more likely to mention hate. Women, on the other hand, were twice as likely as men to choose grief as an emotion associated with their favorite songs (Wells, 1990).

Here is an important point about Wells' study: The respondents were asked to name favorite songs, which, by the very nature of the meaning of "favorite," presupposed that emotional reactions were attached to those songs. Thus, it was not surprising that the respondents did not need to ask for clarification of the emotion terms. The songs were familiar, as were also the emotions they evoked.

Although Wells' study suggests (as is argued later in this book) that old songs can continue to be favorites when they reliably evoke certain emotions, because the songs under scrutiny were well known to at least the respondent who chose them, the results were therefore limited to familiar music.

## CLYNES' MUSIC MOODS RESEARCH

The work of musician and neuropsychologist Manfred Clynes has taken an additional step with his research on emotional reactions to music, by showing that people can react to certain elements in even *un*familiar music. Clynes was able to show that there are certain measurable, repeatable, *physical* reactions to given musical phrases. In addition, Clynes presented evidence that these reactions are cross-cultural—that is, not dependent on Western rules and expectations about rhythm, pitch, timbre, and so on.[2] He made a strong case that our reaction to musical phrases may be a result of biological determinants. Clynes believed that there is a single common

---

[2] For a refutation of this possibility, see Rosner & Meyer (1982).

algorithm (or set of rules) in the brain for producing and recognizing certain kinds of dynamic musical expressions (Clynes & Nettheim, 1982). His research thus tried to answer the following question: "Are there dynamic forms that have an innate meaning, forms that can act upon the nervous system not in arbitrary ways but like keys in a lock, activating thereby specific brain processes to which we react in some sense emotionally?" (p. 47). The answer in Clynes' research seems to be a clear "yes."

**Nonsubjective Measurement Procedures**

Unlike some of the research already reported, Clynes' work does not depend on subjective reports from listeners. Instead, Clynes' subjects learn to use a sentograph, a device that measures both finger pressure and the direction of any movement. Clynes devised ingenious experiments that traced the effects of both the rhythm and the melodic lines in music. Here is a description of how the sentograph was used in studying listeners' reactions to rhythm:

> a subject presses rhythmically with the pressure of a finger on a pressure transducer sensitive to both vertical and horizontal pressure. The seated subject as it were "dances" or "conducts" on his finger, keeping the finger in touch with the transducer all the way through, however, so that the rhythmic impulse is expressed as a pressure impulse produced by the arm. In this way pressure pulse contours are obtained that relate to specific sound rhythms. (Clynes & Walker, 1982, p. 173)

**Predicting Body Movements From Rhythm**

One of the things Clynes and Walker were seeking to do in the study just discussed was to see if a clear parallel could be drawn between rhythms heard and rhythmic body movements produced. If so, then it would be possible to predict (or even specify) which rhythms beget which body movements.

**The Rhythmic Pulse as a Unitary Event**

Clynes' research suggests that when the body's motor responses try to imitate a rhythmic pattern, it does so using a particular algorithm that contains *both* the activity and the rest, stored as a single form in our memory. Clynes referred often to this *pulse*. When the subjects in Clynes' experiments pressed rhythmically on the finger rest/pressure transducer, "pressure pulse contours are obtained that relate to specific sound rhythms" (Clynes & Walker, 1982, p. 173).

This also works in reverse; that is, a person can be taught expressive finger pressure patterns that actually relate to the specific emotions being studied, but he or she learns them as simple motor skills. Then the subject is asked to match the patterns with a list of seven emotions that Clynes isolated. In Clynes' research, there is a remarkably high success rate.

## Essentic Form: Fusion of Rhythm and Melody

Although it is common for musicians to talk of rhythm and melody as separate entities, it is also true that there cannot be a melody without some rhythm to propel it forward, and that rhythm by itself is not usually thought to be a complete musical experience. Clynes' research considers rhythm and melody as a single entity: the dynamic expressive forms that Clynes called *essentic forms*. These forms, developed and confirmed by research, are more than simple tones or rhythmic beats, and they are less than complete melodic phrases. To make an analogy, they are more than the individual words in this sentence, but they are less than the point of the sentence as a whole, and certainly less than the concept of this section of the book. Yet essentic forms are more direct in their impact. According to Clynes and Nettheim (1982):

> Words denoting specific emotions, like the word joy or anger for example, may induce the mind to imagine aspects of joy or of anger to a various and controllable extent. The dynamic expressive sound forms for specific emotions have more direct power to induce this; and this so to the extent to which they precisely express that particular dynamic shape, i.e. one can say, the more "pure" an expression of joy or anger they are. In their pure form they require a special effort, a mental screen, to be ignored: it is difficult to remain unaffected in the presence of a true, authentic expression of grief, or of joy, as it indeed also can be in the presence of very sad or joyful music. Such gripping dynamic emotional "words", or essentic forms, are a means of emotional contagion in daily life, which may be used with a sense of putative power by demagogues and commercial advertisers, or as mutual emotional communication between persons; or in an autocommunicative way as in music and art where the communicative power creates its own rewards.
>
> Essentic form by itself appears to act directly to communicate its quality—no symbolic transformation is required, according to our theory and findings. (p. 51)

## Seven Emotions Isolated, With Their Expression Times

The seven emotions or sentic states that Clynes isolated in his studies are anger, hate, grief, love, sex, joy, and reverence. Each of these has its own unique expressive form. One component of the form is the length of time

TABLE 10.3
Expression Times for Seven Emotions

| Shortest | | (Times in Seconds) | | | | Longest |
|---|---|---|---|---|---|---|
| Emotion: | Anger | Joy | Hate | Sex | Love | Grief | Reverence |
| Expr. time: | 0.7 | 1.1 | 1.6 | 2.0[a] | 5.2 | 9.0 | 9.8 |

[a]Not mentioned in text. Inferred from graphs.
Note. Adapted from "The Living Quality of Music" by Clynes and Nettheim. In M. Clynes (Ed.), *Music, mind, and brain* (p. 56). New York: Plenum. Copyright © 1982 by Plenum. Adapted with permission.

it takes for each expression to occur. That duration is its expression time. Clynes' findings show expression times ranging from a low of 0.7 seconds for anger to a high of 9.8 seconds for reverence (see Table 10.3)

There is good support for the length of musical expressions to fall within this range. For example, according to Paul Fraise, "The slowest adagio in a ¾ bar is no longer than 5 sec. and the longest lines of poetry have from 13 to 17 syllables, the time necessary to recite them being no longer than from 4 to 5 seconds" (Deutsch, 1982, p. 158). Other scholars have studied the *average* length of musical phrases. One found that the average length of a musical bar in a religious hymn was 3.4 seconds. Another found that the average duration of lines of poetry was 2.7 seconds (Deutsch, 1982).

## Inflection (Pitch Changes)

Another component of each form is what might be called its inflection. Clynes referred to it as frequency modulation—that is, the way the beginning frequency (the base frequency at which the tone begins to sound) is modulated up or down by increasing or decreasing finger pressure on the laboratory sentograph.[3] Figure 10.1 shows how vertical and horizontal finger pressure on the sentograph transducer were reproduced on a chart recorder.

Clynes and Nettheim (1982) also found that the modulation depth was very different for different emotions (see Table 10.4):

*Love* had only a small modulation; the sound has a steady secure quality. The downward modulation range, although quite small (less than a semitone), was essential to the expression of this quality.
*Anger* an upward modulation range of approximately a minor sixth.
*Hate* a very small downward modulation—the quality of its hard containment not permitting more modulation.

---
[3]A soundsheet containing recordings of the seven essentic forms is included in a pocket on the inner back cover of Clynes' book *Music, Mind, and Brain*. It is helpful in understanding the modulation that becomes the "melody line."

*Grief* a downward modulation range of about four semitones.
*Sex* an upward modulation range of approximately three semitones.
*Joy* initially a downward modulation followed by a swing upwards, which then subsides to the starting point. Total perceived modulation range—one octave—a third down, an octave up, and a sixth down.
*Reverence* an upward modulation of approximately 2 to 4 semitones.

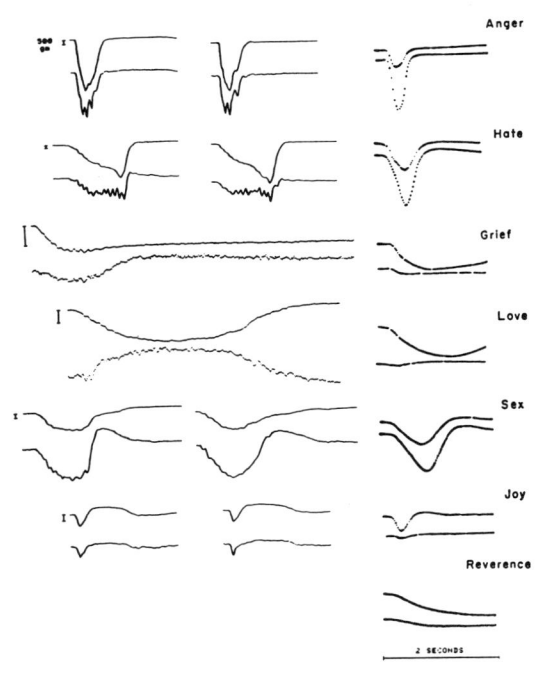

FIG. 10.1. Examples of "sentograms" of the essentic form of emotions. From M. Clynes (Ed.), *Music, mind, and brain* (p. 55), New York: Plenum. Copyright © 1982 by Plenum. Reprinted with permission.

TABLE 10.4
Modulation of Base Frequency During Expression of Each Emotion

| Emotion: | Anger | Joy | Hate | Sex | Love | Grief | Reverence |
|---|---|---|---|---|---|---|---|
| Direction: | up | [a] | down | up | down[b] | down | up |
| % change: | 59% | [a] | 5% | 14% | 2.4% | 21% | 9% |

[a]One octave: biphasic 20% down then 61% up.
[b]Note the very small modulation—almost steady.
*Note.* From "The Living Quality of Music" by Clynes and Nettheim. In M. Clynes (Ed.), *Music, mind, and brain* (pp. 56, 62–63). New York: Plenum. Copyright © 1982 by Plenum. Reprinted with permission.

TABLE 10.5
Expression Times and Modulation of Base Frequencies

| Emotion: | Anger | Joy | Hate | Sex | Love | Grief | Reverence |
|---|---|---|---|---|---|---|---|
| Expr. Time: | 0.7 | 1.1 | 1.6 | 2.[b] | 5.2 | 9. | 9.8 |
| Direction: | up | [a] | down | up | down[c] | down | up |
| % change: | 59% | [a] | 5% | 14% | 2.4% | 21% | 9% |

[a]one octave: biphasic 20% down then 61% up.
[b]Not mentioned in text. Inferred from graphs.
[c]Note the very small modulation—almost steady.
*Note.* From "The Living Quality of Music" by Clynes and Nettheim. In M. Clynes (Ed.), *Music, mind, and brain* (pp. 56, 62–63). New York: Plenum. Copyright © 1982 by Plenum. Reprinted with permission.

Notice that each of the emotions has both a frequency direction (up or down in pitch), and a frequency depth. *When* these changes occur during the emotion's expression time is of critical importance in distinguishing one emotion from another, but for now, it is useful to just present a table showing the direction and depth of each emotion's frequency modulation.

Recall that what the words *up* and *down* referred to in Table 10.5 is the way the pitch of the original tone changes over the expression time, and that the percentage figure shows in a general way how much change there is.

For the purposes of advancing future arguments, Table 10.5 combines the two previous tables. Clynes did not present his results this way; Table 10.5 is an amalgam of my own design.

## Expressions in the Psychological Present

One of the things to note about the *length* of the essentic forms Clynes isolated is that none exceeds 10 seconds. That means, according to several psychologists, that all but the longest will probably seem to the listener to be happening entirely in the present moment. William Stern defined the psychological present this way:

> Within the "present" . . . falls the immediate aftermath or development of the experience, the perpetuation of which cannot yet be regarded as the product of an act of memory or recall. The "psychological present" has been assigned values of between five and seven seconds; even a trained expert musician will scarcely be able to extend it beyond nine seconds. (Rosing, 1984)

Thus, Clynes' assertions that these forms operate in very direct ways, without the need for the listener to think about them, would appear to have good support.

Having developed this foundation of research into the moods and physiological responses that music engenders, we can now proceed in the next chapter to explore the specific elements of a mood-evoking music progression.

## MAJOR POINTS

1. Music produces kinaesthetic responses in most listeners, and that physical reaction becomes part of the pleasure of hearing it. Music listeners react to such elements as the alternation of tension and relaxation that comes from our expectations being frustrated and then fulfilled. Many prefer music that contains just enough "information" to make it both novel and predictable at the same time.

2. Music listeners can be classified two ways: as music mood stability seekers (who hop from station to station because they feel no single popularity-based format supplies a mood consistently enough), and as music mood novelty seekers (who hop from station to station because they feel any given popularity-based format supplies too much of the same mood).

3. The listener can find both complex, original music and obvious, familiar music appealing. Familiar music in particular must be reliable in the effect that it has on the listener.

4. Hearing *either* familiar *or* novel music could satisfy either the music mood stability seeker or the music mood novelty seeker. Novelty of mood is not the same as novelty of the music played. Stability of mood is not the same as familiarity of the music played.

5. A station need not attempt to try to match a new listener's mood, because that person would not stay tuned if the music were not already appealing. However, it is important for *succeeding* songs to attempt to extend, grow, and subtly redevelop the existing mood, to keep that listener tuned in.

6. High-pitched music is generally perceived as playful and happy; low-pitched music is felt to be serious and sad. Perceived pleasantness is most affected by pitch, whereas the degree of activation (from tense to relaxed) is most affected by tempo (rhythm).

7. According to Mendelsohn, desire for a specific kind of music is generally more dependent on the immediate mood of the individual than on some preordained taste. Pop music is enjoyed primarily because it serves to create a desired mood, change an undesirable one, or sustain and accompany a mood already established. Pop music listeners are generally accepting of many diverse music genres.

8. Relaxation from psychological tension can result from both quiet and exciting music.

9. Most music research continues to ask "Do you recognize this song?" and "How much do you like this song?" An equally important question should be "How does this music make you feel?"

10. Clynes' research shows there are certain measurable, repeatable, cross-cultural physical reactions to given music phrases that have innate meaning for the hearer. These phrases ("essentic forms") are a fusion of rhythm and melody—more than simple tones or rhythmic beats, and less than complete melodic phrases.

11. Clynes isolated seven "sentic states" or emotions—anger, grief, love, hate, sex, joy, and reverence—each having a typical expression time and inflection. All of these expressions fall in the psychological "present" moment.

# CHAPTER 11

# *The Components of a Mood-Evoking Music Progression*

This chapter builds on the music and moods research in the previous chapters (as well as earlier material, especially on structure and appeals) to establish the structural bases of a mood-generating music progression. The words *music progression* are used because they are intended to be less encompassing than the term *music format*. A music progresssion means merely the order in which recorded music is presented to the listener. This chapter shows how the ordering of songs needs to be based on much more than an assessment of the tune's popularity. It also introduces and explains those additional factors that should be included in a music presentation system. A sample music progression is offered in chapter 13.

## MUSIC PRESENTATION BASED ON MOOD NEEDS

### Problems and Strengths

In trying to develop a music progression based on "mood needs," at least two pitfalls become apparent fairly quickly. The first is that one listener's mood needs at a given moment are likely to be different from another's. A second is that how a piece of music makes one person feel may be somewhat different from how it makes another feel. There seems to be far too much chance of individual differences in both cases.

Yet the basis for some commonality also exists. First, we know that different audiences make themselves available to listen at different times of the day, and as a result, stations daypart accordingly. The findings about circadian rhythm patterns presented in chapter 4 suggest it may also be possible to track certain mood rhythms that coincide with the biological clocks we all share. And in chapter 10, it was shown that the majority of listeners—whether in an active or passive mood—prefer succeeding music to fit the mood that they were in when they began listening.

Second, we know that there are considerable variations in the way persons from the same demographic background will react to a given piece of music. Yet, research—especially that by Clynes, presented earlier—indicates that there are certain universal factors that operate even across widely varying cultures to allow classification of certain musical phrases into mood categories.

## Recognizing Listeners' Mood Needs

As we begin to try to structure a mood-evocative music progression, it is necessary to reaffirm that a radio music listener does not listen just to hear some abstraction called "music"—he or she listens for certain kinds of music that serve certain kinds of mood functions for that person. Those mood functions are generally not simple, and presenting them well is not easy.

One of the things that killed Disco as a format was its continual "upness"—not just in terms of the number of beats per minute, but its mood. It was always electric, always bright and glittery. And after a while, that one mood, that one stimulus, stopped being a stimulus. The Disco format needed a few ballads, blues, and harder rock in order to provide the contrast that would let us realize the good stuff at the heart of the format. Disco showed that providing a single consistent mood and style was not sustainable as a format, even though there were plenty of people who enjoyed the mood for the first few minutes they tuned in.

Ultimately, developing a music presentation system that recognizes listeners' mood needs becomes "a search for meaning" on behalf of the audience. But most stations do not attempt such a search. The audience brings its searching to the radio, and it hears meanings being sung at them in 3- and 4-minute songs, but the meanings come and go with no particular interpretation or flow from one song to the next. So the programmer's job is to figure out a method of presentation—a structure—that maximizes the music's appeal to a target audience having certain mood needs.

The word format is not used here because for most radio people it conjures up visions of "hot clocks" and other hit rotation systems. The arguments to this point have tried to put to rest the notion that a song's popularity should be its major claim to airplay (reread chapters 9 and 10 if you are not convinced). The structure being offered in this chapter makes popularity only one among several measures of a song's airworthiness. Thus, "rotations" take a back seat to other, broader systems of music presentation that allow for satisfaction of both the music mood novelty seeker and the music mood stability seeker. Structure is not the enemy of the music mood novelty seeker any more than chaos is his or her ally. And the same is true for the music mood stability seeker: Structure is simply a consistent method for pursuing a desired outcome.

Once "hit-ness" is stripped away as the prime reason for airplay, most stations are left with very little else in the way of a structure for music presentation. The question then becomes, "What rational bases are there for choosing to play this song next?" The answers lie in an examination of musical structure itself, from the smallest component parts of sound to the larger concepts of sound hours and dayparts.

*Structure,* as the term is used here, starts with the given that most human beings strongly prefer order over disorder. So intense is the drive that we sometimes try to impose an arbitrary order on events that may not have any internal consistency. That is what a hit rotation does: It imposes the arbitrary order of hit position in the Top 40 or the Hot 100 (or in all-time airplay, for oldies) instead of trying to discern the internal links among songs that would cause them to be played in succession.

Linkages among songs are, by definition, structural. At the same time, a discernible structure within a single song is an appeal, of sorts. Because we take pleasure in orderliness, we also delight in the recognition of a familiar sequence or phrase. Thus, it is not surprising that virtually every popular song likely to be played on the radio has a structured—rather than a random—form.

Once again, the stage movement terms *time, space,* and *force* are the windows we look through to frame the discussion in this chapter. This is appropriate because, in many ways, the popular song is the ultimate spoken gesture. A system that seeks to present a series of spoken gestures so that they have a cohesiveness and integrity of their own is then just a logical extension of what the song itself already does.

## TIME

### Body Rhythms

In a discussion of *time,* we begin by considering the heartbeat and breathing rhythms of the human body, which R. Murray Schafer showed to be highly influential of our speech and music. Schafer (1977) said that the human heartbeat is the first and perhaps the most influential of all the natural body rhythms and that, before the metronome was invented, musicians determined the tempo at which music was played by reference to the speed of a beating heart. He contended that because of this rather obvious rhythm in our bodies, music with a beat that is close to that of the human pulse has a natural appeal. The rhythm of the "Ode to Joy" from Beethoven's Ninth Symphony and the basic drumbeat of Australian aborigines are both close to that of the normal human pulse. It is happenstance that Schafer mentioned the "Ode to Joy," but Clynes found "joy" to have an expression time of about 1.1 seconds—virtually at the same rate as a slow-normal heartbeat.

Breathing is another body rhythm that is probably highly influential of the tempi we set in music. Schafer affirmed that the rhythms of spoken literature and poetry are usually related to breathing patterns. Even more than the heartbeat, the breathing rate varies with exertion. Normally, a person breathes between about 12 and 20 times per minute, taking roughly 3 to 5 seconds for each complete inhalation–exhalation (Schafer, 1977). It is worth noting that a breathing rate of 12 to 16 cycles per minute corresponds well to Clynes' finding of an expression time for "love" of about 5.2 seconds. That would put it on the long, relaxed end of the inhalation–exhalation duration.

Paul Fraise, in an essay on rhythm and tempo, made a strong case for walking as an important rhythmic component:

> The duration of the step is about 550 msec, and corresponds to a frequency of 110–112 per minute. . . . This frequency depends a little on anthropometric differences between individuals, age, and environmental conditions. This spontaneous activity, which is similar to a reflex, is a fundamental element of human motor activity. It plays an important role in all of the rhythmic arts. (Fraise, 1982, pp. 151–152)

## Time as a Structural Element in Sound: The Sound Envelope

Next, we consider time as a structural element by making an analogy between the structure of a song and the "sound envelope" that describes the individual component sounds of the song.

Any sound can be described in terms of its sound envelope. A sound envelope is comprised of at least four parts: the sound's attack, the decay of that attack, the sustain of the main sound, and the release of the sustain. These four phases are often identified by the acronym *ADSR* standing for *Attack–Decay–Sustain–Release* (see Fig. 11.1). What ADSR values stand for is *timing* information: What is the duration of the attack, the duration of its decay, the duration of the sustain, the duration of the release?

```
       Attack              Decay              Sustain             Release
```

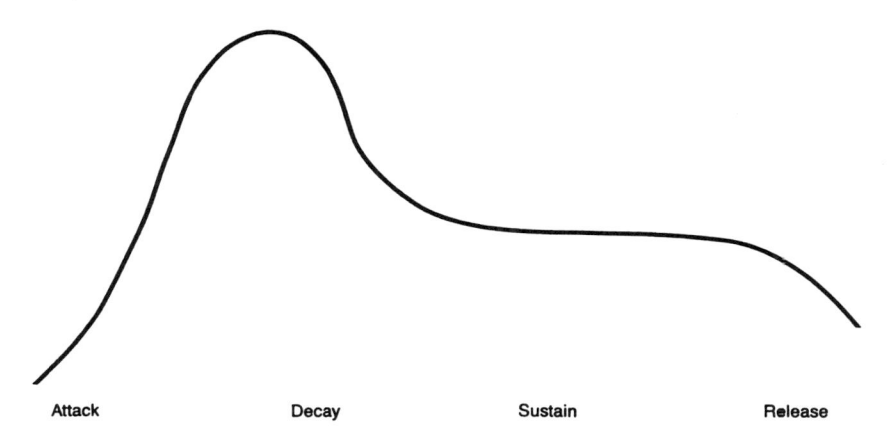

FIG. 11.1. ADSR model showing duration of each mode.

## ADSR Analogized to an Automobile

The terms *attack* and *decay* are really flip sides of the same coin, in the sense that they are the front edge and back edge of the initial part of the sound: the front bumper and grillwork on a car, as it were. Over time, the great bulk of the sound exists in the "sustain" portion, which could be analogous to the main body of the car. The release, although often much longer than the attack–decay, can be thought of as analogous to the taillights and rear bumper. Thus, in microtime, a sound has a fairly rapid onset, a long sustain, and a release of the sustain that can be of almost any speed.

## ADSR Applied to Popular Songs

Popular songs have a similar structure. They generally do not take long to get the overall feel and direction of the tune established—usually no more than 10 to 20 seconds. The body of the song will generally last at least 3 minutes, but seldom more than 5 or 6 minutes. Most pop songs these days do not end abruptly, but rather they fade out over a period of 5 to 20 seconds, which is analogous to the release of the sustain. Using Mendelsohn's terms, the song's beginning creates a new mood (or changes an old one), whereas the body of the song serves to sustain the mood that the beginning established.

Now consider the pop song again through the wider lens of Aristotelian structure. We trace the growth and development of individual songs, and the way those songs' internal timing and structure contribute to the growth and development of a sound hour.

## Aristotelian Structure and the Popular Song

Recall from chapter 4 that the four elements of Aristotelian dramatic structure are exposition, development, building to a climax, and resolution. An individual song will usually display most—if not all—of the elements of Aristotelian structure. The structure may be realized through the rhythm, the melody, and/or the lyrical content. Often, the instrumentation used, the arrangement, or the production techniques influence the sense of forward movement in the song. All of these factors are explored later.

An individual song may fit the Aristotelian model in a single sweep from beginning to end. These are likely to be "story" songs that recount what is already a dramatic event anyway.

More often, the chorus of a given song is a sort of climax, and the verse is the exposition and/or development that leads up to it. Later choruses in the song are often done with additional instruments or voices added, or are performed in a higher key, to increase the sense of climax.

## The Lack of Resolution in Pop Music Structure

Often in popular music, there is little or no resolution—the climactic chorus is simply repeated and fades out. It is probably not too far-fetched to say that as music creators and listeners, we seem loathe to let go of our climaxes, and to admit that there is some period of time when we are on our way "down" instead of building up. It is the rare pop song heard on the radio that fades after a full resolution, rather than fading out the repeat of the climax. We tend not to notice this because the next song coming along generally begins at an exposition stage, which is at a low point in the building process, too. Thus, in much pop music, we really only deal with three of Aristotle's four structural elements: exposition, development, and building to a climax/climax. The next song's exposition substitutes for the last one's lack of resolution. Perhaps the failure of much pop music to resolve completely is merely a reflection of our culture's anxiousness to get on with new things and to skip the weighing of what has gone before. It may be a reflection of our desire to "live in the now"—to be in the state of "flow" in which we relish not having the time to reflect on what has just happened. Or maybe the lack of resolution is a reflection of how our society turns to entertainment media like radio and recorded music to assist in achieving and maintaining a sort of perpetually climactic high, rather than dealing with the true ups and downs of life. Whatever the case, it is important for the programmer to realize that the resolution of the song playing now is usually in the exposition of the song that is to be played next.

TABLE 11.1
Expression Times and Modulation of Base Frequency

| Emotion: | Anger | Joy | Hate | Sex | Love | Grief | Reverence |
|---|---|---|---|---|---|---|---|
| Expr. Time: | 0.7 | 1/1 | 1.6 | 2.0[b] | 5.2 | 9.0 | 9.8 |
| Direction: | up | [a] | down | up | down[c] | down | up |
| % change: | 59% | [a] | 05% | 14% | 2.4% | 21% | 09% |

[a]One octave: biphasic 20% down then 61% up.
[b]Inferred.
[c]Note the very small modulation—almost steady.
Note. After Clynes, M., & Nettheim, N. (1982). The living quality of music. In M. Clynes (Ed.), *Music, mind, and brain* (pp. 56, 62–63). New York: Plenum. Copyright © 1982 by Plenum. Reprinted with permission.

## Rhythms in Programming Sets of Songs

All of the structural elements just mentioned generally are presented at a consistent tempo *within* a song. When songs are placed in juxtaposition to each other, rhythms are likely to vary. Now, the case must be made that tempo/rhythms are an essential consideration in programming sets of songs during some smaller unit of time such as an hour. This is because there is a strong correlation between the mood of a song and the time it takes for that mood to be expressed. Recall from chapter 10 the discussion of Clynes' work on essentic forms—short phrases wherein rhythm and melody are expressed as a single entity. In that chapter, a table was offered that listed the seven emotions Clynes studied, along with their "expression times" (see Table 11.1). As was hinted earlier, expression times are at least partly tied to tempo, and in general, moods with longer expression times such as reverence and grief match up well with slow tempo music; moods with average expression times such as love, sex, and hate match up well with a wide range of medium tempos; and moods with short expression times such as joy and anger match up well with fast tempos. This makes logical sense as well: Joy and anger are emotions that we experience "in the moment" with very little reflection or analysis, whereas we may only come to a sense of grief or reverence when we have devoted some time to thinking about the subject.

## Combining Expression Times/Mood Categories With Aristotelian Dramatic Structure

Although it was stipulated earlier that most pop tunes sustain the same tempo throughout a given song, certainly there can be great variety in tempo among a set of songs. An analogy needs to be made again to the drama. There, an analysis of the length of scenes, or speeches, or the number of transitions, would usually show a rising curve that is consonant with the rising curve of tension as the drama develops, builds, reaches a climax, and then resolves. In other words, the closer to the climax, the briefer the speeches, the shorter the scenes, the greater the number of transitions. The overall rate of presentation speeds up.

Because reverence and grief have the longest of the expression times, it seems logical to assign to them the structural function of carrying out the exposition. Hate, love, and sex, with their average expression times, seem approriate as the bearers of development; and joy and anger, with their quick expression times, seem best associated with climactic structure. As was pointed out already, most pop music does not offer real dramatic resolution, and instead the exposition elements (reverence and grief) found in the beginning of the next song serve as the *de facto* resolution of the old one.

Thus, within a theoretical radio music hour that intended to run the mood gamut from low expression times to high and back again, there might be one or several sets or cycles of music such as the following: The set would begin (not necessarily at the top of the hour) in the slow expositional tempo associated with reverence and/or grief; increase in tempo as the mood shifts to the development phase featuring love, sex, or hate; reach a musical climax in the expression of joy and/or anger; and then begin the cycle again with the resolution/exposition of reverence and/or grief.

Adapting expression times to fit Aristotelian structure allows radio music to be presented in a classic dramatic framework, at least theoretically. However, classic dramatic structure is not sufficient. The expectations that grow out of musical conventions should also be considered.

## Phrasing

One of the attributes of a song, as performed, is phrasing. We think of phrasing—which is defined here as the inflection given certain musical passages by a change in the rate of delivery—as applying mostly to the lyric as sung. But phrasing applies to instrumental music, too. It starts with tempo or beats per minute (BPM) as a base, but then that basic rhythm is modulated by the melody line or the lyrics, so that certain especially important or poignant moments are emphasized. Phrasing is one of the elements that distinguishes expression times from BPM.

Just as phrasing is essential to the communication of important points within a song, so is it important within a mood-evoking music presentation system. A sound hour that gave every tempo or expression category equal emphasis would end up sounding like a vocalist who pronounces everything clearly but who—because of a lack of phrasing—seems devoid of commitment and verve. In other words, the mood-evoking sound hour needs to operate as an orchestra conductor does—using *two* hands. One marks the beat—the obvious, surface tempo, the BPM. The conductor's other hand gives the underlying emotion, the expression. In leading an orchestra, the two hands are sometimes complementary, sometimes at war. For example, a bass beat is continued with one hand, while the other diminishes, builds, or sustains a different line. Although the basic rhythm is what drives the music forward, it is the expression—the phrasing—that modifies that forward motion and gives music (and by extension, sound hours) the desired impact.

### Movement as Growth

There is more to understand about the "forward movement" that takes place as a musical idea develops over time.

Music, like life, is usually perceived as moving forward toward some goal. The pulse of life is mirrored in music's rhythm. A single tone that sounds constantly has no meter, but once silences are interspersed or other tones are mixed in, then we have no choice but to perceive a rhythmic pulse. And because rhythm happens over time, we understand that pulse to be an analog of some portion of our own life span. Every sound has a beginning, a sustain, and a decay, mirroring in microcosmic seconds the decades spanning our own birth, life, and death. While we live, we have no choice but to continue moving forward in time. We may have no idea of the goal our lives eventually will attain, but we can survey the past and discern the shape that our movement through time has produced. If in no other way than in the piling up of seconds ticking off the clock, our life is one of growth, whether we have willed it that way or not. So it is with music. Because music unfolds over a span of time, it is inevitably about growth—growth that is engendered by movement and that results in a certain shape.

### Four Options for Continuation

But once a melody and rhythm are established, the composer is confronted with the question of what to do next. Jan LaRue (1970) in his book *Guidelines for Style Analysis,* suggested (in reference to classical music especially) that there are four basic "options for continuation: recurrence, development, response, and contrast" (p. 15). Those same terms can be applied to popular music, and to the music progression we are constructing. Listed here are my paraphrases of LaRue's definition, associated with radio music formats:

*Recurrence* An immediate repetition, or one that happens after an intervening change.

*Development* A continuation closely related by melody. (Development is not usually done in radio because melodies are catalogued and rotated by radio programmers. A change in key is the closest radio analogue.)

*Response* A continuation unrelated melodically. (Rhythmic response continuation is common in radio music formats, but probably needs still more emphasis.)

*Contrast* A complete change, usually following (and confirming) a heavy articulation by cadences and rests. (In the case of a radio sound hour, the cadences and rests could be something as obvious as a commercial set, or as subtle as an ID jingle that begins with one key or rhythm and ends with another.)

In his book *Emotion and Meaning in Music,* Leonard B. Meyer (1956) also discussed continuation, and was careful to distinguish it from repetition. Meyer underscored the sense in which musical growth must mean movement toward a goal, and how, when that motion is obscured, we expect change. The idea can be applied to formats and rotations as well: So long as the listener can sense that there is movement toward some goal, he or she will not have a sense of repetition. Conversely, change (as an antidote to perceived repetition) will be expected when motion toward a goal is not clear. Meyer made the point in more detail later in his book:

> A stimulus series, then, is well-shaped when its progress, its articulation into phases of activity and phases of rest, its modes of continuation, its manner of completion and closure, and even its temporary disturbances and irregularities are intelligible to the practiced listener and enable him to envisage with some degree of specificity and accuracy what the later stages of the particular musical process will be. Because good shape is intelligible in this sense, it creates a psychological atmosphere of certainty, security, and patent purpose, in which the listener feels a sense of control and power as well as a sense of specific tendency and definite direction. (p. 161)

What Meyer offered in the quote is a rebuttal to those who might argue that a mood-evoking music progression would be too "predictable." Music that is in some way familiar exhibits a coherent growth that becomes its shape. The shape, in turn, gives the listener a sense of security and certainty. Genuine predictability—being able to guess 100% correctly which song will be played next—goes against the necessary appeal of musical complexity that was discussed in chapter 9 (especially the work of John Booth Davies).

## Expectation

Meyer also explored the concept of *expectation* in individual musical works, pointing out that expectation depends on memory:

> As we listen to a particular musical work we organize our experience and hence our expecations both in terms of the past of that particular work, which begins after the first stimulus has been heard and is consecuently "past," and in terms of our memories of earlier relevant musical experiences.
>
> As noted earlier, the norms developed in the memory are not rigidly fixed but change with the addition of each new memory trace: to the extent that the norms have changed, a rehearing of a work is a new hearing, yielding new insights. (p. 90)

What Meyer said is congruent with additional points made in chapter 9—that a song with fairly high complexity may not be as immediately enjoyable as a simple song; but with repeated hearing, the complexities become normalized and enjoyment increases.

There surely needs to be continuation in a mood-evoking music presentation system, but does there also need to be expectation (not just within each song, but throughout the hour)? The answer is "yes," but again, positive expectation is not the same as negative predictability. Every week during radio's first network "Golden Age," it was absolutely predictable that Fibber McGee would open the hall closet and endure the ensuing avalanche of junk, but the audience looked forward to it with great expectation anyway, because the event fit the character and the storyline so well. Predictability did not detract from the audience's positive expectation. Waiting for the thunderous pedal of a huge pipe organ in the finale of the Saint Saens Symphony # 3 is part of the pleasure of sitting through the first movement and half of the second. The same expectancy is the fun of hearing the Big Bopper say into the phone "Do I what? Will I what?" (Expectant pause) "Oh, baby, you KNOW what I like!"

As it is with individual musical works, so it is with overall music presentation: positive expectation about what is to be aired next is fueled by the growth of what is being played now; the shape or mood of the present moment predicts the emotions to come.

## SPACE

In chapters 7 and 8, it was argued that radio air personalities needed to be heard in real acoustic spaces—that the listener longs for audio cues that allow her or him to imagine an actual place where the personality is speaking. The use of the venerable "remote broadcast" is one way of supplying that aural ambience (although remotes usually have been offered more for their commercial than their entertainment value). It at least provides a sense of space because of other sounds in the environment. The typical close-miked announcer in a studio is trapped in a very small place, psychoacoustically just a few inches from your ears. The background silence and the closeness may give a sense of security, even intimacy, but that is not always the intended vocal impact.

If not much thought has been given to the sense of place surrounding the air personalities at most stations, even less has attention has been paid to the acoustic spaces in which music was recorded, and the places in which radio listeners are likely to hear it.

## Concert Halls

R. Murray Schafer made a strong case that concert halls have always influenced the way music is perceived. Pop music, when performed in a large arena or stadium tends to emphasize bass frequencies and thus generates a sound that is diffused and enveloping. In contrast to that is chamber music, which is performed in smaller concert halls where directionality and high frequenices predominate. Dynamics, which are sacrificed for loudness in the arena seting, are also much more controllable in the smaller space. Schafer said that in music intended for performance in concert halls, a sense of distance is important. The "virtual space" of the dynamics of the music is reflected in the actual space of the hall. He equated quiet passages with sounds occurring at the distant horizon, and loud ones with sounds played up close. Because the concert hall allowed music to be heard well even when played quietly, it became a place where silence was the normal mode of audience behavior. Music intended for concert hall performance thus became much more intellectual than it might otherwise have been, for the reason that focused listening and close examination were possible.

Schafer went on to contrast the concentrated listening that is possible in a concert hall with the much more diffused sound of music intended for performance outdoors, such as folk music. Perhaps because folk music is less complex, it does not require the level of attention nor the focus that concert hall music does. Schafer predicted that the popularity of outdoor (and by extension, stadium or arena) rock concerts would bring about a decline in concert hall listening manners, "as concentrated listening gives way to impressionism" (Schafer, 1977, p. 117). It is distressing to note how accurate Schafer was in regard to the deterioration of concert manners, although I would also blame television viewing. People can talk or even scream at each other in front of their TV sets, and the video performance is not disturbed, so the same self-centered behavior gets carried into the concert hall.

Schafer said that arena concerts and much of the pop music heard on the home stereo is designed to flood the listener with sound, with little regard to distance and directionality. He identified this kind of listening condition with the classless society that is pop music.

## Spacial Cues in Recorded Music

Schafer made the point several times that pop music is seeking to immerse the listener in a blend of sound rather than allowing him or her to examine it from both an aesthetic and physical distance. But as was shown already, the radio studio is also a place from which distance and directionality are absent. And what the disc jockey says is obviously not meant to be critically examined like a Mozart opera. The fact is, the music on radio—however much it lacks clarity and focus—is the only place where a listener is going to hear cues as to directionality and distance. And because at most stations music fills far more airtime than any other element, it is important to be *intentional* about presenting the spacial cues that are in the music; that is, there needs to be a rational scheme for the successive presentation of differing acoustic spaces. In regard to questions of distance especially, most stations have done the same with their music presentation that they have done in regard to moods: They jerk the listener all over the place from one song to the next. At one moment, we are in a huge arena hearing a rock band in concert; the next, we are "up close and personal" with a love ballad. The spacial cues are utterly random. There is no attempt at continuity and logical movement in space.

## The Dynamic Sound Plane/Three-Stage Plan

In a later part of his book, Schafer described the work of a sound effects technician to illustrate what he called the *dynamic plane*. The dynamic plane is the aural equivalent of the concept of figure/ground in gestalt psychology, and it is also like the foreground/middleground/background of TV picture composition. The dynamic plane is a most useful concept that is employed later in analyzing acoustic spaces as heard in recorded music. Schafer quoted a sound effects technician as saying that the problem is always to select those few precise sounds which will best portray the scene while also supporting the narration or dialogue. To accomplish this, the technician had developed what he called a "three-stage plan," whose goal was twofold: to restrict the number of sound effects to be included in the scene to a reasonable and practical number and to determine just how recognizable and important each should be compared to the others:

> The "three-stage plan" divides the whole sound-scene (called "scenic") into three main parts. These are: The "Immediate," the "Support," and the "Background." The chief thing to bear in mind is that the "Immediate" effect is to be *listened* to while the "Support" and the "Background" effects are merely to be heard. . . .
>
> The "Support" effect refers to sounds taking place in the immediate vicinity which have a direct bearing on the subject in hand, leaving the "Background" effect to its normal job of setting the general scene.
>
> Take, for example, the recording of a commentary at a fun-fair. The "Immediate" effect would be the commentator's voice. Directly behind this would come the "Support" effects of whichever item of fairground amusement he happened to be referring to, backed, to a slightly lesser degree, by the "Background" effect of music and crowd noises. (Schafer, 1977, p. 157)

The sound technician's three-stage plan of "immediate," "support," and "background" sounds is probably a better way to describe the dynamic sound plane in a popular music performance than "foreground/ middleground/background." The reason is that "foreground/middleground/background" seems to force events into neat little thirds according to where sound sources would be arrayed *visually*. Visually, it is obvious that the lead singer in a band is in the foreground, other guitarists and keyboard players are generally in the middleground, and the drummer is usually in the background. But aurally, the mix does not necessarily work that way. When the lead singer stops singing and a guitar solo takes over, the guitar solo becomes foreground sound even though the guitarist might still be in the middleground visually. The terms *immediate* and *support*, because they do not refer to visual space, are thus better for describing what is aurally prominent and what is secondary. In the preceding example, the lead singer is "immediate," and then the guitar solo takes that position. The guitarist who had been performing a "support" function becomes "immediate" aurally.

Often, bands employ a small chorus of additional (backing) singers who "fatten" the vocals or who sing the latest equivalent of "sha-la-la" or "doo wop doo wop" while the main lyric is being sung by the band members. Such a backing chorus would be an example of a "background" sound element.

## Recording Site Ambience

Beyond the "background" in all cases is the ambience of the recording site. Oftentimes, how much ambience is perceivable is controlled by the distance between the performer and the microphone: the closer the miking, the less sense of acoustic place. Thus, there is an inverse relationship between "immediate" sound sources and the amount of ambience. If the "immediate" sound source is very close-miked, the listener generally receives less sense of place in the musical performance.

### The Three-Stage Plan Can Describe the Listening Place

The terms *immediate, support,* and *background* are also useful in describing the listening place and situation where the radio music is ultimately consumed. An *immediate* listening environment would be inside portable stereo-type headphones, or with the volume turned up high on a loudspeaker system relatively close by, such as in a car. The middle-distance *support* situation would cover most other listening environments where the radio or stereo is being monitored intentionally, but where the volume level is "normal." *Background* listening would pertain just to those situations where levels are so low that the music is not really meant to be listened to in an intentional way.

In the "playback" environment, acoustic differences between rooms can have effects analogous to changes in mike-to-performer distance. Music played back in a room with very little carpet or furniture will be much more reverberant than in a carpeted, draped room with lots of overstuffed chairs. A close-miked "immediate" performer can sound quite intimate in the latter space—approaching the directness of the headphone experience. Played back over loudspeakers in a "starving" college student's bare flat, the intimacy would be mostly missing. Similarly, intimate-sounding performances remain so in a high-end luxury car with plush carpets, softly cushioned seats, and sound-absorbent ceiling material, but would be more like the cold-water-flat experience in an inexpensive car with vinyl seats and rubber floormats. Thus, knowing where the majority of the target audience will be hearing the station at a given time of day becomes increasingly important.

## FORCE

In the previous portion of this chapter, the space in which a song was recorded and the space in which it is heard by the radio listener were shown to affect the song's impact. And before that, BPM and expression time factors were shown to be closely tied to certain emotional states. In this portion, we look more closely at the *intensity* of the music both as performed and as perceived.

### Intensity Factors

*Timbre.* Imagine a loud but close-miked, harshly spoken whisper. You will have to imagine it because it happens so rarely—which is good, because it is frightening. What is frightening about it is not that the voice is close-miked: We expect whispers to be that way. What makes it frightening is that it is loud and harshly spoken. The same words said quietly and sweetly might be soothing; spoken loud and harshly, we get the picture of someone just barely keeping a temper under control, speaking through clenched teeth, spitting out the consonants and half-growling the vowels. It is frightening because of the intensity of the performance, which is reflected in the vocal quality.

Or imagine an electric guitar. We can think of one played by Les Paul—or by Metallica. It is the same basic instrument in both cases, but with very different timbres or qualities. Again, the timbre or quality of the sound goes hand-in-glove with intensity.

*Instrumentation/Presentational Style.* Some stations, in trying to focus and restrict their music, make prohibitions. They might restrict steel guitar because it sounds too "country," or strings because they sound too soft and sweet. But the instrumentation is not always the culprit. Just as often, the presentational style is. It is the *timbre* of a heavily distorted guitar or a raspy-voiced singer that are felt to be too "hard" for a station's sound. We know that tempo and melodic line are influential in engendering a mood, and that spacial factors contribute to the overall impact. But it is probably the instrumentation and presentational style, that together produce a certain intensity of performance, which most affect whether—or when—a certain song gets airplay.

There is also the question not only of *what* the instrumentation is, but also of *how many.* There *is* a difference in quality and timbre between the sound of the Mormon Tabernacle Choir and The Indigo Girls, even though they may be singing similar material. Although there can be tremendous energy from either group, there is no getting around the potency of massed voices when singing loud. On the other hand, "beautiful music" albums with the 100 Guitars or the 101 Strings proved that more instruments do not necessarily result in a more forceful presentation when the content suggests a more quiet approach.

*Instrument/Vocal Density.* Phil Spector, with his "wall of sound" production mix, showed that slow ballads like the Righteous Brothers' "You've Lost That Lovin' Feelin'" could have potency. The potency seems to derive from the *density* of the instrumentation. In that recording, many of the sound sources are not "immediate" and up front. Instead, they are in deep "support" range, even during the great climactic moments. The record has become a classic because of a strong vocal performance, the fine arrangement that builds so well to a climax, and because of the *density* of the instrumentation. This "rock" record features no less than a vocal duo, a chorus, strings, tambourine (reverbed), bongos, drums, and what sound like a vibraphone and a bass guitar. The intensity of the Righteous Brothers' vocal duet is matched by the density of their support.

A "wall of sound" is not the only way to achieve presentational impact. Many of James Taylor's, Paul Simon's, and Willie Nelson's most effective records could have been taped in a closet. Their engaging *lack* of vocal intensity is matched by a *spareness* in the instrumentation. The near-bombast of the Righteous Brothers arrangement would have been wholly inappropriate for their style. Taylor, Simon, and Nelson get their impact from the timbre of their voices, the simple spareness of the instrumentation, and of course, what they say.

## Lyrics

Up to this point, we have been dealing entirely with instrumental music in our discussion of how music evokes emotional reactions. Of course, most popular music has lyrics. Lyrics seem potentially more difficult to deal with than instrumental elements for at least two reasons. For one, every word in any language in the world could conceivably be used in a song, making analysis and classification a hopeless task. For a second, the delivery of lyrics by a vocalist can greatly affect their impact, sometimes even altering their apparent surface meaning entirely.

But happily, lyrics are really easier to deal with than instrumental elements, because much of the time the words employed are rather limited— by the subject matter, by the need to rhyme or at least to fit the rhythm, and perhaps by the parochial imagination of some writers. The result is that the vocabulary that actually has to be dealt with is much smaller than the whole universe of words. Moreover, lyrics often are intended to say what they appear to say, so that a reasonably good guess about the feelings they will invoke is often possible from a fairly cursory hearing.

## The Interpretation of Emotions Expressed Vocally

The research literature about the emotions evoked by vocal expression tends to be much more consistent than the research literature surrounding the evocation of meaning via instrumental music. In terms of ordinary speaking, most researchers agree that vocal expression alone can accurately convey emotional meanings. Put in terms of song lyrics, it could be said that there are certain emotional states connected with the words a lyricist chooses, and perhaps the same or a different set of emotional states attached to those words when heard by a listener. Thus, the effect of the words (as read, not spoken) might be very different among several listeners. However, when said aloud, those same ambiguous words can be expressed so that listeners usually correctly identify the emotional state the speaker was trying to convey, even if the listener does not understand the language the speaker is using (Sundberg, 1982)!

Moreover, it appears that such familiar terms as *pitch, rate,* and *loudness* are good descriptors of the vocal characteristics that affect the expression of meaning. Researchers found that listeners can differentiate between such feelings as contempt, grief, and anger on the basis of differences in rate, the length of pauses and speaking time, and the pitch. Vocal expressions of anger, for example, tended to be portrayed at a fairly fast rate; grief had many long pauses. Pitch turns out to be a reliable way to differentiate between happy and sad vocal expressions—happy ones are always higher in pitch than neutral or sad expressions (Davitz, 1964b, p. 25).

In an article titled "Personality, Perceptual, and Cognitive Correlates of Emotional Sensitivity," (1964a) Joel R. Davitz offered a table listing the characteristics that 61 subjects employed to describe what a voice sounded like when it was expressing each of eight emotional meanings. The emotions to be described were affection, anger, boredom, cheerfulness, impatience, joy, sadness, and satisfaction. Each of these was rated for the dimensions of loudness, pitch, timbre, and rate. The subjects were also asked to describe the speech's inflection (see Table 11.2) Some of these

TABLE 11.2
Characteristic Employed to Describe What a Voice Sounded Like When Expressing Each of Eight Emotional Meanings

| Feeling | Loudness | Pitch | Timbre | Rate | Inflection |
|---|---|---|---|---|---|
| Affection | soft | low | resonant | slow | steady & slightly up |
| Anger | loud | high | blaring | fast | irregular up & down |
| Boredom | moderate to low | moderate to low | moderately resonant | moderately slow | monotone or gradual fall |
| Cheerfulness | moderately high | moderately high | moderately blaring | moderately fast | up & down; overall up |
| Impatience | normal | normal to mod. high | moderately blaring | moderately fast | slightly upward |
| Joy | loud | high | moderately blaring | fast | upward |
| Sadness | soft | low | resonant | slow | downward |
| Satisfaction | normal | normal | somewhat resonant | normal | slight upward |

*Note.* After Joel R. Davitz, "Personality, Perceptual, and Cognitive Correlates of Emotional Sensitivity," In Davitz, 1964a, in *The Communication of Emotional Meaning*. Copyright © 1964 by McGraw-Hill. Reprinted with permission of the McGraw-Hill Companies.

TABLE 11.3
Comparison of Davitz and Clynes on Feelings/Emotions, Rate/Expression Times, and Inflection/Frequency Modulation

| Davitz/Clynes Feeling/Emotion | Davitz/Clynes Rate/Exp. Time | Davitz/Clynes Inflection/Freq. Mod |
|---|---|---|
| **Affection**/Love | **slow**/5.2 sec | **steady**/mostly steady |
| **Anger**/Anger | **fast**/0.7 sec. | **upward**/upward |
| **Joy**/Joy | **fast**/1.1 sec. | **upward**/[a] |
| **Sadness**/Grief | **slow**/9.0 sec. | **downward**/downward |

[a]initial 1/3 octave down, then up an octave, then down 1/6.

findings directly parallel the results already described in Clynes' research on the evocation of moods by instrumental music.

I have constructed a table after the one offered by Davitz, employing the emotional terms used by Clynes, but substituting Davitz's vocal expression terms for Clynes' terms where appropriate (see Table 11.3). Either Clynes or Davitz might argue that "affection" and "love" are not equivalent, and neither are "sadness" and "grief." I have grouped them together because the similarities between the vocal expression and the instrumental expression are striking.

Clynes' work did not deal with timbre, and loudness was a factor only in the sense that over some period of time, the sound would range from zero amplitude to some normal loudness and finally back to zero again at its conclusion. (Clynes was measuring the time it took to go from silence to full audibility and back to silence; he was not looking for subjective judgements about which of the tones were louder or softer.) In addition, because of the way he designed his research, Clynes did not believe that starting frequencies were critical, as he felt the same results could be obtained over a "moderately wide range" (Clynes & Nettheim, 1982, p. 62). (In his research, lower starting frequencies were chosen for the tones that expressed anger and hate, with a medium pitch level used for all others.) Thus, the dimensions that can be related are *rate* (which I pair with Clynes' *expression time*), and *inflection* (which here is related to Clynes' *frequency modulation*). In the resulting table, Davitz's vocal expression terms and findings are listed in bold type on the left, Clynes' terms and findings in normal print on the right.

Note that there is good agreement between Davitz and Clynes on the four identical or nearly equivalent emotions. In the chapter that follows, the case is made that music can be tested on the basis of its vocal and instrumental rate/expression time, and on the basis of its vocal and instrumental inflection/frequency.

## THE TIME/SPACE/FORCE COMPONENTS OF RADIO MOOD

This chapter on time, space, and force factors has introduced enough new material that it may be helpful to conclude with several tables that summarize how the concepts presented here fit into the generation of music moods. The sets of factors that appear to affect the mood generated by listening to music on the radio can be summarized as: (a) performer or song characteristics, (b) general audience characteristics, and (c) individual listener characteristics. All three sets of factors involve the concepts of time, space, and force, but they have different meanings in each case.

Performer or song characteristics (see Table 11.4) refer to the traits that are inherent in the performer or in the song. Being inherent, they are stable. For example, the force factors of instrumentation and presentation style affect a station's acceptance of the song.

General audience characteristics (see Table 11.5) are traits that exist in the audience at large, taken as a homogenous mass. As such, they are a mix of stable and variable characteristics. For example, the time factor of a cultural rhythm such as Mother's Day might call for more music with reverential expression times, whereas the Fourth of July suggests music with joyful expression times.

Individual listener characteristics (see Table 11.6) are the final set of factors. Because these refer to traits held by individuals, they are highly heterogeneous and vary widely. For example, the space factor of the place

TABLE 11.4
Performer or Song Characteristics

| Time | Space | Force |
|---|---|---|
| *Song Rhythms* | *Involvement Factors* | *Acceptance Factors* |
| BPM | performer distance | instrumentation   lyrics |
| expression time | recording's ambience | presentational style |

TABLE 11.5
General Audience Characteristics

| Time | Space | Force |
|---|---|---|
| *Communal Rhythms* | *Involvement Factors* | *Acceptance Factors* |
| seasonal rhythms | appeals | performer popularity |
| cultural rhythms | structure | song popularity |

TABLE 11.6
Individual Listener Characteristics

| Time | Space | Force |
|---|---|---|
| *Personal Rhythms* | *Involvement Factors* | *Acceptance Factors* |
| circadian rhythms | listening place | familiarity |
| lifestyle needs | listening situation | drives for arousal/satiation |

in which a person normally listens will influence how involved he or she can be with the programming.

## MAJOR POINTS

1. The ordering of songs needs to be based on more than popularity. A hit rotation imposes the arbitrary order of hit position, instead of trying to discern the intrinsic merits within a song and the internal links among songs.

2. A slow-normal heartbeat is close to the expression time Clynes found for "joy." A normal breathing rate is close to the expression time for "love." These body rhythms are undoubtedly part of our reaction to music performed at these tempi.

3. Most popular songs exhibit a structure comparable to one cycle of sound expresssed as the ADSR sound envelope, or to one dramatic action graphed on the basis of Aristotelian dramatic structure. In the latter case, note that most pop songs lack true resolution. The next song's exposition substitutes for the previous song's lack of resolution.

4. Moods such as reverence and grief match up well with slow-tempo music; moods with average expression times match with love, sex, and hate; and moods such as joy and anger match well with fast tempos.

5. When expression times are matched to the dramatic structure curve, reverence and grief match up with the slow, low curve of exposition. Hate, love, and sex are related to the more elevated part of the curve called development. Joy and anger are associated with building to a climax. Because of pop music's lack of resolution, reverence and grief also match up with resolution, becoming the exposition of the next song.

6. LaRue's four options for continuation of a musical idea are *recurrence, development, response,* and *contrast.* These can be adapted to describe a mood-generating music presentation system.

7. Expectation is an additional factor in a mood-generating music progression. Positive expectation is not the same as negative predictability. Positive expectation about what is to be aired next is fueled by the growth

of what is being played now; the slope or mood of the present moment predicts the emotions to come.

8. The music on the radio is more likely to have directionality and distance (spacial) cues than is talk on the radio. But music is usually presented in such a haphazard way that the listener is thrust "up close and personal" in one song, and is pulled back to concert distance the next.

9. The dynamic sound plane/three-stage plan suggested in Schafer divides the sound scene into *immediate, support,* and *background* areas. This terminology avoids the bias of the visually oriented terms *foreground, middleground,* and *background.* It can be used to describe both the recording site and the listening place.

10. Among the factors contributing to the intensity (force) of a song as performed are the timbre of the vocals and instrumentals, the presentational style, the number of performers, and the density of the instrumentation.

11. It was shown that the emotions expressed in lyrics can be interpreted even by people from other cultures who do not know the language. And the rate, pitch, inflection, and loudness of spoken expression help listeners to identify various emotions. Of these, rate and inflection correlate well with Clynes' findings in the cases of love, anger, joy, and sadness.

# CHAPTER 12

# Factors in MOST—Mood-Oriented Selection Testing

Chapters 12 and 13 take the theory and reasoning in the previous part of this section and move them toward practice, toward the framework of a mood-evoking music order.

The station seeking to apply the strategies to be outlined here and in chapter 13 would do best not to use them literally but rather to think of them as examples of the testing and thinking the station needs to do. The examples that are provided are not meant to be formulas, but instead should be viewed as the artifacts of research that has only recently begun and that must be further refined.

The two problems any music programmer must solve are—given our target demographic—which songs do we play and in what order do we play them? It comes down to questions of selection and order. Happily, the attributes of a song that recommend it for selection in many cases are also useful in determining when it should be presented.

Note the phrase *given our target demographic* in the foregoing problem statement. Some of the attributes of selection and order work best with a specific audience segment—they are not "one-size-fits-all." Before starting to apply the attribute tests, not only would you know your station's target demographic in terms of how many listeners are available in the typical age, sex, education, and occupation breakouts, but you would also have some sense of what that target audience's mood needs are and how they might change from daypart to daypart.

In order to aid recall, easily remembered acronyms have been developed for the music selection factors and for the music presentation factors being offered. The tests to be applied to selecting a song for airplay are called *mood-oriented selection testing* (MOST). The decisions to be made about when the song is presented fall under the term *mood-evoking music order* (MEMO). (In chapter 14, where a truly audience-sensitive format is proposed, mood-evoking respondent-interactive tracking—MERIT—is introduced.

## USING CLYNES' TERMS TO SELECT AIRPLAY MUSIC

Chapter 10 introduced Manfred Clynes' basic research using a Sentograph finger pressure transducer, and his carefully described essentic forms that combined rhythm and melody. But nearly all radio music testing is necessarily applied research. The challenge in attempting to use Clynes' terms to select music for radio airplay was to devise a music testing procedure that would merely emulate and extend standard practices, without unnecessarily complicating them.

### Feasibility Study

Clynes never intended his emotional reaction terms and their associated expression times to be used as a means of selecting music for airplay. But the fact that he had developed seven distinctive emotional terms that together with average expression times might allow a trained programmer to predict a listener's emotional reaction, invited further investigation. Were Clynes' seven terms (anger, joy, hate, sex, love, grief, and reverence) sufficient as labels for the emotions likely to be evoked by hearing popular music? Would radio listeners in an auditorium test be comfortable choosing one or more of these terms to describe their reaction to a song?

Faculty colleague William J. Adams and I, along with other faculty and student helpers, constructed feasibility and pilot studies that attempted to apply Clynes' findings to the problem of selecting music for radio airplay. The feasibility study involved 36 college student respondents, all between the ages of 18 to 24, about half male and half female. Ten instrumental music selections were chosen to represent typical music genres. Each selection was 20 seconds to 40 seconds in length. The respondents were instructed to write down any adjective that came to mind to describe the way the music made them feel. The words chosen by the respondents were later grouped by the researchers with other synonyms under one of Clynes' seven terms. Although the songs were all instrumentals and the responses were completely open-ended, there was fair to good grouping on the Clynes variables. It appeared feasible to offer the seven terms as a forced choice in a larger pilot study.

## Pilot Study

For the pilot study, the researchers purposely chose music that was thought to evoke the seven emotions isolated by Clynes. The concept this time was to test whether respondents would choose the same emotional terms to describe the music that the researchers had chosen. In this pilot study, the respondents would, in effect, act as audience members in an auditorium music test, while the researchers played the role of radio station music directors.

The music chosen for the pilot study included songs that were "pop" in nature, whereas other selections might be classified as "alternative" or "college radio." All of the music was relatively unknown in the month and year when the survey was conducted. This time, rather than being entirely instrumental, the majority of the songs included lyrics, as is typical of most popular music. Some of the selections were expected to evoke a strong, definite reaction, whereas others were thought likely to cause no reaction (such as a cut comprised entirely of rhythmic speaking with no melody line). There was even a rock song in a foreign language. Certain selections were also chosen specifically because they were complex; that is, because they did *not* elicit just a single response from the investigators. Often such songs displayed a strong tension or opposition between the words and music. Some songs went beyond opposition and seemed to the researchers to evoke two or three layered emotions simultaneously.

The sample for the pilot study was 39% male and 64% female. Eighty-two percent of the sample were high school or college students. There were 129 usable sets of responses. The study participants were asked to indicate which of the seven Clynes terms was closest to how the recorded music selections made them feel. *No feeling* was also an available choice.

Results from the study showed responses clustered on the majority emotion (the emotion chosen by the majority of respondents) as much as 90% of the time for a single song. It also appeared that listeners were generally comfortable about using the Clynes terms to report their emotional reactions. However, in response to follow-up conversations with respondents who expressed a need for it, the researchers coined an eighth *non*-Clynes-tested term: *yearning*. No expression time for yearning was calculated.

Interestingly, certain songs that had the lowest percentage of clustering also averaged a much higher percentage of *no feeling* responses than the majority of the other songs. The researchers tentatively concluded that the combination of low clustering and a high percentage of "no feeling" responses could be a useful filter to prevent airplay of "dangerous" songs, that is, songs that would cause tuneout.

In summary, the feasibility and pilot studies showed that respondents generally were able to assign samples of recorded music into categories labeled with Clynes' seven emotion terms. However, the two studies had relied heavily on college-age respondents, and tested music quite different from that played in standard format-based auditorium tests. A more extensive, better designed study was needed to provide proof of the viability of the Clynes terms for choosing airplay music based on emotional reactions to the songs.

## Multimarket, Multiformat Study[1]

The multimarket, multiformat study began in the spring of 1991 with the assembly of tapes of representative music excerpts for five formats (Country, AC, AOR/Classic Rock, CHR, and Oldies), identification of sites for auditorium testing, and finalization of procedures for recruiting representative listeners. The auditorium testing took place between the summer of 1991 and the late winter of 1992.

*Procedure and Sample.* During testing, respondents were played excerpts from both familiar (popular) and unfamiliar music. After each excerpt, respondents were asked to mark data collection cards to indicate their liking for the song, and also to categorize it using the Clynes mood terms previously discussed.

Four factors enhanced the generalizability and utility of this research for music programmers. First, studies were conducted in markets of varying sizes, and in different regions of the United States in order to achieve as much market size and demographic diversity and applicability as possible. Specifically, auditorium tests were conducted in nine widely dispersed test sites.

Paragon Research of Denver, Colorado, graciously supported this research by adding the study's Emotional Responses to Music survey to three of their large market studies: to a survey of 98 female Adult Contemporary listeners aged 25 to 34 in Orlando, to a survey of 37 male and 40 female Country listeners aged 25 to 44 in Dallas, and to a survey of 42 male and 49 female Country listeners aged 25 to 54 in Indianapolis. Separate reports were developed for each market.

---

[1]I am grateful for the many contributions made to this study by Charles A. Lubbers and William J. Adams, faculty colleagues in the A.Q. Miller School of Journalism and Mass Communications at Kansas State University—especially for their work in the post hoc analysis and for suggesting helpful revisions in the reporting of the results.

In addition, the study would have had far less validity and applicability if the professionals at Paragon Research of Denver had not been so helpful in adding our music tests to some of theirs. The reader must keep in mind that Paragon Research was not responsible for the design of the study, for analysis of the data, nor for the conclusions we have drawn from the data.

This research was supported in part by a 1991 research grant from the National Association of Broadcasters.

Meanwhile working with faculty colleagues at other universities and graduate students from Kansas State University, tests were conducted in six small markets: Columbia, Missouri; Douglas, Wyoming; Storm Lake, Iowa; Holyoke and Crested Butte, Colorado; and Broken Bow, Nebraska. Responses in the six small markets were pooled ($n = 124$). There was a 50–50 ratio of men to women in the small-markets in all age categories except for 18 to 24, in which there were twice as many men as women. Ages in the small market studies ranged from 18 to 55+.

In the large markets surveyed by Paragon Research, respondents were preselected as being devotees of the format being tested. They are identified later as "large market/preselected" respondents. The small-market listeners were not identified with any one station or music format. They were recruited with newspaper stories and classified ads about the testing, via radio advertising, and through personal contact, and thus were a self-selected sample. These respondents are identified later with the term "small-market/self-selected."

A second factor that increases the generalizability and utility of this research relates to the music that was chosen for testing. Much of it was selected to be similar to that currently being offered in the major formats under test. On the other hand, because the study was intended to explore whether music was enjoyed for its emotional impact rather than its popularity ranking, some of the titles and artists chosen for testing were not those usually aired by the format. That is, some obscure titles and little-known artists (thus nonpopular music) were chosen because they coincided with the general "feel" of the format, although they had received little or no airplay. For example, the Adult Contemporary format test tape included "Renegade Intellectuals" by Michael Manring, a Wincham Hill New Age artist; "Cryin' Shame" by Lyle Lovett, who is often categorized as a Country singer; "Real Emotional Girl" by Randy Newman, whose admirable music often eludes being pigeonholed; and "Animal" by Def Leppard, a record that was rarely played on most Adult Contemporary stations in the early 1990s. A complete list of the tested music is supplied in Appendix A.

A third factor that makes this research more generally useful is that a substantial portion of the testing was done under the guidance of experienced music testing professionals from Paragon Research, with audiences recruited by them through their normal procedures. They even developed a special optical mark reader coding card following the format of their usual form. The fact that music testing professionals carried out part of this research should make it easier for future researchers to compare these results with future replications.

Fourth, the standard music testing questions were retained. For each song, respondents were asked three questions: Part A asked "What emotion does this song make you feel?" (Possible answers were love, anger, sex, grief, hate, reverence, joy, yearning, and none/don't know.) Part B asked "Are you familiar with this song?" (Possible answers were yes and no.) Part C asked "How much do you dislike or like this song? (Possible answers were dislike a lot, dislike somewhat, neutral, like somewhat, and like a lot.) Part B on familiarity, and Part C on liking for the song are standard measures in the testing of popular music. It is Part A, "What emotion does this song make you feel?" that was the new variable being tested.

*Results.* The study tested 97 songs representing five formats in nine markets. As with typical music testing, each song must be treated as a separate variable with its own special set of attributes relating to the respondents' perceptions. To offer the reader a sense of the detail that can be gathered from the data, anecdotal highlights from the volatile Adult Contemporary format are offered in Appendix B at the end of this chapter. A song-by-song analysis revealed such things as the willingness of respondents to embrace music that "does not belong" in the given format if the song has other values that evoke an emotional response.

In addition to examining pairs of variables in a given format and market, it was possible to apply statistical analysis to general trends across all formats and markets tested. Table 12.1 shows how many songs in the five formats tested produced significant groupings (at the .05 level or less) on each of the cross-tabulations. The number of songs tested in each format is given in parentheses following the format name.

One of the goals of this study was to prove a procedure for testing unfamiliar music. The Adult Contemporary and Country format results are

TABLE 12.1
Number of Songs in the Five Formats
That Produced Significant Groupings on Five Cross-tabulations

| Cross-Tabulations | Country (19) S D I | Adult Contemp. (20) S O | Clsc Rock/ AOR (18) S | Oldies (18) S | CHR (18) S |
|---|---|---|---|---|---|
| Familiarity by Liking | 18 6 11 | 16 9 | 17 | 15 | 14 |
| Emotion by Liking | 17 14 9 | 17 17 | 18 | 16 | 18 |
| Gender by Liking | 4 0 2 | 0 [a] | 5 | 4 | 4 |
| Gender by Emotion | 0 0 0 | 0 [a] | 4 | 1 | 1 |
| Familiarity by Emotion | 0 0 2 | 2 2 | 2 | 3 | 0 |

S = Small market/self-selected sample (68 men, 55 women, aged 18–55+)
D = Dallas preselected Country listeners (37 men, 40 women, aged 25–54)
I = Indianapolis preselected Country listeners (42 men, 49 women, aged 25–54)
O = Orlando preselected Adult Contemporary listeners (98 women, aged 25–34)
[a] = all respondents were female

emphasized here, because much of the music representing those two formats was unfamiliar.

The cross-tabulation of familiarity by liking in Table 12.1 shows that across all formats and markets tested, there was a generally strong relationship between the respondents' familiarity with a song and their liking for it. This confirms the usual findings in standard music testing.

The familiarity by liking cross-tabulation results from Paragon's test of Country station listeners in Indianapolis are typical. All 19 songs were examined for the percentage of those respondents who either liked the song "somewhat" or "a lot." On average, of those who said they were familiar with the song, 73% said they liked it "somewhat" or "a lot." Of those who said they were not familiar with the song, 48% said they liked it "somewhat" or "a lot." Thus, familiarity did relate to higher liking scores, but even those who said they were not familiar with the song said they liked it "somewhat" or "a lot" just under half the time. This shows that respondents were still able to indicate level of liking after hearing only a (nominal) 20-second clip of *un*familiar music.

A cross-tabulation of the familiarity and liking scores of the Country listeners in Paragon's Indianapolis (large market/preselected) study did not produce a statistically significant result on 8 of the 19 songs. However, the same cross-tabulation for the small market/self-selected responses yielded only one case where there was not a significant result. Thus, it appears that in the case of the Indianapolis preselected Country listeners, there was, overall, a relatively weak connection between how well they knew the song and how much they liked it, whereas with small market/self-selected respondents, there was a signficant connection between how familiar the song was and how much it was liked. One reason for such a difference may be that the Indianapolis respondents were regular Country listeners and thus were more likely to indicate high liking for any Country song, whereas the pooling of the the small market/self-selected responses portrayed the aggregate as listening to all kinds of formats. Across all five of the music formats tested, the large market/preselected fans tended to give higher "liking" scores, whereas the small market/self-selected respondents had responses scattered throughout the "liking" range.

Table 12.1 shows that there was a strong relationship between the emotion the respondents chose and their liking for the song. For two formats in the small market/self-selected tests (Classic Rock/AOR and CHR), every song was significant at the .05 level or less in the cross-tabulation of emotion by liking. The same measurement found 16 out of 18 songs in the Oldies format, 17 out of 19 Country songs, and 17 out of 20 Adult Contemporary songs showing significant grouping in the small market/self-selected tests. The Orlando large market/preselected test of Adult Contemporary listeners found signicant groupings on 17 out of 20 songs, whereas the Dallas large market/preselected test of Country listeners revealed 14 out of 19 songs significantly grouped. Only the Indianapolis large market/preselected Country study showed less than a majority of the songs at the .05 level or less.

The results in Table 12.1 showing a lack of significant grouping on the cross-tabulation of gender by emotion is especially striking, and corresponds to Wells and Hakanen's (1991) findings cited earlier; that is, that there were not great gender differences in the emotions that college students associated with their favorite songs. Only the Classic Rock/AOR format, with 4 out of 18 songs at the .05 confidence level or less, seems to offer the possibility that emotional response may have been influenced by gender. All other formats had only one song or none at all.

Statistical analysis also showed that in no case in the three Country studies were respondents choosing emotional responses randomly.

The low number of groupings shown in the cross-tabulation for familiarity by emotion in Table 12.1 is an especially significant finding. The low grouping demonstrates that only rarely was the emotion chosen influenced by the respondent's familiarity with (or ignorance of) the music. Note that the Country and Adult Contemporary tests—which both consisted of mostly unfamiliar songs—had about the same lack of significant groupings as the Oldies test, where all the songs were at least somewhat familiar. Recall, too, that the longest clip played—even of an unfamiliar instrumental—was about 20 seconds.

Additional results were generated thanks to post hoc analyses conducted by faculty colleagues William J. Adams and Charles A. Lubbers. One analysis indicated that for the Adult Contemporary format, all the age groups expressed strong negative correlations between the degree of liking and no expression of emotional reaction. This result mirrored our finding in the pilot study, where we had tentatively concluded that the combination of low clustering and a high percentage of "no feeling" responses might be a useful filter to prevent airplay of "dangerous" songs.

Such a result also offered a partial explanation for the difference found in the overall results between the Country and Adult Contemporary tests. There were significantly more females than males in the Adult Contemporary sample, because the Orlando AC test was comprised entirely of women. In the Country sample, the numbers in each gender were about the same, but the female subjects had a strong negative correlation between emotional reaction and the degree of liking, whereas the males did not have a signicant coefficient for this relationship. It appears that the female subjects viewed an emotional reaction as more important in the assessment of music, but the strong results for the women may have been canceled by the weak scores for males. However, as there were very few males in the

Adult Contemporary sample, the strong scores for the females remained influential.

*Discussion.* Overall, the multimarket/multiformat study showed that small market/self-selected respondents and large market/preselected format fans were able to agree on the emotions they assigned to both familiar and unfamiliar music. The emotion chosen does not appear to have been based on the gender of the listener. However, the relationship between liking and emotion is linked to gender. Also, although respondents were able to react more strongly to songs they know, just under half were able to react to songs they were unfamiliar with. No difference was found in the emotions selected by those who knew the song and those who did not.

The results of the post hoc analysis indicated that age was an important factor in both the Adult Contemporary and Country formats. The younger and older respondents had more significant coefficients with the degree of liking, and appeared to be reacting more strongly than those in the 24 to 34 age group. The difference in the results for the Adult Contemporary and the Country formats appears to be related to gender, specifically the lack of males in the preselected Adult Contemporary sample.

The study demonstrated that the typical auditorium music test need not be confined to brief, easily identified "hooks" from familiar songs, but can successfully test unfamiliar songs for their emotional impact, if slightly longer segments are played. Moreover, nonhit songs can still be strongly liked and can produce clearly delineated emotional reactions. The new procedure succeeded about the same for any of the formats tested.

Among the new findings of this study were that auditorium music test respondents could usually make choices about their degree of liking for an unfamiliar song after hearing only a nominal 20-sec clip, and could usually choose one of the eight emotional reaction terms to describe how it made them feel.

The choice of an emotional "tag" for each song was not made randomly. Most songs tended to be identified by one or two major emotions, whereas others tended to have reactions scattered among the eight emotional reaction terms. Songs with scattered reactions or high "no reaction/don't know" scores tended to be liked less than songs with a few dominant emotions. This finding provides strong support for the original thesis that factors other than song popularity can be used to evaluate music, and that—based on this testing—emotional reaction can be one of those factors.

Some of the songs chosen for testing would not normally have received airplay in that format. Although some of the songs were unfamiliar, a combination of strong "liking" scores and the emergence of one or two dominant emotional reactions indicated that those songs would likely be well-accepted by the typical listener to that format.

The addition of "emotional reaction" to the standard music tests of "familiarity" and "liking" offers a new dimension for choosing and rotating the music within a given format. Emotional reactions evoked by the music that cause listeners to like the record—regardless of the song's position on a popularity chart—can be factored into airplay decision making. Adding a test of emotional reaction makes it more likely that artists who do not fit standard format labels and who thus "fall through the cracks" (such as some of those featured in the Adult Contemporary tests) may receive deserved airplay. Beyond that, the testing procedure proved in this study may be useful for formats (such as Progressive and Adult Alternative) that already select records from several musical genres, or to stations more interested in serving genuine public tastes than the marketing strategies of record companies.

*Questions for Further Study.* Several questions result from the strong relationship found between the emotion chosen by the respondent and their liking for the song: (a) Was strong dislike for a song likely to affect the emotion chosen in the same way as strong liking scores? (b) In a given music format, are certain emotional responses likely to be dominant? Although it would have been tempting to provide totals of the emotional reactions marked most often for each format, the fact that only a few persons were involved in choosing the music to be tested raises the possibility that the songs selected to represent any given format may have inadvertently favored one emotion or another. It will take replication of this study and an aggregation of other song titles before this question can be answered with certainty.

The study seemed to show that age was a factor in the relationship between the emotion categories and the degree of liking for a song. It is possible that the subjects were most affected by certain emotions at different stages of their life. Whatever the explanation, future investigations will have to take into account more fully the effects of subject age. Further testing will also need to control for gender variables, giving special consideration to how to deal with data when radio station clients specifically want to test the reactions of only one gender.

The question of whether certain emotions in music are more *desired* by devotees of one format (e.g., the Country format as compared to AOR) will also have to await the amassing of more data.

Auditorium music tests such as were undertaken in the Multimarket Multiformat Study are clearly the most desirable method of selecting records based on emotional reactions. But if auditorium testing is not feasible, there are other factors that can help the programmer to discern the time,

TABLE 12.2
Audience-Listener Characteristics

| Performer or Song Characteristics | |
|---|---|
| Time | (Song Rhythms) |
| | Expression Time |
| | Scale |
| Space | (Involvement Factors) |
| | Performer-to-Microphone Distance |
| | Recording Site Ambience |
| Force | (Performer/Song Acceptance Factors) |
| | Presentational Style (Timbre) |
| | Instrumentation (Number, Density) |
| | Lyrics |

space, and force factors in potential airplay music, including procedures that can often predict the Clynes terms that will likely be applied to a song.

The list of factors (see Table 12.2) to be considered in this chapter is an amalgamation of the time–space–force components of radio mood found at the end of the previous chapter. The separate categories of general audience characteristics and individual listener characteristics have been combined into a single list of audience/listener characteristics.

## TIME (SONG RHYTHMS)

We begin with *time* as the first area for mood-oriented music selection testing, and specifically with another way to use Clynes' terms.

For the radio music programmer considering embracing evoked emotions as a song selection factor, the salient point to recall about Clynes' research is that the specific expression times for the seven emotions he isolated are expressed in *seconds*. That means that if it is not feasible to conduct an auditorium music test using the Clynes terms as just outlined, the programmer can at least make an informed guess about the mood that any given song might evoke.

### Finding the Expression Time

Programmers familiar with counting BPM need to "shift gears" to classify music using only the Clynes expression times. First, the beats are not counted. Instead, the length of the interval from one "beat" to the next is timed. Note that the word *beat* in the previous sentence is in quotation marks. That is to alert you that the literal beat (the thump of the bass in the rhythm) does not necessarily equal the essentic pulse in Clynes' domain. Recall the portion on phrasing in chapter 11: The orchestra conductor leads a new slow theme with one hand while the other hand maintains the basic rhythm; or the singer holds onto a certain word and "wrings out" its meaning. In both cases, the expression time is likely to be longer than the short interval between thumps from the bass. In a slow ballad, a phrase of just two or three words might be a complete expression, whereas in a faster song, whole sentences can be a single expression.

In actually deriving expression times, it helps to keep the following question in mind: "Is the expression complete?" In my testing, respondents have been asked to simply say "Now" whenever they feel that the expression is finished (that a new one is beginning, or that the old one is being repeated). For music with a slow beat and a probable long expression time, the tester can start a stopwatch with the $n$th "Now" and stop it on the $n$th "Now" + 1. For music with a faster beat and a probable quick expression time, the tester starts a stopwatch on the $n$th "Now" and stops it 10 seconds later, noting how many times "Now" was said in the interval. Dividing the number of "Nows" into 10 seconds yields the expression time, expressed in seconds or portions of a second.

Some respondents seem to do better at feeling the length of a complete expression because they just have a better sense of musical phrasing—they let themselves get caught up in the flow. The worst are those who make literal counts without investing any of their own emotions. Averaging responses among several listeners is helpful.

## Relating Expression Times to Major, Minor, and Blues Scales

When the expression time is fairly different from the times Clynes found, or when there are other difficulties in classification, a simple correlation with major and minor scales is often helpful. To understand the correlation to be presented, we must briefly review rhythm as it relates to *melody*—a term otherwise avoided in this chapter because it is so vast and hard to concretize.

Pure rhythm—for instance, a drum solo—can exist apart from melody, but melody always goes hand-in-hand with rhythm. This is because once a first tone is succeeded by any other tone, the length of the first tone is made finite and comes to be perceived as some rhythmic unit. (See LaRue's discussion of continuation in chapter 11.) A succession of tones becomes a melody. Melody occurs absolutely on the basis of rhythm.

The first and main note on which a melody begins is known as the *tonic* of a key—the "main note" of the melody is (almost always) in one of 24 keys, such as E-flat or C-major. (Matching of keys is one venerable device for ordering the presentation of radio music, but order of presentation is

TABLE 12.3
Expression Times and Terms Related to Major, Minor and Blues Scales

| Reverence | Grief | Love | Sex | Hate | Joy | Anger |
|---|---|---|---|---|---|---|
| 9.8 | 9.0 | 5.2 | 2.0 | 1.6 | 1.1 | 0.7 |
| major | minor or blues | major or blues | major minor or blues | minor or blues | major or blues | minor |

the subject of the next chapter.) The terms *major* and *minor* are often interchanged with the word *key*, but a more accepted word in music is *scale*. Since the 17th century, the two major modes in western music have been the major and minor scales. About a hundred years ago, the blues added a third scale. Today, most U.S. popular music is in the major, minor, or the blues scale.

In 1935, Kate Hevner published a study that employed an adjective checklist to confirm the traditional attitudes that music in the minor scale was perceived as gloomy, depressing, or sad, whereas major mode pieces were judged to be happy, cheerful, joyous, and so on. (Hevner, 1953). Most music listeners in the western hemisphere associate the major, minor, and blues scales with certain kinds of emotions as strongly as they associate high-pitched music with joy and low-pitched music with grief; or high-pitched, fast-rate melodies with small, light objects like birds, and low-pitched, slow-rate melodies with large, heavy objects like elephants.

Clynes' seven essentic forms, in my view, each carry an association with the major, minor, or blues scale. In Table 12.3, they are listed left to right along with my interpretation of expression time, in seconds (longest expression time to the left, shortest to the right). Table 12.3 lists the usually expected musical scale.

Again, the reader must be cautioned that Clynes did not make these assertions about major and minor scales, or the way one expression time flows into another. They are my interpretations and assumptions. It is just handy to have the major/minor/blues scale correlation as an additional means of classification.

Once you have an average expression time in seconds (perhaps corroborating the apparent emotion using the major, minor, and blues scales), you should be able to label most songs with a mood they are likely to evoke.

### The Dangers of "Emotionless" Songs

In the preliminary research that led up to using the Clynes terms in auditorium music tests, a few songs were found that—when tested on an open-ended basis—did not evoke any emotion at all. That is, when the respondent was not presented with the Clynes list of seven terms, but was instead asked simply to tell what the song caused him or her to feel, the songs left respondents feeling no reportable emotion. Similarly, in the multi-market, multiformat auditorium testing, certain songs elicited relatively high *no reaction/don't know* scores. Obviously, these are "dangerous" songs to play on the air. Using the previously explained expression time classification, these songs *would* fit under one of the seven emotional categories, even though actual listeners are unmoved by them. Thus, it seems sensible to balance the counting of expression times with additional open-ended testing to be sure the theoretically possible mood is actually perceived by the listener.

## SPACE (INVOLVEMENT FACTORS)

The two involvement factors to be discussed here—performer-to-microphone distance and the ambience of the recording site—were described in chapter 11. The three-stage dynamic sound plane, with its categories of *immediate, support,* and *background,* is a central consideration (see Table 12.4).

### Testing for Spacial Factors in Vocals and Instrumentals

In testing for spacial factors in the voices and/or instrumentation, programmers auditioning music need simply to decide which aural elements are immediate, which are in support, and which are in the background. As pointed out earlier, some voices and instruments shift position during a song. If the shift seems crucial, probably that voice or instrument should be listed in both its old and new positions. Otherwise, it can just be listed under the position where the majority of its time is spent.

### Testing for Spacial Factors in the Recording Site's Ambience

Similarly, the music audition process needs to assess the recording site's apparent ambience, using a simple three-part scale: words like *dry* or *dead* are used for spaces with no or very low reverberation, whereas *live* or *reverberant* can be used for spaces with relatively long sound reflections. *Moderate* can be used for spaces in between the two extremes. (Actual *echo*—the discrete *repetition* of whole syllables—is not acoustic ambience; it is a special effect, and does not deserve to be counted as live or reverberant.)

TABLE 12.4
Three-Stage Dynamic Sound Plane

| (Listener) | Immediate | Support | Background | (Site ambience) |
|---|---|---|---|---|

TABLE 12.5
Intensity Checklists for Timbre, Number, and Density
of Voices or Instruments

|  | Descriptor | Intensity |
|---|---|---|
|  |  | Gentle  Moderate  Powerful |
| Timbre of voices or instruments | Harsh/Gritty |  |
|  | Moderate/Medium |  |
|  | Soft/Smooth |  |
| Number of voices or instruments | Many |  |
|  | Moderate/Medium |  |
|  | Few |  |
| Density of voices or instruments | Dense |  |
|  | Moderate/Medium |  |
|  | Sparse |  |

## FORCE (ACCEPTANCE FACTORS)

The factors to be tested under the *force* heading are presentational style (timbre), instrumentation, and lyrics, all of which were discussed in chapter 11. There, in considering presentational style and instrumentation, the timbre, number, and density of voices or instruments were explored.

### Intensity Matrices for Timbre, Number, and Density of Voices or Instruments

Three simple "intensity" checklists can be completed by programmers auditioning music for radio airplay. These checklists track vocal and instrumental force factors. They are *timbre intensity, number intensity,* and *density intensity.* A check mark in the appropriate columns is all that is required (see Table 12.5). In each case shown in Table 12.5, the record listener decides which of the three left-hand attributes best describes the sound he or she is hearing (say, "Harsh/Gritty" for timbre), and then selects a gentle, moderate, or powerful intensity level to describe that attribute's presentational force (for example, *powerful* for a metal-type rock song).

## LYRICS

Chapter 11 also introduced research about the emotions evoked by song lyrics, and showed similarities between Clynes' expression times and frequency modulations, and Joel Davitz's findings about rate and inflection of speech. It was clear from that comparison that instrumental expression and vocal expression had a similar list of emotions, similar rates or expression times, and similar inflections.

Here, we need to consider the lyrics themselves. We do so using a matrix that treats narrative action and reality/fantasy imagery along one axis, with levels of meanings along the other. What Kenneth Burke (1967, pp. 5–6, 36–37) referred to as *jingle* (the pleasure from just the sound of the words) is here labeled as *sound,* and it is a separate single-row check-off.

The empty matrix of Table 12.6 invites the reader to place single lines of lyrics on its grid. For instance, the opening line from the old Steve Winwood hit "While You See a Chance" is "Stand up in a clear blue morning." It would be listed on the vertical axis (narrative action) at the "personal" level. Because it works on the horizontal axis of reality/fantasy imagery in every category, it would be listed once under "actual," once under "wishes," and again under "dreams." Such multiple appearances are not errors or flaws. The inability to be confined to a single cell indicates a lyric that has the advantage of working on several verbal levels.

Such a lyric, in turn, should translate into appeal across several different demographics. It also means that the song has at least a greater *lyrical* complexity than some. As shown in earlier discussions on complexity, that could help prevent early burnout for this song.

There is no intention of minimizing the importance of the sound of words by moving *jingle* to its own area and renaming it *sound.* The fun

TABLE 12.6
Narrative Action and Reality/Fantasy Imagery

|  | *Actual* | *Wishes* | *Dreams* |
|---|---|---|---|
| Abstraction |  |  |  |
| Dictionary |  |  |  |
| Personal |  |  |  |
| Sound |  |  |  |

TABLE 12.7
Lyrics Descriptive of Arousal/Fantasy/Satiation

| Arousal | Fantasy | Satiation |
|---|---|---|
| stimulate | unusual | relaxation |
| excite | uncommon | satisfaction |
| inflame | unfamiliar | full |
| energize | incredible | plenty |
| animate | rare | redundance |
| invigorate | imaginary | saturation |
| active | visionary | abundance |
| potent | utopian | lavish |
|  | ideal | affluent |
|  | legendary | profusion |
|  | fabulous |  |
|  | illusory |  |
|  | extravagant |  |
|  | dreamlike |  |

of saying and hearing certain sounds plays an important part in the appeal of such songs as the Crystals' oldie "Da Doo Ron Ron."

Clearly, "Da Doo Ron Ron" does not have the lyrical complexity and breadth of narrative action and symbolic meaning that "While You See a Chance" does. Fully half (15) of the (30) lines analyzed would fall into the actual (realistic)/dictionary (ordinary definitions) category. Strong narrative action, symbolism, and richness of meaning are at a minimum. Only four lines move away from the literal language: two that use the metaphorical "my heart stood still" as a better way of saying "I was impressed" and two that dream of "making him mine." But the song succeeds anyway, on the strength of the 11 repetitions of "Da Doo Ron Ron Ron, Da Doo Ron Ron." It is such fun to say and sing that however pedestrian the other lyrics are, it does not matter.

The point is, that not every song's lyrics need to rise to a level of epic action, symbolism, and imagery, nor to the wit of an Ira Gershwin. Phrases that are just fun to say will always be an important part of pop lyrics.

Strongly visual lyrics may be one way for radio to compete against music videos. Lyrics that evoke strong mental images allow music stations to move a little closer to being "theater of the mind."

One other way to look at lyrics is in terms of the way they describe arousal, fantasy, and satiation (refer back to Milkman and Sunderwirth in chapter 4). If these are indeed the main psychological states most people crave to be in, then we should expect to find lyrics that help the listener "hook into" one, two, or all three of them. Table 12.7 lists the three terms, each followed by a list of synonyms from a thesaurus.

A person auditioning music for radio airplay would not necessarily expect to hear any of the listed words verbatim; instead, he or she would probably hear a word or phrase whose emotional content suggests one of the three terms or their synonyms. Whichever of the three terms winds up with the most phrases connected to it would then be the one tagged to the song: arousal-oriented, fantasy-oriented, or satiation-oriented. These are important in identifying potential target listeners, and they are also influential later in determining the ordering of the songs for airplay.

## SPECIAL CONSIDERATIONS

The same tests that have been recommended so far in this chapter should also be applied to the special cases listed here, but with the following additional guidelines also considered.

### Recurrents

As alluded to in earlier chapters, there is very little agreement about what constitutes a "recurrent" song. The bewildering variety of approaches to airing recurrents in part reflects the differences in audience targeting among various formats, competitive strategies in different markets, and divergent methods of tracking music popularity. But in my view, the *age* of a record is largely irrelevant to airplay decisions. As was stated earlier, measures of familiarity and continued popularity are not as important as *reliability*—that the song still generates nearly the same emotional reaction in the listener as it originally did. Given this way of thinking, powers, currents, recurrents, and oldies can theoretically all have equal weight—and can share rotation with new music and album cuts.

A heavily played song that has very recently dropped off the charts could be burned out to the point of being "toast." It has lost its emotional reliability. It is especially important to avoid exposing such a recurrent to the high-risk groups in the station's audience. For a hit-music station, that group is the heavy listener (typically younger), for whom the original hit would have become very familiar, or might even have burned out. Playing the song in a recurrent rotation as it begins to slide off of the current hit charts is a big risk with the heavy listening groups. It is less of a risk with older, occasional listeners, who would not have heard it so often originally.

As pointed out in chapter 9, performers go through popularity cycles that are very much like product cycles. Again, especially with a younger audience, unsure of its values, there can be a great fickleness about who is cool and who is not, quite apart from the continuing value of the music. It might not be a singer's music that is death as a recurrent; it might be the singer. Sometimes the best music testing will try to discover attitudes about the performers.

## Oldies and Memory

One reason why there is great latitude in the age range of what constitutes a recurrent song at various stations is because there is also not much agreement on when a former hit becomes an oldie. But the field of psychology has a possible answer. Jonathan Winson (1985), in a chapter on "Memory, Perception and Emotion" in his book *Brain and Psyche,* detailed cases of psychosurgery in which memory capabilities were altered. Winson summarized as follows:

> Apparently a slow neural process occurs in the human brain over a period of approximately three years, by which recent events become stabilized as long-term memories. The hippocampus appears to be central to the process, for unless the structure is present and functioning during the three-year period, memories cannot be recalled at a later time. . . . However, once three years have passed, memories are stored in a form that no longer requires the hippocampus for recall. (pp. 15–16)

What this summary of recent memory research appears to say is that in the human brain, *long*-term memory begins at roughly 3 years. Short-term memory, then, covers anything that happened 1 second ago up to 3 years ago. It makes sense, therefore, to define *oldies,* or *gold,* as being at least 3 years old, for most audiences.

For teenagers, especially because they have been alive such a relatively short while, 3 years seems like a very long time. If teens are the station's target, the gold library should probably begin more recently than that.

## Predicting Burnout

Songs with simple choruses, or several back-to-back repetitions of a typical chorus can be trouble. Some listeners can hear a record just once, and because the chorus is either very simple or is repeated often, they can sing the chorus verbatim by the time the record is over. The chorus, then, is going to burn out first, long before the verses do. That fact should cause the music programmer to either lower that song's level of exposure, or have it spend less time in a heavy rotation.

It is possible to try to predict burnout based on a number of the song attributes studied in this chapter. The scoring scheme was suggested in an article in *Road & Track* magazine titled "Beauty Is the Button Just to the Right of Square Root" (Simanaitis, 1986). We can then look at each characteristic according to the amount of effort that it takes us to understand or appreciate it. Score a 1 for the easiest/least effort; score a 10 for the hardest to understand/most effort.

First, look at the rhythm. If the rhythm is extremely regular, and is maintained throughout (as in a Disco or Rap tune), we might give it just a 1. If the rhythm is 5/4 time as in Dave Brubeck's classic "Take Five," it deserves a 10.

Then consider the melody, both in the chorus and the verses. The 1988 hit by Toto, "Pamela," is an example of a song deserving high marks in both areas for its melodic novelty. Does the song modulate into another key?

Go on to analyze the lyrics of the chorus and the verses for the amount of effort needed to understand them. Compare "While You See a Chance" (high marks) and "Da Doo Ron Ron" (low marks). How many different verses are there?

Finally, consider the complexity of the overall presentation, as we did in chapter 11 with the Righteous Brothers' "You've Lost That Lovin' Feelin'," which would get a high score. How many recognizably different instruments and voices are there?

Add all the scores together and you get a complexity score. Divide the score by the number of times the song will be exposed to its target audience and you get the song's burnout index for that audience on your station. The higher the score, the longer the song should take to burn out.

## MOST—An Afterword

What has been proposed in this chapter is far more music testing than most stations care to do, or would be able to do with limited staff. But these tests for song selection are offered because they are important to consider in making airplay decisions—often at least as important as a song's popularity. Rothenbuhler and McCourt (1992) said that standard auditorium and callout music testing are designed so that they "elicit passive, rather than active participation from audiences.... In the process, the audience is expected to respond to, not determine, what is played" (p. 112). Given their complexity, at least the procedures that have been outlined in this chapter are more listener-centered. It may not seem practical to worry about all the foregoing nuances of music selection. But the more competitive the radio market, the more music selection and presentation comes down to getting the details right.

Clearly, the use of respondents' emotional reactions to music based on Clynes' terms can be an important tool in selecting music for airplay. But understanding what mood is evoked in a listener is only the first step along the path to deciding whether to play that record. The list of other factors (see Table 12.2) included in this chapter on MOST is based on a condensed version of the "Time/Space/Force Components of Radio Mood" found at the end of the previous chapter. That summary's separate categories of "General Audience Characteristics" and "Individual Listener Characteristics" have been melded into a single list of "Audience/Listener Characteristics." This amalgamation reflects the fact that a programmer can never have very much data about individual listeners as compared to information on the general audience. The Audience/Listener Characteristics are used in chapter 13.

## APPENDIX A:
## COMPLETE LIST OF SONGS TESTED
## IN ALL FIVE FORMATS

*Adult Contemporary*
1. Let Her Dance—Marshall Crenshaw
2. Stranger in a Car—Marc Cohn
3. Taken by Surprise—The Outfield
4. Fires of Eden—Judy Collins
5. Love Is Our Cross to Bear—John Gorka
6. Every Time You Walk in the Room—Paul Carrack
7. Renegade Intellectuals—Michael Manring
8. Cryin' Shame—Lyle Lovett
9. Real Emotional Girl—Randy Newman
10. Animal—Def Leppard
11. Telling Me Lies—Linda Ronstadt
12. The Night Ain't Over—The Outfield
13. Drifting—Harry Connick, Jr.
14. My Head's in Mississippi—ZZ Top
15. Stand and Deliver—Mr. Mister
16. Sung to Sleep—Michael Manring
17. And the Night Stood Still—Dion
18. It Feels Like Rain—John Hiatt
19. 29 Ways—Marc Cohn
20. Home Before Dark—Judy Collins
21. Forever for Now—Harry Connick, Jr.
22. The Blues—Randy Newman
23. Mercury Blues—David Lindley
24. Downtown Tonight—John Gorka

*Country*
1. You Can't Take It With You—Gene Watson
2. Who Can She Turn To—Daniele Alexander
3. Every Now and Then—Marty Brown
4. Rockin' the Boat of Love—Normaltown Flyers
5. Remember Me—The Statler Brothers

6. My Ex-Life—Mel McDaniel
  7. Do Me a Favor—Jo-El Sonnier
  8. You Don't Miss a Thing—Eddy Arnold
  9. The Twang Factor—Charlie McDaniels
 10. He Comes Around—Molly and the Heymakers
 11. Navajo Rug—Jerry Jeff Walker
 12. Learning the Game—Black Tie
 13. Hillbilly Blue—Neal McCoy
 14. Straight and Narrow—Wild Rose
 15. What Goes With Blue—Neal McCoy
 16. All You Really Want to Do—Michelle Wright
 17. Paradise Knife and Gun Club—Jerry Lansdowne
 18. I've Got That Old Feeling—Alison Krause
 19. Baby Take a Piece of My Heart—Kelly Willis

*Classic Rock/A.O.R.*
  1. The Spirit of Radio—Rush
  2. Hocus Pocus—Focus
  3. Traveling Riverside Blues—Hindu Love Gods
  4. Hot Dog—Led Zeppelin
  5. Speed of Life—David Bowie
  6. Dancing with Tears in My Eyes—Ultravox
  7. Bouree—Jethro Tull
  8. Watching the Detectives—Elvis Costello
  9. Travelling East—Eric Clapton
 10. Higher Ground—Stevie Wonder
 11. Volcano—Jimmy Buffet
 12. Night Time—Chickasaw Mud Puppies
 13. Hot Burrito # 2—Flying Burrito Brothers
 14. The South's Gonna Do It Again—Charlie Daniels
 15. Dolly Dagger—Jimi Hendrix
 16. Subdivisions—Rush
 17. A Girl Like You—Smithereens
 18. The House Is Rockin'—Stevie Ray Vaughan

*C.H.R./Top 40*
  1. Yo, Sweetness—M. C. Hammer
  2. It's a Monster—Extreme
  3. Something to Save—George Michael
  4. Razor Blades of Love—The Silencers
  5. Daddy Pop—Prince
  6. I Can Hardly Wait—Nelson
  7. Judgement Day—Van Halen

8. Let It Play—Poison
9. Let Me Know—Bell Biv Devoe
10. It's Just Desire—Nelson
11. Young Lust—Aerosmith
12. Ice Cold—Vanilla Ice
13. Ball and Chain—Poison
14. To Da Break of Dawn—L L Cool J
15. Homebound Train—Bon Jovi
16. The Knowledge—Janet Jackson
17. Monkey on My Back—Aerosmith
18. Cowboys and Angels—George Michael

*Oldies*
1. Touch and Go—The Cars
2. The Way I Feel Tonight—Bay City Ramblers
3. Handbags and Gladrags—Rod Stewart
4. Slow Motion—Johnny Williams
5. All the Young Dudes—Mott the Hoople
6. Peace Will Come—Melanie
7. Movin' On Down the Line—Jerry Lee Lewis
8. She Did It—Eric Carmen
9. The Warmth of the Sun—The Beach Boys
10. Mighty Clouds of Joy—B. J. Thomas
11. Please Mrs. Henry—Manfred Mann
12. She Didn't Do Magic—Lobo
13. California On My Mind—Morning Mist
14. I Need Your Loving—Gardner and Ford
15. Dream Lady—Bread
16. Savannah Nights—Tom Johnston
17. You Make It So Hard—Boz Scaggs
18. No—Bulldog

## APPENDIX B: ANECDOTAL HIGHLIGHTS—ADULT CONTEMPORARY FORMAT

The Adult Contemporary study yielded especially interesting results among the mostly unfamiliar records tested in this format. The song "Renegade Intellectuals" by Michael Manring had the lowest familiarity score of any song in the small market/self-selected Adult Contemporary test—only 7 out of 124 respondents said they were familiar with it. When asked for emotional reaction, that unfamiliarity boosted the "no response/don't know" answer to 29%. Yet the "joy" response was marked by 48% of the small market/self-selected sample, even though this instrumental did not provide any lyrics to cue an obvious emotional choice. No other emotion totaled as high as 7%.

"Strangers in a Car" from Marc Cohn's first album showed a split on the basis of emotional reaction and liking. Those who felt yearning were more likely to like the song "somewhat," whereas those who felt grief were more likely to choose "neutral" for their liking score.

Def Leppard's "Animal" was the most familiar song in the small market/self-selected Adult Contemporary test. (Recall that respondents in the small-market sample skewed toward younger participants, which may explain why the song was so well-known in the "wrong" format. On the other hand, as Philadelphia PD Chuck Knight pointed out, "ACs weren't supposed to play Bruce Springsteen's 'Born to Run.' It was out of the norm, but it became successful;" Kinosian, 1995b, p. 45). Although "sex" might seem the obvious emotional reaction, "joy" was most chosen, because of how the song made the listeners feel.

"The Night Ain't Over" by The Outfield was a possible "problem" song. *No response/don't know* was most often selected from among the emotional responses. But ZZ Top's "My Head's in Mississippi" could be even more dangerous among Adult Contemporary listeners: The most-reported emotion was anger, and the majority of respondents disliked the song or were neutral at best.

Michael Manring's solo piano rendition of his composition "Sung to Sleep" was a completely atypical Adult Contemporary winner. The emotions chosen solidly were love, reverence, and yearning, and the song was well-liked—possibly because of the interplay or layering of the three emotions.

"It Feels Like Rain" by folk/blues artist John Hiatt was liked "somewhat" or "a lot" by 61% of the sample, even though grief and yearning were the most chosen emotions. Randy Newman's "The Blues" did not fool many respondents. Although the lyrics repeated the title, listeners marked joy, not grief; and about twice as many liked as disliked it.

The ability of respondents to react on the basis of emotions rather than obvious cues was perhaps most clearly demonstrated in the case of the song "Cryin' Shame" by Lyle Lovett. Here too, the title was delivered as part of the lyric on the test tape, so those looking for obvious cues might have been expected to mark grief as their choice. But only 5 out of 123 respondents in the small market/self-selected study did so—fewer than 4%. Only 2 of the women aged 25 to 34 in the Orlando large market/preselected Adult Contemporary study chose grief. In both cases, the majority choices were split between the emotions sex (small market/self-selected

# CHAPTER 13

## *Factors in MEMO— Mood-Evoking Music Order*

> What, in fact, is "rationality" but the desire for an accurate chart for naming what is going on?
>
> —*Kenneth Burke (1967, pp. 113–114)*

This chapter offers several charts for naming what could be going on in a music presentation system. What could be going on is the evocation of moods, and that is why the thrust of this chapter is the demonstration of mood-evoking music order (MEMO) systems. The systems are built around the characteristics of general audiences and individual listeners that have already been explored (see Tables 11.4, 11.5, and 11.6).

In regard to time (communal and personal rhythm) factors, these are the questions a programmer might ask when putting together the music order for her or his station: (a) What seasonal and cultural rhythms (such as holidays, celebrations, and so on, should be factored in, (b) What circadian body rhythms are my audience reacting to, and (c), What needs caused by the predominating lifestyles in my community need to be considered?

Relative to space (involvement) factors, the programmer might consider (a) the structure and appeals of a music order presentation system, and (b) how they will impact on the listening place and listening situation.

The force (acceptance) factors to be considered revolve around the arousal/fantasy/satiation drives that propel audience behavior.

Having made all these considerations, what we want to do next is to structure a music presentation system that takes them into account. Figure 13.1 shows Aristotelian dramatic structure, first introduced in chapter 4.

Note the curve illustrating the rising and falling action of exposition, development, climax, and resolution. Figure 13.2 illustrates, once more, the

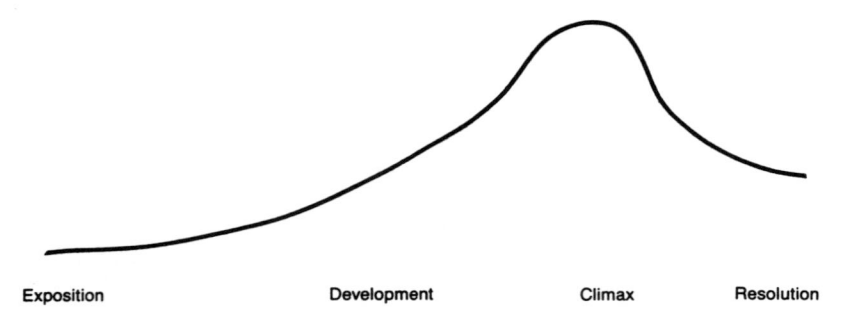

FIG. 13.1. Aristotelian structure expressed as a curve.

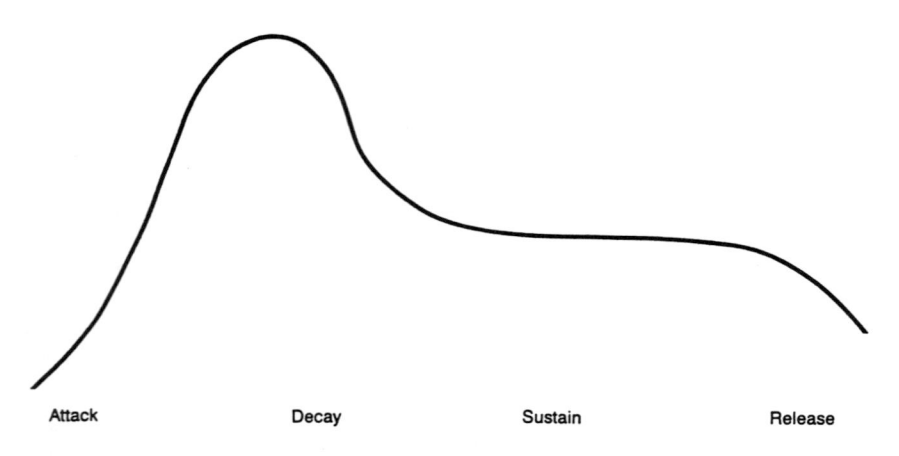

FIG. 13.2. ADSR sound envelope.

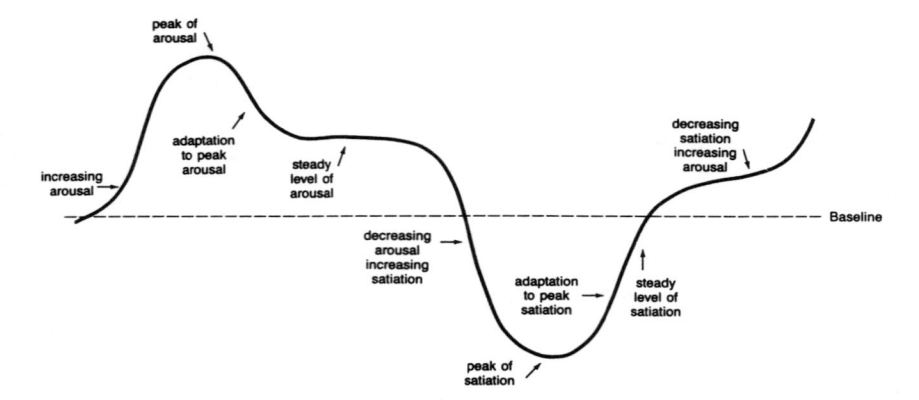

FIG. 13.3. Opponent-process arousal/satiation behavior curve (After Solomon, in Milkman and Sunderwirth) with elaboration by the present author.

ADSR sound envelope of attack–decay–sustain–release. Note how the attack has a rapid rise time and a brief decay, then a long sustain until the release.

Figure 13.3 again takes a look at the opponent-process arousal/satiation behavior curve offered by Milkman and Sunderwirth, this time with added interpretations. Notice how the curve starts to repeat itself on the far right-hand edge, which corresponds to its beginning at the far left. You have already discovered that the curve looks a lot like Aristotelian dramatic structure and ADSR.

Next (in Fig. 13.4), we take the arousal/satiation behavior modes and express them as a continuum, alongside of which we place Clynes' emotion categories and their expression times.

The continuum can also be extended, in effect starting at the end, repeating the behavior term *satiation*. Then the Clynes terms are interpolated to follow the rise and fall of arousal and satiation (see Fig. 13.5).

---

BEHAVIOR:

AROUSAL                                                    SATIATION

EMOTION:

| Anger | Joy | Hate | Sex | Love | Grief | Reverence |

EXPRESSION TIME:

| 0.7 sec | 1.1 sec | 1.6 sec | 2.0 sec. | 5.2 sec. | 9.0 sec. | 9.8 sec |

---

FIG. 13.4. Arousal/satiation behavior modes expressed as a continuum, with Clynes' expression times.

---

BEHAVIOR:

Satiation                         Arousal                         Satiation

EMOTION:

| Rev. | Grief | Love | Sex | Hate | Joy | Anger | Joy | Hate | Sex | Love | Grief | Rev. |

EXPRESSION TIME:

| 9.8 | 9.0 | 5.2 | 2.0 | 1.6 | 1.1 | 0.7 | 1.1 | 1.6 | 2.0 | 5.2 | 9.0 | 9.8 |

---

FIG. 13.5. Arousal/satiation behavior modes expressed as an extended continuum, with Clynes' expression times.

## COMPOSITE MOOD CURVE

Finally, all the previous graphs and curves can be combined into a Composite Mood Curve (CMC; see Fig. 13.6) to show how Aristotelian dramatic structure, the ADSR sound envelope, the arousal-satiation behavior curve, and Clynes' expression times and categories can all coincide. Figure 13.6 is *not* a formula for a "hot clock." It is merely a way of showing the commonality among previous curves. For it to work as a music order presentation system, various refinements and caveats (given later) need to be observed.

What the CMC shows are nine cells, the ninth repeating the first as the curve starts over.

### ADSR Sound Envelope

The ADSR sound envelope terms are the first text line under the cell number. In sound, an attack is virtually instantaneous, and the decay begins immediately, but this does not leave any time at the peak (how like life!), so the ADSR terms break at the peaks. Also note that the time of release coincides with a new attack.

### Arousal/Satiation Behavior Modes

The second text line gives an interpretation of the behavior modes corresponding to arousal and satiation. Notice that I have decreed that decreasing arousal and increasing satiation happen simultaneously in Cell 5, just as do their opposites (decreasing satiation and increasing arousal) in Cell 9. Notice, too, that all of the curve in Cells 5, 6, 7, and 8 are very close to being a reversed, upside-down version of the arousal curve, as if satiation were almost the flip side of arousal.

### Aristotelian Dramatic Structure

The third text line lists the familiar Aristotelian dramatic structure terms. In case it seems odd that "development" in Cell 5 should describe a *downward*-pointing curve, remember that depths of emotion can be developed just as well as heights.

### Pitch-Related Feelings

At the left of the chart, the words *pitch-related feelings* appear, heading a column of words labeling those feelings. You may want to reread the research by Hevner, reported in chapter 10, that found people tending to describe high-pitched music as playful and happy, and low-pitched music

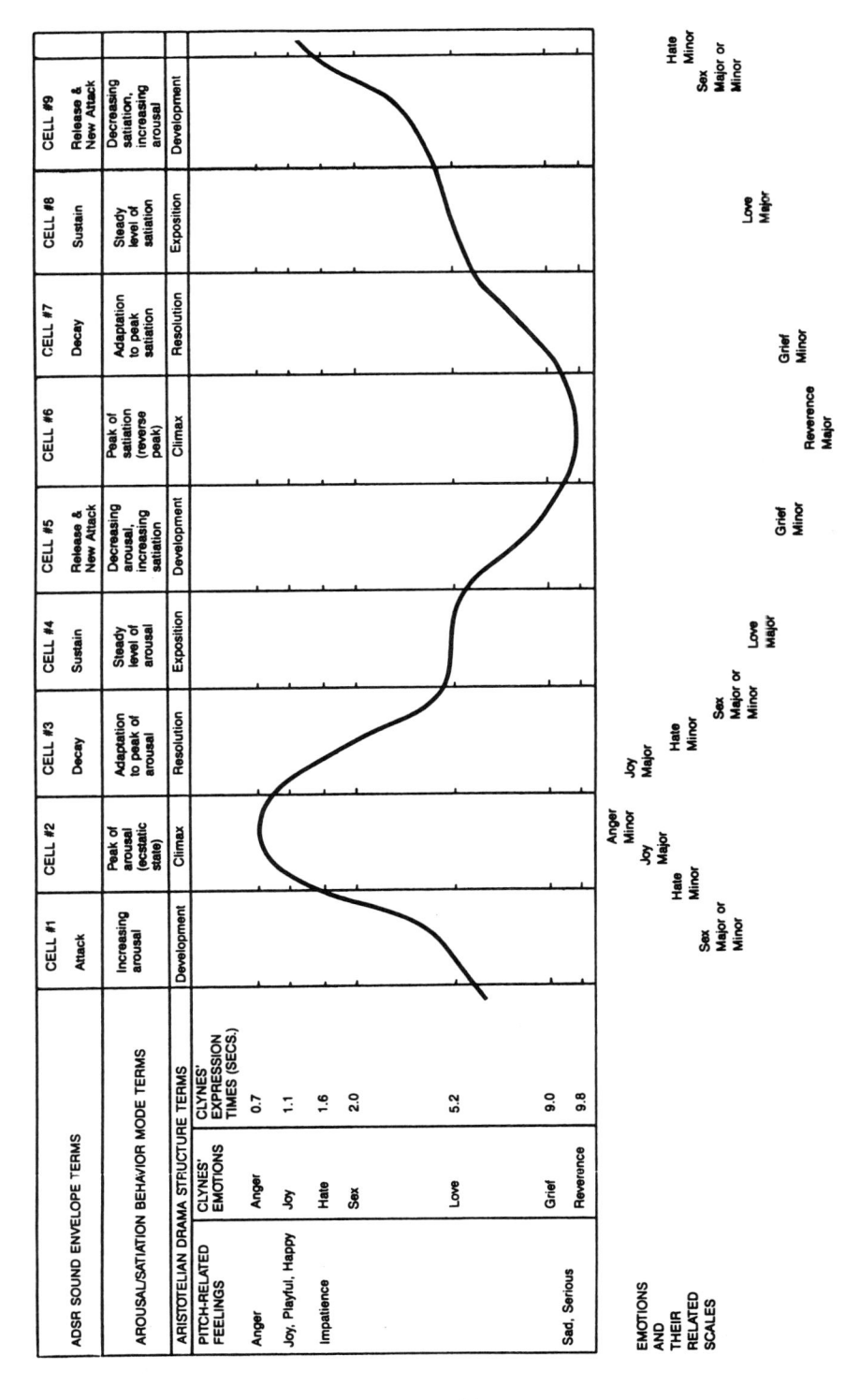

FIG. 13.6. Composite mood curve.

as serious and sad (although tempo was the single most important factor in determing the mood). Also cited there was the research by Thayer et al. that found that reactions to music on a "pleasantness" continuum (which ranged from happiness at one extreme to sadness at the other) were most affected by the pitch, whereas "activation" was most affected by tempo. In regard to lyrics, chapter 10 reported research that found that the pitch of expressions of happiness was higher than the pitch of either neutral or sad expressions. And the work of Joel Davitz in relating pitch to vocal expression found the feelings of anger and joy related to a high pitch and the feeling of affection linked to a low pitch. As a consequence of all these findings about pitch, the pitch-related feelings terms have been placed in either a high or low position, reflecting their relationship to a high or low pitch. Recall that pitch applies both to instrumental music and to music with lyrics.

## Clynes' Emotions and Their Expression Times

The second and third columns in from the left side of the CMC list Clynes' emotions and their expression times in seconds. The longest (slowest) times (corresponding to reverence) are at the bottom; the shortest (fastest) times (corresponding to anger) are at the top. The approximate expression time of each emotion is marked by a dash across columns. For clarity, the emotions are listed again, in order from left to right, at the bottom of the chart, along with the scale (major or minor) that has been related to them.

The Clynes categories and expression times are the single element displayed from the time/space/force triumvirate because expression times (tempo, rhythms, etc.) have been shown to be the single most influential factor in determining the emotion evoked by music. Space factors (such as mike-to-performer distance and the ambience of the recording site), and force factors (such as the timbre of voices or instruments, and the number and density of the voices or instruments), are more important in determining *continuation*—that is, what song should be played next—than in evoking a mood. We take up the question of continuation shortly.

## Emotions and Their Related Scales

Twelve emotions are listed across the bottom of the chart (14 if you count the repeats in Cell 9). Just as the curve is a theoretical model, so is that list of song moods. For instance, suppose the station made the simple rule that only songs in the major scale would be played. Immediately, songs with expression times corresponding to hate, anger, grief, and some sex would drop off the air. The resulting curve would not reach quite so high as when anger was the mood projected for the peak, although it would still drop as deeply into reverence. But the big change would be in the length of time spent at any one expression time level. In fact, with most changes in the curve, that is the major consequence—not so much a change in height or depth, but a difference in how long any one emotion is sustained.

## Using the CMC to Target Specific Demographics

Of course, most stations target a particular segment of the audience. Doing so virtually forces a change in the time spent in various parts of the curve. For example, in the fantasies survey cited in chapter 4 ("Fantasies and Daydreams"), men were shown to be more arousal-oriented, especially in terms of participation in physical activities, whereas women were found to be more interested in the satisfaction (satiation) of social acceptance. Keep that in mind while considering the ancient wisdom that (especially younger) men like faster, harder music, whereas women like slower, softer music. If we now link a quicker desired expression time to male arousal needs, and a slower desired expression time to female satiation needs, then it appears that controlling the amount of the sound hour spent at a given expression time level would operate not only to evoke the mood, but would also differentiate by sex. Thus, a station that lengthens the time spent in the arousal part of the CMC by playing more quick expression time songs will tend to get more men; a station that lengthens the time spent in the satiation part of the curve by playing more slow expression time songs will tend to get more women.

Now, suppose the target audience is young men, who we will define as mid- to late teens and early 20s. Maybe the reason some young men like to listen to hour upon hour of high BPM music is not just about expressing "anger" in the mood sense. Maybe it is a way of saying (by association with the music) that they have the youthful potency to sustain and extend the moments of climax.

Next, imagine that the target is men in their late 20s and early 30s. In this age range, when men become less anger-oriented, and as the hormone-driven need to prove virility slacks a little, we would expect to find the time men desire to remain at "orgasmic" beat intensity also declining. For these men, the time spent at the peak BPM should be shorter (the peaks more pointed). Women in their 30s are no less interested in sex than before, but a more mature understanding of love is probable. For both sexes, desired expression times simply lengthen out (slow down) with increasing age.

In general, playing more music having short expression times would lengthen the amount of the curve spent in the region of joy and anger. This would increase the appeal of the music for those listeners seeking enhancement of an aroused state. Similarly, playing more music having long expression times would lengthen the amount of time the curve remained in the region of grief and reverence. This would increase the appeal of the music for those listeners seeking enhancement of a satiated state.

Playing more music at one extreme high or low part of the curve is a way of serving the music mood stability seeker whom we met earlier. On the other hand, moving along the curve fairly rapidly is a way of pleasing the music mood novelty seeker. These assertions are consonant with the findings of Washburn and Dickinson more than a half-century ago, that music that was either much more exciting than usual or much more relaxing and soothing than usual was appreciated more than music that straddled the middle ground. Straddling the middle of the curve (in a vertical sense) would lead to listener indifference.

## Using the CMC to Optimize Daypart Impact

The material in chapter 4 about circadian rhythms can be applied to make changes in the curve that would have the effect of fitting the music more closely to some average listener's lifestyle. This can be accomplished by dropping some mood categories entirely, or by presenting desired mood categories for longer periods. When some categories are left out, there will be a more abrupt jump from one mood to another, if no other elements are introduced as buffers. This is okay, because the CMC is not intended to imitate a dance mix—it is *not* supposed to be all at one BPM level. The more nonmusical (talk) elements in an hour, the less nuance there should be in dramatic structure. For example, between 7 A.M. and 8 A.M., when there is usually heavy information/talk, each of the four parts of dramatic structure should probably be represented only once before the cycle repeats. In slack times (as at night), the cycles can be much longer and can emphasize any of the structural elements.

A day might go like this: Mornings are a "fresh start." It tends to be the most optimistic time of day for many people—"Today, anything is possible." Morning programming could enhance that emotion by emphasizing the positive emotions: joy, sex, love, and reverence. But because morning radio listeners have always seemed to gravitate to stations that play music that acts like a percolator or battery jumper cables, the music should get you going. In the morning daypart, then, faster tempi should predominate. Thus, more time would be spent with joy and sex, less with love and reverence.

In mid- and late morning, and early afternoon dayparts, the programmer might add grief, and slow and soften the overall sound by reducing the ratio of joy songs. The net effect will be an increase in the sex, love, grief, and reverence moods.

In mid afternoon, the programmer might add to the joy category, and in afternoon drive, he or she might increase (or begin to play) the hate category.

In early evening, more joy songs might be added. By midevening, when teens predominate as listeners, the programmer might delete reverence and add songs in the anger category. In late evenings, still more anger songs might be played.

## CONTINUATION

What song should be played next? That is the question that a continuation scheme seeks to answer. We have already explored the pros and cons of continuing the present mood versus moving on to the next area of the curve. Clearly, how much of any one mood to offer at a given time is heavily dependent on the target audience.

But what about the other methods of "growth," the other ways of moving forward? If mood is related most of all to expression time, what about space and force factors? And what about that slipperiest of all musical factors, melody?

Recall from chapter 11 LaRue's four basic options for continuation. They were summarized this way:

*Recurrence*  An immediate repetition, or one that happens after an intervening change.
*Development*  A continuation closely related by melody. (Development is not usually done in radio because music rotation systems do not track melodies per se. "Key" is the closest radio music programmers get.)
*Response*  A continuation unrelated melodically. (Rhythmic response continuation is common in radio music formats, but probably needs still more emphasis.)
*Contrast*  A complete change, usually following (and confirming) a heavy articulation by cadences and rests. (In the case of a radio sound hour, the cadences and rests could be something as obvious as a song that takes off in a completely different direction or a commercial set, or as subtle as an ID jingle that begins with one key or rhythm and ends with another.)

### Recurrence

First, do not confuse the continuation term *recurrence* with the music-library term *recurrents*. Recurrence would not mean a literal repetition of the song, but rather repetition of at least one of its time, space, or force factors. For example, the programmer—using recordings tagged with information generated by the MOST system—would be able to select a song with the same kinds of voices and instruments in the "immediate" space. Or, the programmer could approximate the same general recording site ambience, matching "dry" with "dry," and so on. Among the force factors, an example of one that could be repeated is timbre intensity, wherein the "edge" or "feel" of the vocal in the previous song is offered again, with slight variation.

## Development

LaRue (1970) said development is a continuation closely related by melody. Because the incredible variety of melodies makes them just about impossible to track, the best we can hope for is matching the key: for example, C minor to C minor. Matching *scales* (major with major, minor with minor) is a given within a certain mood. Changing scales probably also generates a change in mood (except possibly with sex).

## Response

Response, according to LaRue (1970), is a continuation that is unrelated melodically, so this is where we would expect to find developmental (not wholesale) changes. Responses should grow logically and organically out of what came before. This is the place where radio music programming can work most profitably to improve. Much of the time, what is heard instead of response is contrast—LaRue's fourth continuation option—in which there is a complete change. But those complete changes are usually unmotivated. They do not necessarily occur only at natural breaks in the program flow, where LaRue said they would confirm cadences or rests (which were earlier analogized to stop sets). Many times, contrast is employed as continuation when response is what should occur.

Examples of response in terms of space would include a move of a voice or an instrument that was in the "immediate" aural position to a "support" position, or a change from a dry ambience to a slightly livelier one.

Examples of response in terms of force might include a change from a sparse density of instrumentation to a more moderate one, or from just a few voices to a moderate number of voices.

## Contrast

Contrast is what happens accidentally much of the time in standard music rotations where hit ranking is more important than flow. But there is nothing wrong with contrast if it is motivated. In fact, as Ed Shane (1991) found, contrast in tempo, texture, style, instrumentation, and so on, is an important contributor to the sense that a station plays a good variety of music. Variety is not just about the titles played; the listener perceives variety in how the songs are ordered.

## Lyrics

Only the recurrence and development continuation options could also be adapted to lyrics. You would not want to air a literal recurrence, and development is related to melody, not words. That leaves response and contrast as areas of possible lyric continuation.

Response might mean moving from a song whose lyrics are mostly dictionary-based to one with more abstractions, or from one heavy on wishes to one more reflective of actual events. Or, if the lyrics were tracked for their arousal/fantasy/satiation components, it might be possible to construct a sound hour in which the lyrical responses also follow the CMC in terms of the Milkman and Sunderwirth behaviors.

The CMC could also be a model for varying lyrical complexity, with more demanding lyrics at one point of the curve, and less demanding ones at another.

Finally, lyrics can simply correspond to the moods on the CMC. As already stated about lyrics, they often mean what they seem to mean. If the lyric seems to be about love, maybe the simplest thing to do is to air it at the "love" part of the curve, assuming that other factors will correspond as well.

## POPULARITY AND THE CMC

This presentation would be incomplete if we did not discuss popularity as part of CMC. Popularity gets too much emphasis at most stations, but it would be naive to think song popularity is just going to go away and hide.

Popularity probably should not be superimposed on the curve in a literal way: by playing the big hits only at the peaks. The problem with using that approach would be that there is an awful lot of the curve that is not at a peak.

Instead of laying popularity rankings over the curve, perhaps *reliability* would be a better factor to consider (see chapter 9 for a discussion of how *reliability* extends the concept of familiarity). Reliability would cover current hits, oldies, new music, and recurrents. Only one of those four music categories is literally "popular"—the current hits. Tracking the degree of reliability would turn things around somewhat: It could be argued that many oldies are actually more familiar and reliable than some current hits. On a reliability curve, then, oldies might appear at the peaks, newcomers in the troughs, and current hits in the places in between.

Finally, there is no reason why popularity needs to fit the CMC at all. Popularity is an arbitrary, constantly changing factor. The more stable components of the CMC are interrelated so that they produce a logical continuation from one element to the next. A station could have a good air sound using the Composite Mood Curve and do so with very little thought to popularity. Indeed, one of the most appealing attributes of the CMC is that any music type is theoretically possible.

## USING THE CMC FOR OTHER ELEMENTS

In designing sound hours (or perhaps 90-minute hours in circadian time), the programmer might also want to consider elements beyond the tunes. For instance, what is the expression time of spoken material in a stop set? Is it as slow as grief or reverence? If so, could spoken stopsets substitute for grief and reverence songs? Or suppose music beds are prominent in the station's productions. Then the music bed of a stopset element can be measured for *its* expression time, and the stopset element could then fit into the curve at the appropriate point. In following this practice, a programmer might even decide that stopset elements need not be played according to any particular clock or cluster. Instead, they could be inserted wherever and whenever the expression time of the spot's music bed fits the CMC. If this were done, stopsets would no longer exist as unrelated clusters, but would instead be inserted where they match the surrounding mood. Then, where there is a gap between expression time levels in the music (as in the morning drive example, where neither anger nor grief were played), stopset elements could fit between the two levels, acting as a sort of buffer.

### The CMC and Standard Music Rotation Systems

Having read this far, you should now have a new set of tools for selecting and ordering music for radio airplay. Whether or not you use the CMC at your station, from now on you will probably have some doubts about the efficacy of standard methods of music selection, and typical systems for presenting it.

The usual music rotation systems do make sense if your station wants to help make a hit, or respond to genuine audience demand to air a hit. But rotation systems based on standard popularity measures will always present the kind of problems that these three radio practitioners reflect:

> I don't want to drastically change my current/recurrent/library percentages and add too much new music. By trying to rotate too many currents, I wind up not doing justice to anything. It's become a big problem because there are many new songs out there I'm very comfortable with and would like to play . . . . On many weeks, I usually struggle and keep currents in rotation

# CHAPTER 14

## Toward MERIT

### SHOULD RADIO LEAD OR FOLLOW SOCIETY?

The question of whether the mass media lead society or follow society has been debated for decades, so it is not useful to guess which is "true." But the last chapter of this book concludes with the outline of a radio format that tries to both follow society, and to lead it.

The arguments in Part III for a music presentation system based on moods is largely built on concepts that are reflective of the audience's needs, desires, and drives, so MOST and MEMO are schemes that "follow" the patterns society already has. On the other hand, offering music that is chosen to match or evoke a mood is an attempt to "lead" a radio audience into new listening territory, perhaps away from dependence on the hits. An audience that is actually more in control of radio programming would be closer to "leading" society.

Forty years ago, the Top 40 pioneers took a step away from autocracy toward democracy by deciding to play the music that the public—rather than the station owner and the announcers—wanted to hear. But over the years, the system of selecting music for radio airplay has become very industry-oriented, with only faint reference today to the desires of the great majority of the potential listening public. MOST and MEMO are music selection and presentation system that could allow radio to break out of that self-referential cycle, to play songs that satisfy the needs of listeners whose musical needs have little to do with keeping up with the hits.

But what if the audience had a still greater role in determining the programming, and through that leadership by the public, the radio station took on an enhanced leadership role in society? At that point, the question of who leads and who follows becomes moot, as radio and society become symbiotically interactive. Imagine a radio station that is continuously, intentionally interactive with its audience.

## A GLIMPSE OF WHAT MERIT MIGHT BE: MOOD-EVOKING RESPONDENT-INTERACTIVE TRACKING

### Begin With News

Perhaps the place to begin is with your news—something this book has passed over until now. Why (beside sponsorship) are newscasts always a predetermined length? Your audience knows that some days there are not 5 minutes of crucial items and that your newscaster is padding to make it sound as if there were. Other days, there are 10 minutes of important events that get butchered into two-sentence stories to get them all in. You would not play truly unimportant music just to fill a time slot, and you would not play just the first 30 seconds of each song. Why do that with the news? Let the length vary by importance.

Beyond that, why schedule newscasts at all (except perhaps in the morning)? If the items are really *news,* they probably should not wait for a whole hour before they are said. Truly newsworthy news can be done like drop-ins.

### Jingles and Liners

Next, consider your jingles and your liners. Even the most limited hot rotation music playlist has more than 10 or so titles, but many stations play just three or four "shotgun" jingles over and over and over. You think you are doing it for logo consistency. The public thinks you are doing it because you are too cheap to buy more. Are you? Shouldn't a variety of jingles and liners be part of the entertainment too? What would it be like if some of your audience played and voiced a few ID jingles to be dropped in very occasionally, just as a way of keeping things fresh, local, and inconsistent?

### Commercials and PSAs

What about spots? Are you ready to turn down a buy that has just one version of a national ad in heavy saturation because airing it would anger your listeners? Are you set up to write and produce multiple versions of a local campaign that will run for more than a few days?

What about PSAs? Are public service announcements basically fillers for unsold time, or are they part of the pulse of your community? Consider eliminating public service material whose content is corporate, distant fact giving (downward flow), and instead begin to conceive of public service announcements as an input-gathering opportunity that processes what the community wants to say about itself.

## Listening to the Community

To accomplish the goal of being the community's voice, the station needs to say "We're listening to you," and mean it. But really listening to the community will lead some radio stations into unfamiliar waters. For listener-supported KUNC-FM, licensed to the University of Northern Colorado at Greeley, listening to the listeners who wrote, called, and e-mailed the station about their music format resulted in raising 125% of their goal during one pledge drive! For urban-formatted WUSL-FM in Philadelphia (Power 99), the needs of the community were realized in free "powerhouse" concerts with serious underlying themes such as "Power Over AIDS," "Power Over Drugs," and "Power Over Violence." (Philly Station Giving Power to the People," 1991, p. 89) For Adult Alternative/Americana station KPIG-FM in Monterey, California, it was the recognition by PD/Music Director Laura Hopper that "composting down" their programming to fit the lowest common denominator was not the way to go:

> There are so many other places where people can get music, and good music. But they can't get it mixed intelligently and with personality and localized to fit the market. Radio ought to be responsive to its listeners, like we are. I don't know how else they're going to survive with all the competition out there. (Jepsen, 1995, p. 27)

That kind of attitude can help a station to succeed in the face of a plethora of other signals that provide narrow formats for "tunable personalities." In short, radio needs input from the listeners that will in fact shape what they get from their radio station.

## Commentlines and Clotheslines

Input from listeners that can result in PSAs and that can be used for internal guidance to actually change the radio station are not the end of it. The end of it is to put your community on the air.

Your station may have tried "public affairs programming" with your audience in the past, and might have found it unsatisfactory. Such programming might take the shape of a talk show with a host, guest, and call-ins. Or a daily topic for audience discussion is announced, and the audience is invited to call a recording line so that a selection of the calls can be played later on the air. Your experience with either of these might have been disappointing. You may have found that your audience was better equipped to talk about getting their wash clean than in expressing opinions on "controversial issues of public importance." But by casting your everyday listeners in the role of advocates and knowledgeable persons (which they know they are not), you narrow the prospective speakers on your air to only a few (perhaps the same few) active "loudmouths" out of the thousands of passives who actually listen.

But maybe the reason you only get 10% call-ins on a talk show is because everybody knows that your talk show is probably not going to change anything. What if the talk show *did* change things?

**Ownership and Feedback**

Most public TV and public radio stations have had to develop a sense of ownership because they now depend even more heavily on the listening public for their financing. And some commercial stations have developed advisory boards and "frequent listener clubs" to generate feedback on programming ideas. But commercial radio stations, because they depend on advertisers instead of the public at large, have generally not *had* to build a strong sense of proprietorship among their audiences.

How many commercial radio stations can you name that have tried to develop a format that reflects the community mind on a continuously interactive basis? The question here is can a radio station be not just a community mirror, not just a socializing force, but a means by which people can help to determine their future, instead of being just a bubble in a tide of huge uncontrollable social movements?

What is being proposed here is nothing less than an entire paradigm shift. The paradigm shift needs to be,

> You don't have to change the dial. We want you stay on the dial where you are with us and we will provide as many ways as we can for you to talk back to us. Tell us what you need. Tell us what you want. Tell us what you dream. We share more than few minutes of your attention. We share the planet and the future. What can we do together to live long and prosper?

And from the calls and letters, the station pulls out keywords, to track the community mood, to help build the community mind. It might seem that radio stations would be natural information processors, because they report the news. But in how many stations does the content of the news help shape the format? If a station really did that, the logs could not be prepared 6 days ahead.

## Winning Versus Community

Helping to build a healthy community mind is tough work. In fact, community building of any sort is tough in modern society, because the industries that advertise on the commercially supported media have a bottom-line stake in encouraging rugged individualism: More units (of products or services) can be sold if they are bought by individuals who keep them to themselves than if they are bought by cooperating groups who share them. Community building, then, might bewilder or anger some of a station's commercial clients, who could see the effort as a subversive activity.

Of course, you are not in business to vex your advertisers. Quite the opposite: Your goal as a station is to win audiences, shares, and dayparts. The station that wins the ratings race gets the big agency buys. To do that, you might even think you need a playlist comprised of winners, played in a winning rotation.

The community of listeners to your radio station does not care much about what it takes to land a new commercial account, or whether all the songs you added last month became hits. Radio is not a game to the community of listeners. It is a service that either meets their needs or does not. Winning is not wrong; it is just not the point of communities. Communities do not try to win. They hope to succeed. If you do your part well, they will wish you every success.

## Toward MERIT

MERIT would be a Mood-Evoking Respondent-Interactive Tracking format. It would use something like MOST to select the music, and a version of MEMO would be used to present it, but the presentation order would not be based wholly on preconceived mood patterns; instead, it would mix in the moods reflected in the station's pulse-taking of the community.

Think of the way stations and networks suspend their formats—even forego commercials—in times of crisis. Until the crisis passes, the whole presentation is centered on the community's needs, with members of that community (or their surrogates on the station/network staff) talking to and for each other. What MERIT suggests is that audiences should be catered to in less traumatic times, too.

MERIT comes down to this concept: that radio people are—whether we know it or not—involved in a dialogue. It is just that for a very long time, radio has not had to be very good at keeping up the listening part of the dialogue, because it was doing most of the talking and the audience was doing plenty of listening. For radio to continue to succeed in the face of many more competing voices, there will have to be more listening to the listeners: at the level of their mood needs on a general, theoretical basis at the least; at the level of the community's psychosocial needs for dialogue with itself at the best. A station programmed under the MERIT concept would be the last one in the market to drill away with a single cut of a boring commercial or promo line, because doing so would be a tacit admission that the station was not really in the dialogue business—that its communication was one-way after all, and the listener be damned.

One definition of religion is that it is a human attempt to make meaning out of the chaos of life. If radio is an information processor (in all its content, not just the news), then it is religious. But for it to be a religion I can practice, radio must program music better than I can do it myself. Radio must be more of a companion to me than all but my best friends and lover. Radio must know where I am in life and be a step ahead of me, helping to push the underbrush out of my way. Radio must lead me to challenges, and show me how to go about winning. Radio must avoid a format that reminds me of how probabilistic, indistinct and chaotic life is, but should instead stress novelty, possibility, and a reason to keep on listening and trying. Radio needs to be a religion I can practice, because this world needs my aspiration. But I need a model.

## MAJOR POINTS

1. A radio station that is continuously, intentionally interactive with its audience is the ideal: A Mood-Evoking Respondent-Interactive-Tracking station (MERIT).

2. Public TV and radio stations have been forced to develop a sense of listener "ownership" because they depend on that sense of loyalty for funding. Commercial stations would do well to take some cues from listener-supported stations in the area of building a true constituency.

3. The MERIT station would want its talk shows to change things. Its role would be not just a community mirror, not just a socializing force, but a means by which people could help determine their future. But for any of this to happen, the station must be much more active in gathering feedback, by being out in—and an integral part of—the community.

4. The MERIT station would present music (and other program elements) in ways that would reflect the station's community pulse-taking.

5. The MERIT station would see itself as being involved in a true dialogue, and would thus do much more listening to its listeners.

6. The MERIT station would help to make meaning out of the chaos of life, by being a model for meaning.

# References

Adkins, G. (1984). What would radio-television critics like us to understand? The critics speak. *Journal of Broadcasting, 28,* 355–359.
Alexander, S. (1993a, Dec. 3). Examining station playlists. *Radio & Records,* p. 34.
Alexander, S. (1993b, October 29). Re-examining 'Alternative'. *Radio & Records,* p. 33.
Alexander, S. (1994a, July 22). The influence of callout research. *Radio & Records,* p. 22.
Alexander, S. (1994b, September 9). Like no otter [SIC] station . . . *Radio & Records,* p. 28.
Allen, M. (1984, June 10). How do you rate (or do you care?). *Manhattan Mercury,* p. E-1.
Archer, C. (1994a, July 8). Targeting the disenchanted. *Radio & Records,* p. 25.
Archer, C. (1994b, August 5). Unique quality provides 'smooth' sailing. *Radio & Records,* p. 33.
Archer, C. (1995a, September 15). Are consultants ruining everything? *Radio & Records,* p. 82.
Archer, C. (1995b, November 24). 'Fire in the belly': BA's Cody responds. *Radio & Records,* p. 67.
Archer, C. (1995c, September 1). From early innovation to success—and beyond. *Radio & Records,* p. 87.
Archer, C. (1995d, November 17). John Gehron: Life beyond NAC. *Radio & Records,* p. 78.

Archer, C. (1995e, December 22). 'NAC is still all about the music.' *Radio & Records*, p. 77.
Associated Press Broadcast Services [advertisement by]. (1988, April 15). *Radio & Records*, p. 13.
Balon, R. (1988, November 25). What listeners don't know can kill you. *Radio & Records*, p. 30.
Beacham, F. (1995a, September). RealAudio: A world market for radio broadcasting? *Radio World Magazine, 19*, 38.
Beacham, F. (1995b, June). Satellite radio services are flying high with digital television uplinks. *Radio World Magazine, 19*, 18.
Bloomquist, R. (1993, December 3). The power and importance of knowledge. *Radio & Records*, p. 23.
Bloomquist, R. (1994, April 22). And now, back to our story . . . *Radio & Records*, p. 35.
Bond, G.H. The Wednesday afternoon format. *The Bond Report*. Flagstaff, AZ: Author.
Boot up the future with MoodMaker software. (1994, Fall/Winter). *Advance*, a publication of Kenwood USA.
Brentar, J., Neuendorf, K., & Armstrong, B. (1994). Exposure effects and affective responses to music. *Communication Monographs, 61*(2), 161–181.
Burke, K. (1996). *Language as symbolic action*. Berkeley & Los Angeles: University of California Press.
Burke, K. (1967). *The philosophy of literary form*. Baton Rouge: Louisiana State University Press.
Burns, G., & Thompson, R. (1987). Music, television, and video; Historical and aesthetic considerations. *Popular Music and Society, 11*(3), 11–25.
Carroll, R., Silbergleid, M., Beachum, C., Perry, S., Pluscht, P., & Pescatore, M. (1993). Meanings of radio to teenagers in a niche-programming era. *Journal of Broadcasting and Electronic Media, 37*, 159–176.
Chichester, P. (1995, January). PC radio charts potential new course for the airwaves. *Radio World Magazine, 19*, 28–31.
Clynes, M. (Ed.). (1982). *Music, mind, and brain*. New York: Plenum Press.
Clynes, M., & Nettheim, N. (1982). The living quality of music. In M. Clynes (Ed.), *Music, mind, and brain* (pp. 47–63). New York: Plenum Press.
Clynes, M., & Walker, J. (1982). Neurobiologic function of rhythm, time, and pulse in music. In M. Clynes (Ed.), *Music, mind, and brain* (pp. 171–216). New York: Plenum Press.
CRB Survey says (March 4, 1994) *Radio & Records*, (pp. 52, 57).
Crisell, A. (1986). *Understanding radio*. London: Methuen.
Davies, J. B. (1978). *The psychology of music*. London: Hutchinson.

Davitz, J. (1964a). Personality, perceptual, and cognitive correlates of emotional sensitivity. In J. Davitz (Ed.), *The communication of emotional meaning* (pp. 57–68). New York: McGraw-Hill.

Davitz, J. (1964b). A review of research connected with facial and vocal expressions of emotion. In J. Davitz (Ed.), *The communication of emotional meaning* (pp. 13–29). New York: McGraw-Hill.

Deford, F. (July 22, 1996). Rings master. *Newsweek, 128,* 53.

DeLuca, M. (1995, September 8). Cashing in on a format boom. *Radio & Records,* p. 53.

Denver, J. (1988a, June 10). The real deal on recurrents. *Radio & Records,* p. 40.

Denver, J. (1988b, February 5). What your slogan really means. *Radio & Records,* p. 42.

Denver, J. (1989, February 24). Station bonding. *Radio & Records,* p. 41.

Denver, J. (1993, July 16). Stopset strategies for today. *Radio & Records,* p. 29.

Denver, J. (1994, March 25). Grow your own hits. *Radio & Records,* p. 25.

Deutsch, D. (Ed.). (1982). *The psychology of music.* New York: Academic Press.

Downey, J. E. & Knapp, G. E. (1968). The effect on a musical programme of familiarity and of sequence of selections. In M. Schoen (Ed.), *The effects of music* (pp. 238–239). Freeport, NY: Books for Libraries Press.

Drake, B. (1988, October 7). Drake: CHR is very very healthy. *Radio & Records,* p. 28.

Eckels, H. (1983, November). New game in town. *Technology Illustrated,* p. 18.

Fears and fantasies of the American male. (1987, August). *Men's Fitness,* p. 49.

Fink, E., Robinson, J., & Dowden, S. (1985). The structure of music preference and attendance. *Communication Research, 12,* 301–318.

Fisher, G. (1994). *Arbitron radio futures think tank session.* Columbia, MD: The Arbitron Company.

Fletcher, J. (1987). *Music and program research.* Washington, DC: National Association of Broadcasters.

Fraise, P. (1982). Rhythm and tempo. In D. Deutsch (Ed.), *The psychology of music* (p. 158). New York: Academic Press.

Fuller, J. (1996, July 11). Muzak looks to compose itself. *Kansas City Star,* p. B-5.

Furlong, W. (1976, June). The fun in fun. *Psychology Today, 10,* 35.

Gronau, K. (1995, October). NAC jazzes up ratings of age-old radio genre. *Radio World Magazine, 19,* 34.

Harris, G. (1994, January 14). Busting radio's myths. *Radio & Records,* p. 15.

# REFERENCES

Heeter, C., & Greenberg, B. (1985). Cable and program choice in Dolf Zillmann & Jennings Bryant (Eds.), *Selective exposure to communication* (pp. 203–224). Hillsdale, NJ: Lawrence Erlbaum Associates.

Helton, L. (1995a, November 3). KRG study: We're still the 800-lb. gorilla. *Radio & Records*, p. 46.

Helton, L. (1995b, December 15). More labels, fewer stations; pressure rises, ratings drop. *Radio & Records*, p. 42.

Helton, L. (1995c, November 10). Station liners through the 90s. *Radio & Records*, p. 44.

Helton, L. (1995d, May 26). Women and music: Valid input. *Radio & Records*, p. 48.

Hevner, K. (1953). The affective character of major and minor modes in music. In R. W. Lundin (Ed.), *An objective psychology of music* (pp. 145–146). New York: Ronald Press.

Hollabaugh, L. (1994, March 4). Stations selective with special programming. *Radio & Records*, p. 42.

"I got fired everywhere." (1995, October 6). *Radio & Records*, p. 54.

Immel, A. (1982, June). Chris Crawford: Artist as game designer. *Popular Computing, 1*, 57.

In-car listeners more impatient with radio spots. *Radio & Records*, July 29, 1994, p. 1, 16.

Jepsen, C. (1995, November). 'Fat' KPIG feels free to be itself with mix of music and fun. *Radio World Magazine, 19*, 25, 27.

Kabrich, R. (1993, June 25). CHR & AC—More in common than you ever imagined. *Radio & Records*, p. 20.

Kassoff, M. (1993, August 13). Is CHR still a viable format? *Radio & Records*, p. 28.

Kelly, T. (1994, April 22). New music takes over. *Radio & Records*, p. 32.

Kennedy, D. E. (1981). *Listener perceptions as dimensions of radio station positioning: A multivariate analysis.* Unpublished doctoral dissertation. Bowling Green State University, Bowling Green, OH.

Kinosian, M. (1988, July 22). Is less talk more appealing? *Radio & Records*, p. 49.

Kinosian, M. (1994, April 1). On-air PDs lead by example. *Radio & Records*, p. 35.

Kinosian, M. (1995a, November 17). Compromising positions. *Radio & Records*, p. 62.

Kinosian, M. (1995b, September 1). New hybrids 'reinvent the format.' *Radio & Records*, p. 45.

Kinosian, M. (1995c, August 25). PDs ill at ease over 'radioese'. *Radio & Records*, p. 34.

Kojan, H. (1988, January 29). Abrams: AOR in serious crisis. *Radio & Records*, p. 44.

Land, H. (1957, May). The Storz Bombshell. *Television Magazine, 14,* 3.

Lang, G. (1995, January 19). Just take those old records off the shelf: Why is Oklahoma City radio reeling in the years? *Oklahoma Gazette*, p. 4.

Larson, R., & Kubey, R. (1983). Television and music: Contrasting media in adolescent life. *Youth and Society, 15,* 13–31.

LaRue, J. (1970). *Guidelines for style analysis.* New York: Norton.

Leader, J. (1980, April 4). Programmer's notebook: Are you predictable? *Radio & Records*, p. 18.

Lichty, L. & Ripley, J. (1969). Analyzing broadcast programs: Appeals. in L.W. Lichty & J.M. Ripley (Eds.), *American broadcasting: Introduction and analysis* (pp. 141–149). Madison, WI: College Printing & Typing Co., Inc.

Listeners love radio at home. (1993, July 30). *Radio & Records*, p. 3.

Love, W. (1993, May 14). The importance of format clocks. *Radio & Records*, p. 27.

Lull, J., Johnson, L., & Edmond, D., (1981). Radio listeners' electronic media habits. *Journal of Broadcasting, 25* (1), 25–36.

Lull, J., Johnson, L., & Sweeny, C., (1978). Audiences for contemporary radio formats. *Journal of Broadcasting, 22* (4), 439–453.

Lutz, R. (1978, November 17). Media marketing: Right down the line. *Radio & Records*, p. 12.

MacFarland, D. (1990). *Contemporary radio programming strategies.* Hillsdale, NJ: Lawrence Erlbaum Associates.

MacFarland, D. (1993). *The development of the Top 40 radio format.* North Stratford, NH: Ayer.

Marcus, G. (1987). Review of *The Billboard Book of Number One Hits. Popular Music, 6* (1), 110–112.

Maxwell, C. (1993a, July 30). New music: Testing the waters. *Radio & Records*, p. 28.

Maxwell, C. (1993b, June 11). Winter's winners and losers almost even. *Radio & Records*, p. 27.

Maxwell, C. (1994a, August 5). Plays per week: How they've changed the industry. *Radio & Records*, p. 31.

Maxwell, C. (1994b, September 22). Progressive evolves to adult alternative. *Radio & Records*, p. 86.

Maxwell, C. (1994c, April 8). Progressive format debuts. *Radio & Records*, p. 27.

Maxwell, C. (1994d, January 14). The singles vs. multi-cut debate. *Radio & Records*, p. 32.

Maxwell, C. (1995, December 15). Format struggles with growing pains. *Radio & Records,* p. 74.

McClellan, S. (1995, July 17). Out-of-home, sweet out-of-home. *Broadcasting & Cable, 125,* 23.

McLendon, G. (1962). Radio: The years to come. Presentation given at the World's Fair of Music and Sound, Chicago, IL.

McLendon, G. (1969). The time before this. Presentation given at the Alpha Epsilon Rho broadcasting honorary, Detroit, MI.

McVay, M. (1994, October 14). The PD's guide to directing talent. *Radio & Records,* p. 54.

Melton G., & Galician, M. (1987). A sociological approach to the pop music phenomenon: Radio and music utilization for expectation, motivation, and satisfaction. *Popular Music and Society, 11*(3), 35–46.

Mendelsohn, H. (1966). *Mass entertainment.* New Haven, CT: College and University Press.

Metropolitan soars with Kluge at helm (1959, May 25). *Billboard, 71,* 8.

Meyer, L. (1956) *Emotion and meaning in music.* Chicago, IL: The University of Chicago Press.

Milkman, H., & Sunderwirth, S. (1987). *Craving for ecstasy: The consciousness and chemistry of escape.* Lexington, MA: Lexington Books.

Mix stations target growing adult market niche. (1990, September 17). *Broadcasting, 119,* 28.

National Association of Broadcasters (Research and Planning Department). (1985). *Radio W.A.R.S: How to survive in the 80s.* NAB Services, Washington, DC.

National Association of Broadcasters (1985). *Radio in search of excellence: Lessons from America's best-run radio stations.* NAB Services, Washington, DC.

Negroponte, N. (1995). *Being digital.* New York: Vintage Books.

Novia, T. (1995a, September 8). A CHR/Pop national auditorium test. *Radio & Records,* pp. 66, 68.

Novia, T. (1995b, September 1). The mid-90s state of the format. *Radio & Records,* p. 34.

Novia, T. (1995c, November 17). Rick Cummings sells it like it is. *Radio & Records,* p. 34.

Ohlgren, T.H. & Berk, L.M. (Eds.). (1977). *The new languages.* Englewood Cliffs, NJ: Prentice-Hall.

Ortman, O. (1968). Non-auditory effects of music. In M. Schoen (Ed.), *The effects of music* (p. 128). Freeport, NY: Books for Libraries Press.

Oxenford, L. (1952). *Design for movement.* New York: Theatre Arts Books.

Panzarella, R. (1980). The phenomenology of aesthetic peak experiences. *Journal of Humanistic Psychology, 20,* 69–85.

Parker, M. (1991). Reading the charts—making sense with the hit parade. *Popular Music, 10*(2), 205–217.

Peters, T., & Waterman, R. (1982). *In search of excellence*. New York: Harper & Row.

Petrozzello, D. (1994, December 12). Fragmentation the key to music formats. *Broadcasting & Cable, 124,* 75.

Philly station giving "power" to the people. (1991, January 7). *Broadcasting, 120,* 89.

Piirto, R. (1994, May). Why radio thrives. *American Demographics, 16,* 42–45.

Pirsig, R. (1975). *Zen and the art of motorcycle maintenance*. New York: Bantam Books.

Pollack, J. (1988, December 16). Satisfying the complicated consumer. *Radio & Records,* p. 36.

Polskin, H. (1988, February 13). Keep your eye on Pirmin Zurbriggen—and other hot tips for your viewing pleasure. *TV Guide, 36,* 8.

The Psychology of Formats. (1993, September 5). *Broadcasting, 123,* 50.

Ries, A. & Trout, J. (1986). *Positioning: The battle for your mind*. New York: McGraw-Hill.

Robinson, D. (1991, September 9). A buyer's eye view of rehashed radio. *Mediaweek, 1,* 30.

Roschke, R. W. (1987) Dream/brain/text: The media–brain connection in mental processing of texts. In K. H. Richards (Ed.), *Society of biblical literature 1987 seminar papers*. Atlanta, GA: Scholars Press.

Rosenfeld, A. (1985, December). Music, the beautiful disturber. *Psychology Today, 19,* 50.

Rosing, H. (1984). Listening behavior and musical preference in the age of "transmitted music." In R. Middleton & D. Horn (Eds.), *Popular Music 4* (p. 129). Cambridge, England: Cambridge University Press.

Rosner, B.S., & Meyer, L.B. (1982). Melodic processes and the perception of music. In D. Deutsch (Ed.), *The psychology of music* (p. 320). New York: Academic Press.

Ross, S. (1993) Music radio—the fickleness of fragmentation. *Media Studies Journal, 7*(3), 93–103.

Rothenbuhler, E. (1985). Programming decision-making in popular music radio. *Communication Research, 12,*(2), 227–230.

Rothenbuhler, E., & McCourt, T. (1992). Commercial radio and popular music: processes of selection and factors of influence. In J. Lull (Ed.), *Popular music and communication* (2nd ed., pp. 101–115). Newbury Park, CA: Sage Publications.

Rubin, A.M. (1986). Uses, gratifications, and media effects research. In J. Bryant & D. Zillmann (Eds.), Perspectives on media effects (pp. 281–301). Hillsdale, NJ: Lawerence Erlbaum Associates.

Sabo, W. R., Inc. [advertisement by]. (1988, January 22). *Radio & Records,* p. 29.

Schafer, R. M. (1977). *The tuning of the world.* New York: Knopf.

Schlosberg, J. (1991, September 9). Format monotony. *Mediaweek, 1,* 26.

Schoen, M., & Gatewood, E. (1968). Problems related to the mood effects of music. In M. Schoen (Ed.), *The effects of music* (p. 154). Freeport, NY: Books for Libraries Press.

Shalett, M. (1988, May 20). Music videos: Heard but not seen? *Radio & Records,* p. 36.

Shane, E. (1991). *Cutting through: Strategies and tactics for radio.* Houston, TX: Shane Media Services.

Shane, E. (1995–1996). Modern radio formats: Trends and possibilities. *Journal of Radio Studies, 3,* 3–9.

Sharkey, B. (1994, October 10). Radio for people who think. *Mediaweek, 4,* 22.

Shaw, R. (1993, May 3). Fragmentation! *Mediaweek, 3,* 24.

Simanaitis, D. (1986, July). Beauty is the button just to the right of square root. *Road & Track, 37,* 174–175.

Sklar, R. (1988, August 26). Talk on FM: Mining the "new frontier." *Radio & Records,* p. 38.

Smart-Radio targets PC users. (1995, November 27). *Broadcasting & Cable, 125,* 98.

Starr, M. (July 22, 1996). The man who really knows the score. *Newsweek, 128,* 51.

Stephenson, W. (1967). *The play theory of mass communication.* Chicago, IL: University of Chicago Press.

Straw, W. (1988). Music video in its contexts: Popular music and postmodernism in the 1980s. *Popular Music, 7*(3), 247–266.

Strover, S. (1987, October). *Research and planning: The impact of music video on radio.* Washington, DC: National Association of Broadcasters.

Studies portray the passionate, the impassive. (1987, March 26). *Kansas City Times,* pp. B-4, B-6.

Sundberg, J. (1982). Speech, song, and emotions. In Clynes, M. (Ed.), *Music, mind, and brain* (pp. 137–149). New York: Plenum Press.

Survey sees radio taking on middle-age bulge. (1993, June 18). *Radio & Records,* p. 1.

Tannenbaum, P. (1985). 'Play it again, Sam': Repeated exposure to television programs. In D. Zillmann & J. Bryant (Eds.), *Selective exposure to communication* (pp. 225–241). Hillsdale, NJ: Lawrence Erlbaum Associates.

Tarradell, M. (1996, June 24). Lyle Lovett's on the road to yet another hit. *Kansas City Star,* p. D-6.

Wallis, R. & Malm, K. (1988). Push-pull for the video clip. *Popular Music, 7*(3), 267–284.

Washburn, M., & Dickinson, G. (1968). The sources and nature of the affective reaction to instrumental music. In M. Schoen (Ed.), *The effects of music* (p. 126). Freeport, NY: Books for Libraries Press.

*We see farther.* (1983). Advertising brochure from Electronic Arts (n. p.).

Wells, A. (1990). Popular music: Emotional use and management. *Journal of Popular Culture, 24,* 105-117.

Wells, A., & Hakanen, E. (1991). The emotional use of popular music by adolescents. *Journalism Quarterly, 68,* 445–454.

Weston, L. (1979). *Body rhythm: The circadian rhythms within you.* New York: Harcourt Brace Jovanovich.

"Why listeners switch from one music station to another." (1994, February 4). *Radio & Records,* p. 1.

Wilkie, M. (1994, October 17). Radio on demand touted at NAB. *Advertising Age, 65,* 43.

Winson, J. (1985). *Brain and psyche.* Garden City, NY: Doubleday.

Wonsiewicz, S. (1995, November 10). Blues-based rock headed into the pink? *Radio & Records,* p. 20.

Zillmann, D., and Bryant, J. (1985). Affect, mood, and emotion as determinants of selective exposure. In D. Zillmann & J. Bryant (Eds.), *Selective exposure to communication* (pp. 157–190). Hillsdale, NJ: Lawrence Erlbaum Associates.

Zillmann, D., & Bryant, J. (1986). Exploring the entertainment experience. In J. Bryant & D. Zillmann (Eds.), *Perspectives on media effects* (pp. 303–324). Hillsdale, NJ: Lawrence Erlbaum Associates.

# Index

## A

"Aberrant" songs, 152
Abrams, Lee, 95
AC format, 66, 68, 70, 71, 76, 161, 208–214
　recent trends, 77–78
　survey (Orlando. FL), 208, 211–212
Acceptance factors and emotional reactions to music, 219–220, 231
Acoustic environment, natural, 105
Acoustic space applied to a music progression, 193–197
Adams, William J., 206, 208, 212
ADSR (sound envelope), 186–187, 232–233
　analogized to an automobile, 187
　and the composite mood curve, 234
　applied to popular songs, 187
Adult Album Alternative, see Adult Alternative format
Adult Contemporary format, see AC format
Adult Alternative format, 77–80, 214, 247
　recent trends, 78–80
Agenda-setting function, 23
Aging of radio audience, 74
Airchecking, 131, 132
Airplay
　decision-making, factors in, 151–152
　music, selecting using Clynes' terms, 206–215

Album Oriented Rock format, see AOR format
Algorithms, 3
Alice in Chains, 161, 162
All News format, 70
Alternative format, 77, 156–157
　recent trends, 77
Ambience
　of recording site, factor in a music progression, 196–197
　of a remote, 112–113
*American Graffiti*, 126
"Animal", 209
Announcer
　as actor, 128–131
　as ideal mate, 127–128
Announcing styles, 31
AOR format, 67, 69–71, 95, 107, 151, 156, 208, 211, 212, 214
　recent trends, 78–80
Appeals, 50–51
　of complex, original music, 167
Appendix A, 225–227
Appendix B, 227–229
*A Prairie Home Companion*, 136
AQH audiences, 78
A. Q. Miller School of Journalism and Mass Communications, 208
Arbitron, 22
Aristotelian structure, 48–50, 232

*260*

and the composite mood curve, 234
and the popular song, 188
Aristotle, 2
Arledge, Roone, 135
Armored cocooning, 23
Arousal, 41–43
Arousal/fantasy/satiation, 231
Arousal/satiation behavior modes and the composite mood curve, 234
ARTS '82 National Music Preferences Study, 71–73
Associated Press Broadcast Services, 134–135
At-home
  audience, 12
  listening, 89
At-work listening, 89
Atari, 36
Atkins, Chet, 75
Attention to and usage of competing media, 54
Audience
  and control (as portrayed in magazines), 52
  characteristics and radio mood, 202
Audiences
  attracted by various formats, 69
  studio, 137
Audio processing, 107
Auditorium music testing, 150–151
alternatives to, when using Clynes terms, 214–215
"Aural wallpaper", 12
Automated stations, special problems of, 96–99

## B

"Background" (position on three-stage sound plan), 196
Balon, Rob, 68
Barbershop music, 71–73
Beatles, 160, 174
Beautiful music, 70–71, 78
"Beauty is the Button Just to the Right of Square Root", 223
Because of what you aired yesterday, today must be different, 94
*Being Digital*, 11
Benatar, Pat, 161
Best radio is radio that sells, 119
Big Band format, 71–72
Big Bopper, 193
*Billboard List of Number One Hits*, 150
Biondi, Dick, 126
Biorhythms, 45

Bluegrass, 12, 71–73, 79
Blues, 79
Blues scales (keys) and expression time, 216–217
Body rhythms, 45–48
  related to songs, 185–186
*Body Rhythm: The Circadian Rhythms Within You*, 45–48
Bolton Research, 157
Bond, Gary, 131–132
"Boomer-oriented lifestyle triggers", 83
Box, Alan, 21
BPM, 215, 237
*Brain and Psyche*, 223
Brentar, Neuendorf & Armstrong, 158
Bricks and mortar (of a format), 67
Broadcast Architecture, 80
Broadcasting is a service business, 101
Broadway musicals and show tunes, 66, 71–72
"Brown Eyed Girl", 161
Building
  song preference, 157
  to a climax, 49
Burke, Kenneth, 23, 220
Burnout, 66, 87, 160–162
  can begin between 8 and 16 plays, 158
  predicting, 223–224
Burns & Thompson, 18
Burns, George (programmer and consultant), 93–94
Burns' five-stage model of format innovation, 93–94

## C

C-band satellite audio services, 21
Cable-delivered audio, 20
Call-out music research, 150
Calls to station, using on air, 136
Can radio listening be a "flow" activity?, 57
"Candy" (computer game thrills), 36
Car radio listening, 89
Carpenter, Edmund, 10, 118–119
Carroll et al., 144
Casper, WY, 80
CD changers, 11
CDs, desired features of, 20
Challenge
  and control (in computer games), 34–35
  of change, 16
  of radio performance in a visual era, 118–120
Chapman, Tracy, 80
Charts, specialized music genre, 73

Children and TV, 25
"Chinese" music format, 21
Chocolate sundae in Lake Michigan, 33
Choosing radio, 11
CHR format, 1, 68, 154, 159–161, 208, 211
CHR-Urban/"Churban", 81
Christian format, 82–83
Chronobiology, 45
Circadian rhythms, 45–48
Circulation, 10
Clark, Dick, 126
"Classic", 68
Classic Rock format, 78–80, 160–161, 208, 211–212
Classical/chamber music, 71, 73
Climax, in pop music structure, 188
"Clock-thinking", 86
Clones, 94–95
Close-miking of announcers, 112
Closure, 33
Clynes' emotion terms, 177–180, 233
    and music moods research, 175–181
    and the composite mood curve, 236
    and the Multimarket, Multiformat Study, 208–215
    using to select airplay music, 206–215
Clynes, Manfred, 175–181, 184, 189, 201, 206–208, 215–218, 220, 224
Clynes & Nettheim, 176–179, 201
Clynes & Walker, 176
CNN, 16
CNN Headline News, 15–16
Cocooning, 23
Commentlines and clotheslines (at the MERIT station), 247–248
Commercial
    loads, 20, 88
    presentation, 88–90
Commercial-free hours, 133
Commercials (at the MERIT station), 246
Community, 23
    building, 249
    listening to (at the MERIT station), 247
    mind (at the MERIT station), 248
Complex music,
    appeals of, 167
    elicits more attention, 166
Composite mood curve, 234–241
    and standard music rotation systems, 242–243
    chart of, 235
    using for other elements, 242–243
    using to optimize daypart impact, 238–239
    using to target specific demographics, 237–238

Compression and limiting (audio processing), 107
Computer
    age, 24
    games, lessons about entertainment values from, 34
    screen, 24
Concentration, 57
Concert halls (acoustic space in a music progression), 194–195
Confirmation/consistency/predictability, 131–132
"Consensus cut", 151
Consistency, 13–14
Consistent quality, 14
Contemporary Hit Radio, *see* CHR format
*Contemporary Radio Programming Strategies*, 1
Continuation
    and the composite mood curve, 239–241
    four options for, in a music progression, 191–192
    in a mood-evoking music progression, 193
Continuous sounds, 106
Contrast (in a music progression), 192
    and the composite mood curve, 239–240
Control: appearance versus reality, 53
Control rooms and studios, 112–113
Core beliefs (announcer attribute), 133
Costas, Bob, 135
Countdown shows, 64
Country format, 71, 73, 76, 102, 208, 210–214
    recent trends, 74–76
Country Radio Broadcasters, 153
Country surveys (Dallas, TX; Indianapolis, IN), 208, 211
*Craving for Ecstasy: The Consciousness and Chemistry of Escape*, 40
Crawford, Chris, 36–37
Creative flux, 91
Crisell, Andrew, 137
Crossfade, 114
"Cryin' Shame", 209
Crystals, The, 221
Csikszentmihalyi, Mihaly, 56
Cultivation function, 23
"Current" music category, 155–156
Currents, 242–243
*Cutting Through*, 11, 123
Cybercommunity, 23

# D

"Da Doo Ron Ron", 221, 224
Dagwood Bumstead, 125–126, 128
Daily rhythms, 46

# INDEX

Dallas Country survey, 208, 212
"Dangerous" songs related to "no feeling" response, 207
D'Arcy Masius Benton & Bowles, 39, 74
Davies, John Booth, 141–142, 165–166, 192
Davitz, Joel R., 174, 200–201, 236
Daydreams (table), 39
Daypart
  impact, optimizing with the composite mood curve, 238–239
  restrictions, 12
Daytime dreaming, 19
Dees, Rick, 150
Def Leppard, 209
Deford, Frank, 135
Delivery business, 10
Demographics, targeting with the composite mood curve, 237–238
Dependability, 15
Development
  and the composite mood curve, 239–240
  Aristotelian structure, 49
  in a music progression, 188, 192
*Development of the Top 40 Radio Format*, 1
Differentiation
  via oldies, 66
  via presentational style, 66
Digital
  audio, 16, 19
  audio broadcasting, 20
  Cable Radio, 21
  cellular phone service, 16
Direct broadcast satellites, 2, 16, 20
DirecTV, 21
"Dirtiest Words on Radio", 133
"Disco Duck Part 1", 150
Disco format, 168, 184
Distance from the microphone, 123–124
DMX music service, 21
"Don't fix it if it ain't broke", 92
Don't just imitate the form—understand the function, 95
"Don't tell me what I already know", 134
Downey & Knapp, 167
"Downhome" music style, 72–73
Drake, Bill, 133–134
Dramatic structure, 48–50
*Dream/Brain/Text*, 18, 33–34
Dreams and fantasies, 19, 39
"Drop-in", 115
Dylan, Bob, 150
Dynamic range
  audio processing, 107
  sound plane/three-stage plan, 195–196

## E

"Ear candy" (adolescent-appeal music), 36
Ebersol, Dick, 135
Echostar broadcast satellite, 21
Ecological or geographical base of musical style, 71
Editing rates of radio production, 114–115
Editors and inventors, 95–96
Electronic Arts, 35, 37
Electronic media habits related to various formats, 69–71
Emmis Broadcasting, 77
*Emotion and Meaning in Music*, 192
Emotion term to describe a song, liking, and gender, 213
Emotional
  meanings in favorite songs, 174–175
  reaction added to standard music testing, 214
"Emotional Use of Popular Music by Adolescents", 145
"Emotionless" songs, dangers of, 217–218
Emotions
  assigned to music using Clynes terms, 213
  expressed vocally, interpretation of, 199–201
  scales (keys), and the composite mood curve, 236–237
Emulate the analysis, not necessarily the style, 121–125
Entertainment, 3
Enya, 80
Essentic forms: fusion of rhythm and melody, 177–180
Esteem needs, 51
"Eureka!" event in format innovation, 90
Exchange of effort (between audience and announcer), 129–130
Excitatory homeostasis, 45
Excitement, 40
Exciting or relaxing songs preferred, 170
Expectancies and novelties in music, 165–166
Expectation (in a music progression), 193
Exploring time/space/force, rewards of, 55
Exposition, 49
  in pop music structure, 188
Expression times (Clynes' term), 177–180, 189, 201
  and Aristotelian dramatic structure, 189–190
  finding the, 215–216
  related to major, minor, and blues scales, 216–217
EZ Communications, 21

# F

Factors
   in airplay decision-making, 151–152
   intrinsic to the song (how it makes you feel), 148
Fade to black (radio's pause), 114
Familiarity (of airplay music), 156, 160–162, 241
   and novelty of airplay music, 167
   not a prerequisite for liking a record, 156
   plus certainty equals reliability, 168
Fantasies and daydreams, 33–36, 38–43
"Fat synth" sound, 169
Favorability, familiarity and burnout (music research), 160–162
Feasibility study, using Clynes' terms to select airplay music, 206
Feedback, need for, 136–137
Female PDs and MDs at Country stations, 75
Fibber McGee's closet, 193
Fink, Robinson, and Dowden, 71
Fisher, Gary, 22
"Flat" (linear) frequency response, 112
"Flemish" music format, 21
Fletcher, James E., 155, 166
"Flow" experience, 35–36, 56–58, 130, 137
FM, appropriateness for talk format, 20
Folk music, 71, 79
Force (acceptance) factors, 231
   for predicting emotional reactions to music, 219–220
   in a mood-evoking music progression, 197–201
Form vs. function, 3
Formality and complexity of music, 71—73
Format
   as a safety net, 74
   clocks, 85–87
   copying, 95
   failure and the wide exploration of alternatives, 91
   preference, 70
   structure, 15
   success and the narrow repetition of a formula, 91
Formats, 10
   and research, 100
   history of, 63
   suspending in times of crisis, 249
Fox News Channel, 16
Fraise, Paul, 178, 186
"Freak Me" by Shai, 82

Freberg, Stan, 33
Freshening recorded elements, 98–99
Ft. Pierce, FL, 80
"Full-service" stations, 83
Full-time, off-air Program Director, 103

# G

Gaither, Roger, 136
"Gatekeepers" in the radio music business, 151–153
Gehron, John, 80–81
Gender, liking for song, and emotion term chosen, 213
Gershwin, Ira, 221
Godfrey, Arthur, 30–31, 120–127, 130
Going live (automated stations), 97
"Gold" (oldies), 66, 68
Goldstein, Avram, 164
Grammy Awards, 154
Graphical user interfaces, 24
GRP Records, 158
*Guidelines for Style Analysis*, 191

# H

Hall, Edward T., 123
Hard to master, 35
Harris, George, 87
Hartenstein, Eddy, 21
Harvey, Paul, 121, 122
Hassle-free consistency, 13
Hawkins, Willam, 35–36
"Headcount" ratings, 73
Headphone listening, 108
Heavy Metal, 167–168
Heavy rotation, 66, 158
Heeter & Greenberg, 145–146
"Help me when I need it, not when I don't", 134
Herb Woodley, 126
Heuristics, 3
Hevner, Kate, 169, 217
Hi-fi/Lo-fi soundscapes, 106
High audience formality and performance complexity, 72
High-fidelity sound environment, 105
High song repetition grates on audience's TSL tolerance, 157
Hispanic format, 82–83
Hit
   charts, 73
   rotation systems, 184–185

"Hit-ness", 185
Homogenous audiences, 13
"Hooks"
  in airplay music, 168–169
  in auditorium testing of unfamiliar songs, 213
Hopper, Laura, 247
Hornsby, Bruce, 80
Host (alternative term for "announcer"), 118
Hot AC, 76–77
"Hot clocks", 65, 184
"Hot Hits", 68
Houston, Whitney, 75, 161
"How does this music make you feel?", 174
"How it makes me feel", 144, 148, 162
How listeners choose a music radio station, 143–148
How music stations currently choose their music, 148–155
Howard, Bruce, 79
Huntington, Steve, 158
Hymns/gospel, 71–73

I

"I Have Nothing", 82
"I Will Always Love You", 161
Icons (computer), 24–25
ID jingles, 67–68, 114–115
Ideograms, 25
If programming is "product," then invention must be the norm, 185
Image packages, 68
"Immediate" (position on three-stage sound plan), 196
Immersion (computer), 24
"Impact of Music Video on Radio", 16
"In-car Listeners More Impatient With Radio Spots", 89
*In Search of Excellence*, 99
Inattention, 34, 36, 57
Inconsistency, 14
Indianapolis Country survey, 208, 211
Indigo Girls, 198
Inflection (pitch changes), 178, 201
Information, 3, 15–16
  -on-demand, 16
  -seekers, 16
"Informer", 82
Innovation of format elements, 85–96
Instrument/vocal density in a music progression, 198
Instrumentation/presentation style in a music progression, 198
Intellectual talk, 83

Intense concentration, 130–131
Intensity
  checklists, 219
  matrices for three music peformance factors, 219–220
Interaction, rewards of, 54
International or urban roots (of music), 72
Internet, 2, 11, 16, 21, 23
  Underground Music Archive, 21
  Intimate distance, 123–124
Involvement factors and emotional reactions to music, 218–219, 231
Isreal, David, 132

J

Jazz, 71, 73
Jingle (pleasure from merely the sound of the words), 220
Jingles, 25, 113–114
  (at the MERIT station), 246
Joel, Billy, 161, 174
John, Elton, 174
"Joy and Pain", 161
"Jump", 169

K

Kasem, Casey, 128
Kassoff, Mark, 77
Keep fixing what isn't broken, 91–92
Keillor, Garrison, 136
Kennedy, David E., 14–15
Kenny G, 78, 80
Kenwood CD changer, 11
Key (scale) related to expression time, 216–217
Kinaesthetic responses, 57–58, 164–165
Klein, Paul, 13
KLIF, Dallas, TX, 67
Kluge, John, 149
KOTR, San Luis Obispo, CA, 79
KOWH, Omaha, NE, 65
KPIG-FM, Monterrey, CA, 247
KSCA, Los Angeles, 79
KUNC-FM, Greeley, CO, 247

L

Lack of vocal variety, 98
Lang, George, 153
Lange, Joseph, 124
Lanz, David, 80
LaRue, Jan, 191, 240

Laughter as a cue to the audience, 137
Leader, John, 94
Least objectionable
   lunch, 13
   program, 13, 147
Led Zeppelin, 174
Lewis, Beth, 158
Lichty, Lawrence, & Ripley, Joseph, 50
Liking
   and popularity (of airplay music), 155
   for songs
      is linked to gender, 213
      is related to emotional reaction, 213
Limbaugh, Rush, 83
Limited playlist, 64–65, 90, 149
Liners, 87–88
   (at the MERIT station), 246
Linkages among songs (in a music progression), 185
Listener
   characteristics, music, and mood, 213
   -supported, 247
*Listener Perceptions as Dimensions of Radio Station Positioning*, 14
Listener's agenda: enjoying the process, 55
Listeners do not care about the radio business, 10
Listening
   as work accompaniment, 28
   becoming "up close and personal", 124
   environment, 105–110
   place can be described by three-stage sound plan, 197
   to the community (at the MERIT station), 247
Lite Jazz, recent trends, 80–81
Lite/soft AC, 78, 79
Local daily newspaper example, 9
Local or rural roots (of music), 72
Local/Rural/Downhome scale, 72
Logos (TV network), 24
Long stopsets, 90
LOP, *see* Least objectionable program theory
"Losing the frame", 130
"Love Is a Battlefield", 161
Lovett, Lyle, 209
Low ambient noise level, 106
Low audience formality and performance complexity, 72
Lowest common denominator of inoffensiveness, 13
Lubbers, Charles A., 208, 212
Lucas, George, 95
Lujack, Larry, 128
Lull, Johnson, and Edmund, 69
Lull, Johnson, and Sweeny, 69

Lutz, Richard J., 92
Lutz's Programming Idea Life Cycle, 92–93
Lyrics
   and continuation (using the composite mood curve), 241
   descriptive of arousal/satiation/fantasy, 221
   in a mood-evoking music progression, 199
   in mood-oriented music selection testing, 220–222
   narrative action and reality/fantasy imagery in, 220

# M

MacFarland, David T., 1
Machines as scapegoats, 97
"Machines should work. People should think", 96
"Magic", 68
Major scales (keys) and expression time, 216–217
Mama Cass, 15
"Man in the Box", 161
Managing
   emotions with music (teens and young adults), 145
   perceived acoustic space, 109–110
Management, primary tasks of, 99–103
Manipulating the listener, 87
Manring, Michael, 209
Marcus, Greil, 150
Maslow's needs pyramid, 51
Mass appeal, 13
   need not mean doing what the other guys do, 15
*Mass Entertainment*, 27
Matching the listener's mood, 171
McDonald's, 13
McLendon, Gordon, 16, 63–64, 67, 99, 100
McLuhan, Marshall, 23
McMahon, Bill, 132–133
McVay, Mike, 132
Measuring music popularity
   via call-out and auditorium music tests, 150–151
   via record sales and airplay by other stations, 149–150
Meeks, Bill, 67
Melodic tracks, 80
Melton & Galician, 17–18
Mendelsohn, Harold, 27–30, 171–175
   music moods research, 171–175
   positive values of mass entertainment, 27

Merriman, Tom, 67
Metallica, 198
Meyer, Leonard B., 165, 192–193
Microsoft, 21
Milkman, Harvey, & Sunderwirth, Stanley, 40–41, 43–44, 49, 221, 232–233
Minor scales (keys) and expression time, 216–217
Modern Rock format, recent trends, 77
Mood/easy listening, 71, 73
Mood
   -evoking music progression, 183–184
   -evoking respondent-interactive tracking (MERIT), 246–250
   maintenance or change, desire for, 170
   needs, recognizing listeners', 184
MoodMaker PC software, 11
"More music, less talk", 11
Mormon Tabernacle Choir, 198
Morrison, Van, 161
MTV, 16–19, 23, 42, 119
   and music video influence on radio music selection, 154
Multimarket, multiformat study to select airplay music, 208–215
Music
   clocks, 149
   monitors, 149
   mood
      and desire for variety, 173
      and individual predispositions, 172–173
      created, changed, or sustained, 172–173
      novelty or stability seeker, 170–171
      novelty seeker, 185
      stability seeker, 185
      style or genre less important than the mood, 173–174
   presentation systems, 116
      based on mood needs, 183–185
   progressions, 183–184
   research (Country format), 153–154
   rotation
      categories, 149–150
      systems, 65, 113
         and the composite mood curve, 242–243
   sweeps, 88, 133
   trade magazines, 73
   videos, 16–17, 154
*Music and Program Research*, 155
Music-and-news, 63
Music Choice music service, 21
*Music, Mind and Brain*, 178
"Music utility", 11

Muzak music service, 21

## N

NAB, *see* National Association of Broadcasters
NAC format, 77, 80–81, 107, 158
   recent trends, 80–81
Nashville Network, 17
National Association of Broadcasters, 27, 71, 99, 208
National Public Radio, 83
Natural acoustic environment, 105
Need for feedback, 136–137
Needing Arthur Godfrey again, 120–127
Negroponte, Nicholas, 11
Nelson, Willie, 199
New Adult Contemporary/Lite Jazz, *see* NAC
New Age music, 80–81, 209
New Country format, 79
Newman, Randy, 209
New music,
   repetition of, to increase familiarity, 156–157
   testing of, 156
   *see also* Unfamiliar music, 80, 211, 213
New Rock format, 66, 77
News copy, uses for, 135
"News from Lake Wobegon" stories, 136
News-Talk format, 83
Nielsen Media Research, 12
Ninety-minute hour, 47
"No feeling" response on airplay music test, 217
Nonradio listening, 12
"No reaction/don't know," in airplay music test, 217–218
No-science audience survey, 12
Nostalgia format, 71, 82
Novel versus familiar "hooks", 168–169
Novelty of airplay music, 166–167
Number One record, 82

## O

100 Guitars, 198
101 Strings, 198
"Ode to Joy", 186
"Off-mike", 113
Oldies, 66, 68, 208
   and memory, in mood-oriented music selection testing, 223

Oldies format, 83, 160, 212
  recent trends, 81–82
Opera, 71, 73
Opinion-flaunting talk, 83
Opponent-process
  arousal/satiation behavior curve, 232–233
  model, 43–45
Organization of the book, 4
Originality (of airplay music), 156
Orlando, FL, AC survey, 208, 211, 212
Ortman, Otto, 164
Other audience needs and desires, 51
Other opinions about the music selection process, 153
Ownership and feedback (at the MERIT station), 248


P

"Pamela", 224
PAMS, 67
Panzarella, R., 145
Paragon Research, 88–89, 208–209
Patrick, Lou, 157
Paul, Les, 198
PD, see Program Director
Performer characteristics and radio mood, 202
Personal distance, 123–124
"Personality, Perceptual, and Cognitive Correlates of Emotional Sensitivity", 200
Peters & Waterman, 99–101
Petri dish for daydreams, 40
Petty, Tom, 161
Phillips, Wally, 136–137
Photoperiodism, 45
Phrasing (in a music presentation system), 190–191
Pilot Study, using Clynes' terms to select airplay music, 207
Pink Floyd, 174
Pirsig, Robert M., 129–130
Pitch
  of announcer's voice, 122
  of music
    helps to determine emotional reaction, 169
    relates to its pleasantness rating, 169
    -related feelings and the composite mood curve, 234, 236
Plain talk, 132
Play, definitions of, 31

"Play It and Say It" campaign, 133–134
*Play Theory of Mass Communication*, 30
Playing
  actions, not emotions, 128–129
  objectives, 128–129
Playlist history (lack of with NAC), 80
Pleasantness and activation reactions to music, 169
Pleasure 32
  as product, not by-product, 42
  of play, 30
  sources of, 39
  -seeking, 40
"Point-of-view" cameras, 110
Pop music listeners accept many diverse music forms, 172
Popularity, 160–162
  and the composite mood curve, 241–242
  of music not related to mood, 174
  versus familiarity (of airplay music), 155–157
Positioning, 14–15
  liners and statements, 77, 87–88
"Power", 68
Predictability, 193
  of a music progression, 192
Predicting
  body movements from the rhythm of music, 176
  burnout, 223–224
Preselection (of music for airplay), 152
Presentation style/instrumentation in a music progression, 198
Primary tasks of management, 99–103
Problems of automated and syndicated stations, 96–99
Producer (listener as), 10–11
Product Life-Cycle Model, 92
Production personnel
  and spot loads, 102
  off-air, 102
"Productivity Through People", 100
Program choice model, 146–147
Program Director, 12
  as chronobiologist, 45
  full-time, off-air, 103
  of Progressive format station, 17
  of Top 40 station, 17
  typist as, 97
Programming consultants (selecting music for airplay), 151
"Programming Decision-Making in Popular Music Radio", 151–152
"Programming Idea Life Cycle", see Lutz's
Progressive AOR, 157
Progressive format, 214

recent trends, 78–80
Proxemics, 123
PSAs (at the MERIT station), 246–247
*Psychology of Music, The*, 141–142
Psychological present, emotional reactions in, 180
Public
    distance, 123–124
    smile, 127
"Pull" media, 11, 21
Pushbutton radio tuning, 89
"Push" media, 11, 21

## Q

Qualitative audiences, 13
Quality, *see* Exchange of effort
Questions raised by control rooms, 112

## R

"Race music", 74
Radio Advertising Bureau, 33, 74
Radio Broadcast Data Service, *see* RBDS
Radio
    as a sound wall, 108–109
    "connection", 42
    editing rates, 115
    guides, 52
    performers are salespeople, 119–120
    studio must not be the monk's cell, 137
*Radio In Search of Excellence*, 99
Radio is
    a fertilizer of fantasies and daydreams, 33
    encompassing, 32
    low-demand, 32
    open-ended, 33
Radio's
    arena, 9
    attributes, 27
*Radio W.A.R.S: How to Survive in the 80s*, 71
Raitt, Bonnie, 154
Rantel Research, 160
Rap, 81, 167
Rate (production elements), 113–116
RBDS, 21–22
RealAudio, 21
"Real Emotional Girl", 209
Real talk, 132–133
Reality therapy, 137
Recent trends in selected formats, 74–83
Receptive and active fantasy, 41

Record companies, 66
Record distributors, 151
Recording site ambience, considered in a music progression, 196–197
Recurrence
    and the composite mood curve, 239–240
    in a music progression, 192
Recurrent records, 159–160, 242–243
    in mood-oriented music selection testing, 222
    no consensus on definition of, 159
Relaxation, 40
    not escape, 28
Reliability, 241
    emotional, 222
    of airplay music, 168
    takes continued effectiveness into account, 168
Remote broadcasts, 194
"Renegade Intellectuals", 209
Repetition of new music to increase familiarity, 156–157
Research
    and formats, 100
    on how and why music affects us, 165–171
Research Director, Inc., 12
Resolution, 49
    lack of in pop music structure, 188
Response
    and the composite mood curve, 239, 240
    in a music progression, 192
Reverberation
    in recorded music, 112
    -station audio processing, 107
Rewards
    of exploring time/space/force, 55
    of interaction, 54
"Rhythm and Blues", 74, 81
Rhythm durations, 46
Rhythmic Contemporary/Hip-Hop, 81
Rhythmic pulse (Clynes term), 176
Rhythms,
    circadian (body), 231
    communal, 231
    cultural, 231
    of the human body related to songs, 185–186
    personal, 231
    seasonal, 231
Ries, Al, 15
Righteous Brothers, 198–199, 224
Riker, Greg, 21
Rob Base & DJ EZ Rock, 161–162
Robinson, David, 89–90
Rock, 71–73, 79

"Rock and roll", 66
Role of radio in an increasingly visual electronic society, 22
"Roll With It", 162
Rolling Stones, 79
Roschke, Ronald W., 18–19, 33
Ross, Sean, 76
Rothenbuhler & McCourt, 152–153, 224
Rothenbuhler, Eric, 151–152

## S

Sade, 80
Saint-Saens Symphony # 3, 193
San Jose, CA (music video study), 17
Satellite-delivered music services, 21
Satellite Music Network, 96
Satiation, 41–43
Scales (keys),
    related to emotions and the composite mood curve, 237
    related to expression time, 216–217
"Scenes From an Italian Restaurant", 161
Schafer, R. Murray, 105–106, 108–109, 185–186, 194–196
Schlesinger, Dr. Laura, 83
Schlosberg, Jeremy, 100
Schoen & Gatewood, 170–171
Sebastian, John, 80–81
Segue, 114
Selectivity, 70
Self-referential emotions, 127
Selling the music, 133–134
Sense of place
    in acoustic space, 110–113, 194
    lacking in studios, 112
Sentograms, 179
Sentograph, 176, 178
Serving the machine, 96
Shane, Ed, 11, 67, 75–76, 83, 116, 123–124, 170, 240
Shane Media Services, 77
Shaw, Russell, 82
"Shazzam!", a very slow, 90–91
Shift from discrete to continuous sound, 106
Shotgun jingles, 115
Signal processing, 107–108
Silence, 114
Simon, Paul, 199
Singers and song delivery (analogized to announcers), 120
Singing commercials, 67
"Single" record
    reinstitution of, 19

renewed importance because of music videos, 154
Sleep cycle, 47–48
Slogans and station characteristics, 68
Small-market/self-selected survey, 209
Smart-Radio, 21–22
Smooth Jazz format, 77, 80, 107
Social or consultative distance, 123–124
Socially controlled publics and existential mass audiences, 30
Soft/lite AC, 78, 161
Solitary versus social listening experiences, 29
Solomon, Richard, 43, 232
Something you walk away with, 37
Song
    characteristics and radio mood, 202
    preference, building, 157
    rhythms for predicting emotional reactions to music, 215–218
Soul/Blues/Rhythm and Blues, 71–73
Sound envelope (in song structure), 186–187
Soundscapes, 105–106
Sound walls (radio as a "force field"), 109
Space
    announcer's use of changes in distance, 124–125
    involvement factors, 231
    for predicting emotional reactions to music, 218–219
Spacial
    cues in recorded music, 195
    factors
        in the recording site's ambience, testing for, 218
        in vocals and instrumentals, testing for, 218
Speaking to the audience individually, 120–121
Special
    audio services, 20
    considerations in mood-oriented selection testing, 222
    problems of automated and syndicated stations, 96–99
Specialized music genre charts, 73
Spector, Phil, 198
Spot clusters, 88
St. John, Michael, 100
Stabs, 115
Staff as source of ideas and productivity, 100–101
Standard components of record popularity, 155–162
Stanislavsky, 2, 129, 137
Star Wars, 95

Station
   IDs, 25
   identification jingles and image packages, 67
   mission, 2
   productivity, 101–103
   search patterns, 145–146
   selection, 143–148
"Stationality", 67–68
Staying fresh, 98–99
Stephenson, William, 30–32
Stereo television receivers, 19
Stern, Howard, 83
Stern, William, 180
Stewart, Bill, 64–65, 90–91
Stopsets, 88–90
Stories
   in popular music, 19
   on radio, 135–136
   telling, 18
Storz station group, 67–68
Storz, Todd, 64–65, 90–91, 99
Street Pulse Group, 17
Strover, Sharon, 16–17
Structure, 48
   desire for in songs, 185
"Structure of Music Preference and Attendance", 72
Studio audiences, 137
Summers, Harrison, 50
"Support" (position on three-stage sound plan), 196
"Swiss Folk" music format, 21
Symbiosis of format differentiation and ratings detail, 73
Syndicated
   programming, special problems of, 96–99
   production collides with local production, 97–98

## T

Talk
   about the community's stories, 135–137
   format, 83, 118
   opinion-flaunting, 83
   vs. music loudness levels, 107
Talking mostly about the music, trap of, 134
Tannenbaum, Percy, 168
Targeting and selling the listener, 125
Taylor, Gary, 132
Taylor, James, 199
Teens, uses of music by, 144–145

Television
   editing applied to radio, 114–115
   gave up space exploration, 110
Tempo
   and expression times, 189
   of music relates to its activation rating, 169
Terminating evaluation (most common station search strategy), 146
Testing new music, 156
Thayer, Tanaka & Winborne, 169
Three-stage sound plan, 195–196, 219
   can describe the listening place, 197
Timbre
   and distance from the microphone, 123–124
   announcer's vocal quality, 123–124
   intensity/force factor in a music progression, 197–198
Time
   and "force" sound parameters, 109
   announcer's rate, 122
   as a structural element in sound, 186–187
"Time shifting" radio programs, 53
Time/space/force components of radio mood, 202–203
Time spent listening, see TSL
TM Productions/TM Century, 67
"Tonnage", 13
Top 40, 1, 16, 64, 66–68, 70, 73, 85, 91, 99, 114, 121, 126, 144, 148–149, 152, 171, 245
   and the limited playlist, 64
Top 40/CHR, 77–78, 85, 88–89
   recent trends, 76–77
"Top of mind" positioning, 67
Toto, 224
Toward another meaning for "productivity" in radio, 101–103
Toward MERIT, 249–250
Trade magazines, 66
Trade paper music charts, importance of, 149–150
Traits of the ideal mate (compared to announcer), 127
Travelling Wilburys, 154
Trout, Jack, 15
Trying things, 99–100
TSL, 75, 78, 85, 148, 156–157
Tuneout, 34
   in spot clusters, 89
   minimizing, 13
*Tuning of the World, The*, 105–106
Turner, Tina, 162
"Turnoff"—early-stage burnout of airplay music, 158

TV
    editing applied to radio, 114–115
    gave up space exploration, 110
"Twist and Shout", 160–161
Two audience expectation guidelines, 134
Typist as Program Director, 97

## U

*Understanding Radio*, 137
Unfamiliar music, 80
    can be auditorium-tested, 213
    indication of liking for in music test, 211
Unistar, 96
Unreliability of phone requests for music, 154–155
"Up close and personal" (Olympics coverage), 135
"Uptown" music style, 72, 73
Urban
    AC, 77
    Adult Contemporary, 81
    Gold, 81
Urban format, 247
    recent trends, 81
Uses and gratifications, 3
Uses
    of music by teens, 144–145
    of radio news copy, 135
Utilities, monopolistic, 14

## V

Van Halen, 169
Variety
    and contrast (complete musical change), 240
    perceived (as a result of announcer talk), 116
VCR, 23
Vega, Suzanne, 80
Verbal Frisbies™, 137
VH-1, 17
Video and computers are changing the commonality of community, 23
Visual
    environments, 25
    gestures, 119
    presentation, manipulating, 24
    society, 25
Vocal
    expression of emotional meanings, 200–201
    or instrument density in a music progression, 198

variety, lack of, 98

## W

Waitress in the bar story, 65
"Wall of sound", 198–199
Washburn & Dickinson, 170, 238
W. B. Doner & Co. agency, 89–90
WCAU-FM, Philadelphia, PA, 76
WDOK, Cleveland, OH, 132
Weather Channel, 15
Wednesday Afternoon Format, 131–132, 136
Wells & Hakanen, 145, 212
Wells, Alan, 174–175
Weston, Lee, 45–48
Wexler, Jerry, 74
WGN, Chicago, IL, 136
What business is radio in?, 9
"What does radio do?", 27
What do listeners really want from radio?, 3, 16, 37
"What emotion does this song make you feel?", 209–210
What factors make a song popular in the first place?, 162
What is the reason for choosing to play this song next?, 185
What is there to talk about?, 131–135
What radio does best, 32
What the title means, 1
What this book offers, 1
"What's Love Got to Do With It", 162
"What's new with you?", 14
"While You See a Chance", 220, 224
Who listens like the listener?, 103
"Why is this song popular, and with whom?", 162
"Why Listeners Switch From One Radio Station to Another", 88–89
Why radio sounds like limbo, 111
Why talk about the music?, 134
Wilson, Sue, 87, 132
Windham Hill, 209
Winning versus community, 249
Winson, Jonathon, 223
Winwood, Steve, 162, 220
Wireless cable, 16
WKKO, Cocoa, FL, 114
WKQB, Charleston, SC, 136
WMCA, New York, NY, 65–66, 171–172
WMT, Cedar Rapids, IA, 15
WNEW, New York, 64
Wolfman Jack, 126
WQAM, Miami, FL, 68, 114
W. R. Sabo, Inc., 133

WUSL-FM, Philadelphia, PA, 247

## Y

Yanni, 80
"Yearning", 8th term added to Clynes' seven emotions, 207
"You Don't Know How..", 161
"You've Lost That Lovin' Feelin", 198, 224
Young, Neil, 79
*Your Hit Parade*, 64
Your neighbor as salesperson, 125

## Z

*Zen and the Art of Motorcycle Maintenance*, 129–130
Zero talk and commercial-free hours, 133
Zillmann, Dolf & Bryant, Jennings, 27, 42, 45, 137, 144, 146–147, 172–173"Zoo" crews, 137
Zoom lenses, 110–111
Zydeco, 12